SEXUAL PREFERENCE

STATISTICAL APPENDIX

SEXUAL PREFERENCE

ITS DEVELOPMENT IN MEN AND WOMEN

STATISTICAL APPENDIX

Alan P. Bell
Martin S. Weinberg
Sue Kiefer Hammersmith

An official publication of the Alfred C. Kinsey Institute of Sex Research

INDIANA UNIVERSITY PRESS
BLOOMINGTON

Manufactured in the United States of America

Library of Congress Cataloging in Publication Data

Bell, Alan P., 1932
  Sexual preference, its development in men and women.
Statistical appendix.

  "An official publication of the Alfred C. Kinsey
Institute of Sex Research."
  1. Homosexuality — Statistics.   2. Homosexuality —
Social aspects — Statistics.   3. Homosexuality — Psycho-
logical aspects — Statistics.   I. Weinberg, Martin S.
II. Hammersmith, Sue Kiefer.   III. Institute for Sex
Research.   IV. Title.
HQ76.B438 Suppl.   306.7'6   81–47006
ISBN 0–253–16674–8   AACR2
1 2 3 4 5 85 84 83 82 81

CONTENTS

PREFACE

In writing Sexual Preference: Its Development in Men and Women, we had to deal with a massive and complicated body of data. The interview schedule included over 500 questions dealing with respondents' social and sexual histories, and the various statistics necessary for the comparative and causal analyses were obtained over a period of several years. The main volume of Sexual Preference includes only the most important and illustrative statistics and interview questions. In this Statistical Appendix we provide other statistics that may be of particular interest.

Part I contains the questions from the interview schedule that were used in writing this report on sexual preference. Each question is followed by the response categories (in the case of closed-ended questions) or coding categories (in the case of open-ended questions) and the percentage distributions for eight categories of respondents. Those categories are white homosexual males (WHMs), black homosexual males (BHMs), white heterosexual males (WHTMs), black heterosexual males (BHTMs), white homosexual females (WHFs), black homosexual females (BHFs), white heterosexual females (WHTFs), and black heterosexual females (BHTFs).

For the reader's convenience, these questions have been grouped according to topic. Consequently, the order in which they appear does not correspond to the order in which the questions were asked in the interview. Nor does the Statistical Appendix include all the questions the respondents were asked, since many questions in the interview schedule pertained to adult circumstances and characteristics and were reported elsewhere.*

Part II contains statistics relevant to the causal and comparative analyses for the white men in the study.

---

*Alan P. Bell and Martin S. Weinberg, Homosexualities: A Study of Diversity Among Men and Women (New York: Simon and Schuster, 1978).

Specifically, it includes the path diagram for the white males; the intercorrelations (Pearsonian r's) between variables in the path diagram, and the means and standard deviations for those variables; the total effects, the standardized path coefficients (beta), and the unstandardized path coefficients (b) for the path model; and finally, the total effects and the standardized and unstandardized path coefficients for a fully recursive path model (i.e., one containing all possible paths, including those that failed to meet our criteria of statistical and substantive significance). Part II also presents the results of our preliminary comparisons, with etas and probabilities obtained from analysis of variance. The statistics in Part III correspond to those in Part II except that they pertain to the white women in the study instead of the white men.

Part IV contains path diagrams and statistics relevant to the path analyses for specific types of homosexual men and women in the study. Included are black men and black women and the following types of white homosexual respondents: effeminate homosexual men, noneffeminate homosexual men, "masculine" homosexual women, nonmasculine homosexual women, bisexuals, exclusively homosexual men and women, homosexual men and women who have had therapy or counseling, and those who have not had therapy or counseling. We also provide tables for the white homosexual respondents that allow the reader to see the percentage and number of respondents falling into each special category as well as the degree of overlap between categories.

Readers who wish other information about the interview schedule or additional statistical analysis that was done in the course of this study should contact the authors directly.

A.P.B.
M.S.W.
S.K.H.

NOTE TO PATH DIAGRAMS

Several of our path diagrams contain paths between mutually exclusive variables. These paths, indicated by broken arrows, are statistically significant but not very meaningful. For instance, one set of mutually exclusive variables (found in Diagrams 1, 5, 8, and 9) is Homosexual Arousal in Childhood and First Homosexual Arousal in Adolescence; a respondent who experienced Homosexual Arousal in Childhood, by definition, cannot experience his First Homosexual Arousal in Adolescence—hence the strong negative path between these two variables. Other sets of mutually exclusive variables are (in Diagrams 1, 5, 8, 9, and 11) Felt Sexually Different in Childhood, and Began to Feel Sexually Different in Adolescence; and (in Diagram 9) Homosexual Genital Activities in Childhood, and Homosexual Genital Activities Began in Adolescence.

In other path diagrams, one of the mutually exclusive variables is incorporated in a composite measure; this also yields paths (represented in broken arrows) which are statistically significant but not very meaningful. In Diagram 2, for instance, Adolescent Homosexual Involvement is a composite measure consisting of Adolescent Homosexual Activities and First Homosexual Arousal in Adolescence—two variables that were combined because they are highly intercorrelated. However, Homosexual Arousal in Adolescence and the variable from which the broken arrow originates—Homosexual Arousal in Childhood—are mutually exclusive. This tautological relationship overshadows any connection which might exist between Homosexual Arousal in Childhood and Homosexual Activities in Adolescence; hence the weak, negative path coefficient.

Similarly, Diagrams 4 and 7 contain Homosexual Feelings in Childhood, which is a composite measure consisting of Homosexual Arousal in Childhood and Felt

Sexually Different in Childhood--two variables that were combined because they were highly intercorrelated. This composite measure is mutually exclusive with two variables appearing in the next stage of Digrams 4 and 7: First Homosexual Arousal in Adolescence, and Began to Feel Sexually Different in Adolescence. Hence we find a strong negative path coefficient linking Homosexual Feelings in Childhood with each of these variables, but these paths are not very meaningful.

Some readers may wonder why these path coefficients between mutually exclusive variables are not exactly -1.00. The reason is that many of our respondents did not experience homosexual arousal, feel sexually different, or engage in homosexual genital activities, during either period. Thus the fact that a particular respondent did not have these feelings during childhood still does not tell us whether he experienced them during adolescence.

PART I

Interview Questions

and Response Distributions

MOTHERS/Mother-Child Relationships

	WHM	BHM	WHTM	BHTM		WHF	BHF	WHTF	BHTF
	(N=546)	(N=101)	(N=279)	(N=52)		(N=219)	(N=62)	(N=100)	(N=39)
During [the time you were growing up], how afraid were you of your mother?									
Not at all	42%	56%	39%	71%		44%	50%	46%	44%
Very little	32	22	41	25		22	21	27	18
Somewhat	18	15	16	2		19	16	22	23
Very much	8	7	4	2		15	13	5	15
	(N=547)	(N=102)	(N=279)	(N=51)		(N=0)	(N=0)	(N=0)	(N=0)
How much did your mother act like a girlfriend or lover to you?									
Not at all	58%	63%	67%	78%		[not asked of females]			
Very little	20	18	24	14					
Somewhat	14	11	7	6					
Very much	8	9	2	2					
	(N=550)	(N=103)	(N=282)	(N=53)		(N=221)	(N=64)	(N=99)	(N=39)
How happy do you think your mother was about being a woman?									
Not too happy	11%	5%	12%	2%		26%	17%	15%	5%
Pretty happy	26	15	38	19		33	27	28	15
Very happy	57	68	38	70		37	42	53	69
Don't know	6	13	12	9		4	14	4	10
	(N=533)	(N=97)	(N=273)	(N=53)		(N=208)	(N=61)	(N=95)	(N=39)
Between the ages of 12 and 17, how much friction or bad feeling was there between you and your mother?									
None	26%	36%	20%	53%		14%	30%	25%	36%
Very little	35	24	35	32		24	28	29	18
Some	24	25	32	11		25	15	28	31
Much	16	15	14	4		37	28	17	15

MOTHERS/Mother-Child Relationships

During the time you were growing up, which parent did you talk most freely and easily with?

	WHM	BHM	WHTM	BHTM	WHF	BHF	WHTF	BHTF
	(N=538)	(N=100)	(N=275)	(N=53)	(N=209)	(N=60)	(N=99)	(N=38)
Father	5%	10%	15%	8%	19%	18%	20%	13%
Mother	81	79	58	75	54	45	53	53
Both	5	2	13	9	4	7	16	11
Neither	9	9	14	8	23	30	11	24

As you think about the relationship you had with your mother during the time you were growing up, I would like you to circle the number at each of these items which indicates best the way she behaved to you. For example, if your mother was extremely involved with you, you would circle 6. On the other hand, if she was extremely detached from you, you would circle 0.

A. Involved with me/ detached from me

	WHM	BHM	WHTM	BHTM	WHF	BHF	WHTF	BHTF
	(N=543)	(N=103)	(N=279)	(N=52)	(N=219)	(N=63)	(N=98)	(N=39)
0 Detached from me	1%	1%	1%	2%	5%	10%	3%	0%
1	3	3	1	0	12	10	3	0
2	5	6	9	4	11	2	7	0
3	16	17	15	15	16	25	20	31
4	22	22	31	23	11	14	20	18
5	24	20	26	17	20	17	20	10
6 Involved with me	29	31	18	38	25	22	26	41

B. Not hostile toward me/hostile toward me

	WHM	BHM	WHTM	BHTM	WHF	BHF	WHTF	BHTF
	(N=543)	(N=103)	(N=279)	(N=52)	(N=219)	(N=63)	(N=98)	(N=39)
0 Hostile toward me	3%	4%	4%	2%	5%	14%	3%	10%
1	5	5	3	2	7	5	3	3
2	4	3	6	10	6	5	6	3
3	10	13	13	12	18	19	15	10
4	9	8	10	4	8	6	6	3
5	22	15	29	13	20	3	12	18
6 Not hostile toward me	47	53	36	58	36	48	54	54

MOTHERS/Mother-Child Relationships

	WHM	BHM	WHTM	BHTM	WHF	BHF	WHTF	BHTF

C. Rejecting of me/ accepting of me

	WHM	BHM	WHTM	BHTM	WHF	BHF	WHTF	BHTF
	(N=543)	(N=103)	(N=279)	(N=52)	(N=218)	(N=62)	(N=98)	(N=39)
0 Accepting of me	43%	55%	31%	56%	27%	37%	43%	56%
1	20	17	27	17	15	6	19	13
2	10	5	17	12	10	6	11	15
3	13	7	13	6	17	19	10	5
4	4	6	5	6	6	5	5	3
5	6	4	6	4	17	15	6	3
6 Rejecting of me	4	7	1	0	9	11	5	5

D. Non-controlling with me/ controlling with me

	WHM	BHM	WHTM	BHTM	WHF	BHF	WHTF	BHTF
	(N=543)	(N=103)	(N=278)	(N=52)	(N=219)	(N=63)	(N=98)	(N=39)
0 Controlling with me	14%	21%	8%	8%	17%	29%	21%	36%
1	13	15	15	15	16	11	12	5
2	16	9	24	17	13	8	19	5
3	28	27	25	31	16	17	18	33
4	8	12	13	19	11	13	7	10
5	11	9	12	8	12	11	14	5
6 Non-controlling with me	8	8	4	2	15	11	7	5

E. Overprotective with me/ non-protective with me

	WHM	BHM	WHTM	BHTM	WHF	BHF	WHTF	BHTF
	(N=543)	(N=103)	(N=278)	(N=52)	(N=219)	(N=63)	(N=98)	(N=39)
0 Non-protective with me	3%	10%	5%	0%	10%	10%	9%	10%
1	7	10	9	6	12	8	9	8
2	10	5	12	13	9	10	10	5
3	24	33	31	42	24	27	20	38
4	13	11	21	25	10	5	24	10
5	19	12	13	8	10	10	12	8
6 Overprotective with me	24	20	9	6	25	32	14	21

F. Fair toward me/ unfair toward me

	WHM	BHM	WHTM	BHTM	WHF	BHF	WHTF	BHTF
	(N=542)	(N=103)	(N=279)	(N=52)	(N=219)	(N=63)	(N=98)	(N=39)
0 Unfair toward me	3%	4%	1%	0%	6%	16%	4%	0%
1	5	6	4	4	6	6	3	5
2	6	3	6	2	12	6	9	5
3	21	12	22	10	23	13	13	18
4	11	14	14	10	11	5	11	10
5	22	22	28	27	11	14	27	18
6 Fair toward me	31	40	25	48	24	40	33	44

MOTHERS/Mother-Child Relationships

In addition to what we have just covered, how would you describe your relationship with your mother, including your own feelings and reactions to her, during the time you were growing up?

	WHM	BHM	WHTM	BHTM	WHF	BHF	WHTF	BHTF
A. Closeness, involvement, close-binding	(N=533)	(N=103)	(N=274)	(N=53)	(N=216)	(N=63)	(N=96)	(N=39)
Felt close to mother	47%	35%	21%	21%	18%	22%	25%	33%
Felt distant from mother	11	14	16	4	23	24	18	18
Closeness/distance varied	5	3	2	0	6	3	3	5
No mention of closeness/distance	38	49	62	75	53	51	54	44
B. Affection	(N=523)	(N=96)	(N=272)	(N=53)	(N=206)	(N=62)	(N=96)	(N=39)
Mentioned love, warmth, etc.	57%	58%	52%	79%	43%	44%	55%	74%
Mentioned dislike, hatred, etc.	7	6	4	4	13	10	6	3
Amount of affection varied	2	2	3	0	3	2	3	0
No mention of affection/dislike	33	33	41	17	41	45	35	23
C. Regard, esteem	(N=539)	(N=103)	(N=273)	(N=53)	(N=216)	(N=63)	(N=98)	(N=39)
Admired, respected mother	18%	21%	16%	40%	12%	14%	19%	10%
Did not admire, respect mother	4	0	1	2	4	3	2	3
Regard-esteem varied	1	1	2	0	3	0	2	0
No mention of regard-esteem	77	78	81	58	81	83	77	87
D. Negative feelings	(N=537)	(N=103)	(N=274)	(N=53)	(N=218)	(N=63)	(N=98)	(N=39)
Mentioned anger, hostility, etc.	28%	27%	21%	8%	42%	29%	23%	31%
Afraid of mother	3	2	1	2	4	3	2	0
Negative feelings varied	3	1	3	0	4	2	3	0
No mention of negative feelings	66	70	75	91	50	67	71	69
E. Similarity	(N=539)	(N=103)	(N=274)	(N=53)	(N=218)	(N=63)	(N=98)	(N=39)
Much or some similarity	6%	3%	1%	0%	2%	0%	1%	3%
Little or no similarity	3	0	1	4	5	2	3	0
Feelings of similarity varied	0	0	0	0	0	0	1	0
No mention of similarity	92	97	98	96	93	98	95	97

5

MOTHERS/Mother-Child Relationships; Identification with Mother

	WHM	BHM	WHTM	BHTM	WHF	BHF	WHTF	BHTF
F. Relationship as a whole	(N=532)	(N=101)	(N=269)	(N=53)	(N=214)	(N=62)	(N=97)	(N=39)
Generally or entirely positive	65%	67%	70%	92%	39%	48%	66%	85%
Neutral or varying	15	12	13	4	15	11	14	5
Generally or entirely negative	22	21	17	4	46	40	20	10
While you were growing up, to what extent did you feel like or similar to your mother?	(N=543)	(N=103)	(N=279)	(N=53)	(N=219)	(N=62)	(N=99)	(N=39)
Not at all	15%	21%	17%	28%	37%	24%	15%	18%
Very little	20	24	31	32	25	37	26	21
Somewhat	39	33	39	38	24	26	43	51
Very much	26	22	13	2	14	13	15	10
To what extent did you want to be the kind of person your mother was?	(N=542)	(N=103)	(N=278)	(N=53)	(N=221)	(N=61)	(N=100)	(N=39)
Not at all	19%	25%	24%	21%	47%	26%	15%	18%
Very little	23	21	31	26	19	25	23	15
Somewhat	34	35	33	42	22	34	33	44
Very much	24	18	12	11	13	15	29	23
How much would you say your father wanted you to be the kind of person your mother was?	(N=0)	(N=0)	(N=0)	(N=0)	(N=200)	(N=57)	(N=93)	(N=34)
In no way	[not asked of males]				27%	18%	8%	9%
In very few ways					22	18	16	9
In some ways					30	44	30	50
In most ways					22	21	46	32

6

MOTHERS/Mothers' Personal Traits

Now, I'd like you to describe, by circling the numbers below, the kind of person your mother was during the time you were growing up. For example, if your mother was extremely adequate you would circle 6. On the other hand, if she was extremely inadequate you would circle 0.

	WHM (N=541)	BHM (N=103)	WHTM (N=280)	BHTM (N=52)	WHF (N=219)	BHF (N=63)	WHTF (N=98)	BHTF (N=38)
A. Adequate/inadequate								
0 Inadequate	2%	1%	1%	0%	6%	5%	3%	5%
1	2	2	3	2	7	2	1	0
2	8	3	6	2	13	6	8	3
3	11	12	14	8	14	14	15	18
4	18	12	21	8	16	19	11	5
5	28	28	35	17	14	21	20	21
6 Adequate	31	43	20	63	29	33	41	47

	WHM (N=543)	BHM (N=103)	WHTM (N=280)	BHTM (N=52)	WHF (N=219)	BHF (N=63)	WHTF (N=98)	BHTF (N=39)
B. Strong/weak								
0 Weak	2%	2%	1%	0%	7%	6%	1%	5%
1	4	5	5	2	5	8	2	5
2	7	6	10	6	8	5	13	3
3	13	12	17	4	15	5	9	15
4	19	12	22	23	13	13	19	8
5	27	21	30	19	18	21	20	15
6 Strong	28	43	15	46	35	43	35	49

	WHM (N=542)	BHM (N=103)	WHTM (N=280)	BHTM (N=52)	WHF (N=219)	BHF (N=63)	WHTF (N=98)	BHTF (N=39)
C. Active/passive								
0 Passive	1%	3%	0%	0%	5%	3%	2%	8%
1	4	6	5	4	4	8	4	3
2	5	3	9	0	13	8	8	15
3	10	9	16	6	12	6	10	10
4	17	17	19	15	12	19	14	10
5	27	25	28	37	20	17	27	10
6 Active	37	37	23	38	34	38	35	44

7

MOTHERS/Mothers' Personal Traits

	WHM (N=543)	BHM (N=103)	WHTM (N=280)	BHTM (N=52)	WHF (N=217)	BHF (N=63)	WHTF (N=98)	BHTF (N=39)
D. Warm/cold								
0 Cold	2%	3%	1%	0%	10%	10%	0%	5%
1	3	0	3	2	9	8	5	0
2	6	3	6	2	8	5	7	10
3	13	10	14	6	16	11	15	8
4	17	11	20	12	9	11	13	5
5	24	23	28	37	20	19	15	21
6 Warm	35	50	29	42	27	37	44	51
	(N=540)	(N=103)	(N=280)	(N=52)	(N=218)	(N=63)	(N=98)	(N=39)
E. Successful/unsuccessful								
0 Unsuccessful	3%	3%	1%	2%	9%	11%	0%	8%
1	6	6	6	0	8	3	3	0
2	6	8	10	0	9	11	10	5
3	19	14	26	12	18	11	18	15
4	24	19	19	13	15	24	15	15
5	22	27	24	33	19	16	23	21
6 Successful	20	23	14	38	22	24	30	36
	(N=543)	(N=103)	(N=280)	(N=52)	(N=217)	(N=63)	(N=98)	(N=39)
F. Pleasant/unpleasant								
0 Unpleasant	1%	0%	1%	0%	3%	3%	0%	3%
1	4	1	1	2	4	5	3	3
2	4	2	6	4	8	10	4	3
3	12	16	12	4	17	5	10	13
4	17	8	22	13	17	17	16	13
5	25	24	31	25	22	19	22	8
6 Pleasant	38	50	27	52	30	41	44	59
	(N=543)	(N=103)	(N=280)	(N=52)	(N=219)	(N=63)	(N=98)	(N=39)
G. Masculine/feminine								
0 Feminine	42%	46%	31%	58%	37%	52%	52%	56%
1	22	21	35	27	21	21	20	21
2	17	16	19	6	12	10	12	10
3	10	9	11	6	15	11	11	10
4	5	3	3	2	8	2	1	3
5	3	2	1	2	5	5	2	0
6 Masculine	1	4	0	0	1	0	1	0

8

MOTHERS/Mothers' Personal Traits

	WHM (N=543)	BHM (N=103)	WHTM (N=279)	BHTM (N=52)	WHF (N=219)	BHF (N=63)	WHTF (N=98)	BHTF (N=39)
H. Relaxed/uptight								
0 Uptight	10%	7%	5%	6%	26%	11%	11%	13%
1	14	6	13	2	18	14	11	3
2	17	12	25	6	16	6	13	13
3	24	22	25	21	17	30	21	28
4	18	23	13	17	9	14	19	10
5	12	21	13	31	7	14	11	18
6 Relaxed	5	9	6	17	7	10	12	15
I. Dominant/submissive	(N=542)	(N=102)	(N=280)	(N=52)	(N=218)	(N=63)	(N=98)	(N=39)
0 Submissive	4%	7%	5%	2%	8%	8%	6%	13%
1	6	12	8	8	7	11	7	0
2	10	8	19	10	12	8	7	8
3	21	21	32	33	17	25	33	38
4	18	15	13	31	14	6	21	15
5	21	15	15	10	14	14	14	13
6 Dominant	19	24	8	8	28	27	11	13
J. Conforming/non-conforming	(N=543)	(N=103)	(N=279)	(N=52)	(N=219)	(N=63)	(N=98)	(N=39)
0 Non-conforming	1%	4%	3%	0%	4%	8%	5%	8%
1	7	7	6	2	6	5	5	8
2	8	8	13	8	10	10	9	10
3	15	23	24	29	20	16	20	31
4	20	21	17	23	9	13	22	15
5	26	21	26	27	25	24	21	5
6 Conforming	22	16	11	12	26	25	16	23
K. Independent/dependent	(N=543)	(N=103)	(N=280)	(N=52)	(N=219)	(N=63)	(N=98)	(N=39)
0 Dependent	7%	6%	2%	4%	10%	5%	12%	8%
1	7	7	12	4	12	5	5	0
2	11	7	18	6	11	8	5	5
3	20	10	22	12	16	21	17	10
4	18	13	21	13	14	21	29	13
5	19	20	16	37	16	33	14	13
6 Independent	19	38	9	25	21		17	51

MOTHERS/Mothers' Personal Traits

	WHM (N=543)	BHM (N=103)	WHTM (N=280)	BHTM (N=52)	WHF (N=219)	BHF (N=63)	WHTF (N=98)	BHTF (N=39)
L. Healthy/sickly								
0 Sickly	3%	5%	1%	0%	7%	5%	2%	8%
1	4	2	3	2	7	5	2	0
2	10	11	8	4	8	2	4	3
3	11	12	15	6	13	8	12	10
4	12	14	16	10	11	14	13	13
5	27	23	30	25	25	22	22	15
6 Healthy	33	34	26	54	30	44	44	51

Now, looking back, if you had one word to describe your mother during the time you were growing up, what would it be?

	WHM (N=544)	BHM (N=103)	WHTM (N=277)	BHTM (N=52)	WHF (N=221)	BHF (N=63)	WHTF (N=99)	BHTF (N=38)
Close, nurturant, involved	7%	5%	8%	2%	5%	2%	7%	3%
Warm, friendly	13	10	13	17	7	8	16	13
Exuberant, fun	2	0	0	2	2	0	3	0
Attractive	4	12	1	2	5	8	4	5
Steadfast	2	4	5	4	2	0	2	0
Happy	1	0	1	10	1	2	1	3
The greatest, the best	7	14	4	6	2	13	9	26
Competent	1	3	3	2	0	0	2	0
A decent human being	13	7	10	15	10	19	17	16
Tranquil, serene	0	1	1	0	0	0	0	0
Other positive word	2	2	1	4	2	0	1	3
Controlling, demanding	10	7	8	2	9	3	0	3
Cold, remote, uninvolved	2	0	4	0	6	3	1	3
Weak, passive, indecisive	1	2	3	2	5	6	2	0
Hostile	0	1	0	2	2	3	1	0
Incompetent	2	1	1	0	1	5	1	5
Irresponsible	0	1	0	0	1	0	0	3
Rigid	0	0	0	0	2	3	0	0
Unhappy	3	4	4	2	5	3	3	5
Messed up, unstable	3	1	3	2	6	3	7	3
Other negative word	7	10	5	4	12	6	5	5
Proper, prim, a lady	2	2	2	0	1	0	2	3
Abused victim	2	0	1	0	2	2	1	0
Glamorous, a movie star	0	1	0	2	0	0	0	0
Rebellious, nonconforming, forceful	3	4	3	13	3	3	2	0
Other ambiguous word	4	5	7	2	5	5	3	3
Neutral word (just plain Mom, young, etc.)	5	6	9	6	4	3	6	5

MOTHERS/Mother Surrogate

Now I am going to ask you some questions about the female who in some sense substituted for your mother. Who was she?

	WHM	BHM	WHTM	BHTM	WHF	BHF	WHTF	BHTF
	(N=61)	(N=25)	(N=16)	(N=3)	(N=25)	(N=14)	(N=9)	(N=2)
Stepmother	26%	24%	62%	0%	20%	14%	0%	0%
Foster or adoptive mother	25	4	12	0	28	29	22	0
Grandmother	18	24	19	33	32	21	33	50
Aunt	13	44	0	33	8	21	33	50
Other female relative	13	0	6	33	0	14	0	0
Some other person	5	4	0	0	12	0	11	0

II

MOTHERS/Mother Surrogate-Child Relationships

	WHM	BHM	WHTM	BHTM	WHF	BHF	WHTF	BHTF
	(N=61)	(N=25)	(N=16)	(N=3)	(N=25)	(N=14)	(N=9)	(N=2)
During the time you were growing up, how afraid were you of your [mother surrogate]?								
Not at all	41%	44%	50%	100%	72%	64%	44%	50%
Very little	31	32	19	0	12	29	22	50
Somewhat	16	16	25	0	4	7	11	0
Very much	11	8	6	0	12	0	22	0
	(N=61)	(N=25)	(N=16)	(N=3)	(N=0)	(N=0)	(N=0)	(N=0)
How much did your [mother surrogate] act like a girlfriend or lover to you?								
Not at all	61%	60%	69%	67%		[not asked of females]		
Very little	23	24	19	0				
Somewhat	8	16	12	33				
Very much	8	0	0	0				
	(N=61)	(N=25)	(N=16)	(N=3)	(N=25)	(N=14)	(N=9)	(N=2)
How happy do you think your [mother surrogate] was about being a woman?								
Not too happy	10%	0%	6%	0%	16%	7%	11%	0%
Pretty happy	28	20	31	0	28	14	56	0
Very happy	54	80	56	100	56	71	22	100
Don't know	8	0	6	0	0	7	11	0

12

MOTHERS/Mother Surrogate-Child Relationships

	WHM	BHM	WHTM	BHTM	WHF	BHF	WHTF	BHTF
Between the ages of 12 and 17, how much friction or bad feeling was there between you and your [mother surrogate]?	(N=59)	(N=25)	(N=16)	(N=3)	(N=23)	(N=13)	(N=8)	(N=2)
None	24%	40%	12%	100%	39%	46%	50%	0%
Very little	36	28	38	0	9	15	0	50
Some	20	20	44	0	13	38	38	50
Much	20	12	6	0	39	0	12	0
During the time you were growing up, which did you talk most freely and easily with, your father or your [mother surrogate]?	(N=27)	(N=10)	(N=11)	(N=1)	(N=5)	(N=4)	(N=2)	(N=1)
Father	4%	0%	36%	0%	20%	0%	50%	0%
Mother surrogate	85	90	45	100	40	75	50	100
Both	4	0	0	0	0	0	0	0
Neither	7	10	18	0	40	25	0	0

As you think about the relationship you had with your [mother surrogate] during the time you were growing up, I would like you to circle the number at each of these items which indicates best the way she behaved toward you.

A.	WHM	BHM	WHTM	BHTM	WHF	BHF	WHTF	BHTF
Involved with me/detached from me	(N=60)	(N=25)	(N=16)	(N=3)	(N=25)	(N=14)	(N=9)	(N=2)
0 Detached from me	3%	4%	0%	0%	12%	0%	0%	0%
1	3	0	19	0	8	0	0	0
2	8	0	6	0	0	0	11	0
3	10	20	31	0	8	0	11	0
4	8	16	6	67	4	29	11	0
5	27	24	19	0	28	21	22	50
6 Involved with me	40	36	19	33	40	50	44	50

13

MOTHERS/Mother Surrogate-Child Relationships

	WHM	BHM	WHTM	BHTM	WHF	BHF	WHTF	BHTF
	(N=60)	(N=25)	(N=16)	(N=3)	(N=25)	(N=14)	(N=9)	(N=2)

B. Not hostile toward me/hostile toward me

	WHM	BHM	WHTM	BHTM	WHF	BHF	WHTF	BHTF
0 Hostile toward me	12%	4%	6%	0%	12%	7%	11%	0%
1	5	0	0	0	8	7	11	0
2	5	8	12	0	8	0	11	0
3	8	8	25	0	0	0	11	0
4	7	8	19	33	0	7	0	0
5	13	12	12	0	36	21	22	0
6 Not hostile toward me	50	64	25	67	36	57	33	100

C. Rejecting of me/accepting of me

	WHM	BHM	WHTM	BHTM	WHF	BHF	WHTF	BHTF
	(N=60)	(N=25)	(N=16)	(N=3)	(N=25)	(N=14)	(N=9)	(N=2)
0 Accepting of me	38%	44%	6%	33%	52%	57%	67%	0%
1	17	16	19	67	24	14	22	0
2	10	0	6	0	4	7	0	0
3	17	20	50	0	0	7	0	0
4	7	8	12	0	0	0	0	0
5	5	4	0	0	8	7	11	100
6 Rejecting of me	7	8	6	0	12	7	0	0

D. Non-controlling with me/controlling with me

	WHM	BHM	WHTM	BHTM	WHF	BHF	WHTF	BHTF
	(N=60)	(N=25)	(N=16)	(N=3)	(N=25)	(N=14)	(N=9)	(N=2)
0 Controlling with me	22%	8%	6%	33%	40%	29%	44%	0%
1	15	12	6	0	16	14	11	0
2	10	16	12	33	12	7	22	0
3	20	24	38	0	12	21	22	0
4	12	4	6	0	0	21	0	0
5	12	20	25	33	8	7	0	100
6 Non-controlling with me	10	16	6	0	12	0	0	0

E. Overprotective of me/non-protective of me

	WHM	BHM	WHTM	BHTM	WHF	BHF	WHTF	BHTF
	(N=60)	(N=25)	(N=16)	(N=3)	(N=25)	(N=14)	(N=9)	(N=2)
0 Non-protective of me	10%	8%	12%	0%	16%	0%	0%	0%
1	0	4	19	0	4	0	0	0
2	10	12	12	33	4	7	0	50
3	38	28	31	33	28	36	33	0
4	15	8	6	33	16	21	11	0
5	12	16	12	0	16	21	0	0

MOTHERS/Mother Surrogate-Child Relationships

	WHM	BHM	WHTM	BHTM	WHF	BHF	WHTF	BHTF
F. Fair toward me/unfair toward me	(N=61)	(N=25)	(N=16)	(N=3)	(N=25)	(N=14)	(N=9)	(N=2)
0 Unfair toward me	5%	12%	6%	0%	12%	0%	11%	0%
1	5	4	6	0	0	0	11	0
2	7	0	12	0	0	7	0	0
3	16	20	25	0	12	14	11	0
4	8	12	19	0	4	7	11	0
5	23	20	12	67	24	21	0	50
6 Fair toward me	36	32	19	33	48	50	56	50

In addition to what we have just covered, how would you describe your relationship with your [mother surrogate], including your own feelings and reactions to her, during the time you were growing up?

	WHM	BHM	WHTM	BHTM	WHF	BHF	WHTF	BHTF
A. Closeness, involvement, close-binding	(N=61)	(N=23)	(N=16)	(N=3)	(N=25)	(N=14)	(N=8)	(N=2)
Felt close to her	36%	35%	0%	0%	24%	21%	12%	0%
Felt distant from her	11	0	38	0	4	0	12	0
Closeness/distance varied	2	0	0	0	0	7	0	0
No mention of closeness/distance	51	65	62	100	72	71	75	100
B. Affection	(N=61)	(N=22)	(N=16)	(N=3)	(N=25)	(N=14)	(N=8)	(N=2)
Mentioned love, warmth, etc.	52%	59%	56%	100%	60%	64%	50%	100%
Mentioned dislike, hatred, etc.	18	5	19	0	20	0	25	0
Amount of affection varied	3	0	0	0	0	7	0	0
No mention of affection/dislike	26	36	25	0	20	29	25	0
C. Regard, esteem	(N=61)	(N=25)	(N=16)	(N=3)	(N=25)	(N=14)	(N=8)	(N=2)
Admired, respected her	25%	24%	12%	33%	32%	36%	25%	0%
Did not admire, respect her	.3	0	6	0	0	0	0	0
Regard-esteem varied	0	0	0	0	0	0	0	0
No mention of regard-esteem	72	76	81	67	68	64	75	100

15

MOTHERS/Mother Surrogate-Child Relationships; Identification with Mother Surrogate

	WHM	BHM	WHTM	BHTM	WHF	BHF	WHTF	BHTF
D. Negative feelings	(N=61)	(N=25)	(N=16)	(N=3)	(N=25)	(N=14)	(N=8)	(N=2)
Mentioned anger, hostility, etc.	25%	20%	62%	0%	16%	14%	12%	0%
Afraid of mother surrogate	3	4	0	0	0	0	12	0
Negative feelings varied	2	0	0	0	0	0	0	0
No mention of negative feelings	70	76	38	100	84	86	75	100
E. Similarity	(N=61)	(N=25)	(N=16)	(N=3)	(N=25)	(N=14)	(N=8)	(N=2)
Much or some similarity	3%	4%	0%	0%	0%	0%	0%	0%
Little or no similarity	0	0	0	0	4	0	0	0
Feelings of similarity varied	0	0	0	0	0	0	0	0
No mention of similarity	97	96	100	100	96	100	100	100
F. Relationship as a whole	(N=61)	(N=25)	(N=16)	(N=3)	(N=24)	(N=13)	(N=8)	(N=2)
Generally or entirely positive	64%	68%	38%	100%	67%	85%	62%	100%
Neutral or varying	8	8	6	0	4	8	0	0
Generally or entirely negative	28	24	56	0	29	8	38	0
While you were growing up, to what extent did you feel like or similar to your [mother surrogate]?	(N=28)	(N=12)	(N=11)	(N=1)	(N=7)	(N=4)	(N=3)	(N=1)
Not at all	25%	17%	45%	0%	43%	50%	0%	0%
Very little	25	17	45	0	14	25	67	100
Somewhat	36	50	9	100	29	25	33	0
Very much	14	17	0	0	14	0	0	0
To what extent did you want to be the kind of person your [mother surrogate] was?	(N=29)	(N=11)	(N=11)	(N=1)	(N=7)	(N=4)	(N=3)	(N=1)
Not at all	45%	27%	45%	0%	29%	25%	0%	0%
Very little	3	18	36	0	0	25	33	0
Somewhat	38	36	18	100	57	25	33	100
Very much	14	18	0	0	14	25	33	0

MOTHERS/Identification with Mother Surrogate

	WHM	BHM	WHTM	BHTM	WHF	BHF	WHTF	BHTF
How much would you say your father wanted you to be the kind of person your [mother surrogate] was?	(N=0)	(N=0)	(N=0)	(N=0)	(N=5)	(N=4)	(N=3)	(N=0)
In no way					20%	25%	0%	
In very few ways		[not asked of males]			20	0	33	
In some ways					20	50	0	
In most ways					40	25	67	
How much would you say your [father surrogate] wanted you to be the kind of person your [mother/mother surrogate] was?	(N=0)	(N=0)	(N=0)	(N=0)	(N=39)	(N=14)	(N=9)	(N=8)
In no way					28%	21%	11%	38%
In very few ways		[not asked of males]			18	14	44	12
In some ways					26	29	22	50
In most ways					28	36	22	0

17

MOTHERS/Mother Surrogates' Personal Traits

Now, I'd like you to describe, by circling the numbers below, the kind of person your [mother surrogate] was during the time you were growing up. For example, if she was extremely adequate, you would circle 6. On the other hand, if she was extremely inadequate, you would circle 0.

A. Adequate/inadequate

	WHM (N=61)	BHM (N=25)	WHTM (N=16)	BHTM (N=3)	WHF (N=25)	BHF (N=14)	WHTF (N=8)	BHTF (N=2)
0 Inadequate	2%	0%	12%	0%	20%	0%	0%	0%
1	3	0	0	0	0	0	0	0
2	5	0	19	0	16	0	0	0
3	10	12	25	0	4	14	12	0
4	15	20	19	33	4	29	12	50
5	28	16	12	33	32	29	0	50
6 Adequate	38	52	12	33	24	29	75	0

B. Strong/weak

	WHM (N=61)	BHM (N=25)	WHTM (N=16)	BHTM (N=3)	WHF (N=25)	BHF (N=14)	WHTF (N=8)	BHTF (N=2)
0 Weak	2%	0%	0%	0%	16%	0%	0%	0%
1	5	4	6	0	0	0	0	0
2	5	4	6	0	12	7	12	0
3	11	20	19	0	4	14	0	100
4	16	16	12	33	28	29	0	0
5	21	16	38	33	40	7	0	0
6 Strong	39	56	19	33	—	43	88	0

C. Active/passive

	WHM (N=61)	BHM (N=25)	WHTM (N=16)	BHTM (N=3)	WHF (N=25)	BHF (N=14)	WHTF (N=8)	BHTF (N=2)
0 Passive	2%	4%	6%	0%	12%	0%	0%	0%
1	3	0	6	0	4	0	0	0
2	7	16	0	0	4	0	0	50
3	7	16	25	0	4	29	0	50
4	21	24	6	0	16	7	38	0
5	16	40	19	67	20	14	12	0
6 Active	44	—	38	33	40	50	50	0

MOTHERS/Mother Surrogates' Personal Traits

	WHM	BHM	WHTM	BHTM	WHF	BHF	WHTF	BHTF
D. Warm/cold	(N=61)	(N=24)	(N=16)	(N=3)	(N=25)	(N=14)	(N=8)	(N=2)
0 Cold	8%	4%	6%	0%	8%	7%	0%	0%
1	3	4	6	0	8	0	12	0
2	2	0	19	0	4	14	12	0
3	15	17	19	0	8	0	0	0
4	13	8	12	0	16	14	25	0
5	20	25	25	67	20	7	25	0
6 Warm	39	42	12	33	36	57	50	100
E. Successful/unsuccessful	(N=61)	(N=25)	(N=16)	(N=3)	(N=25)	(N=14)	(N=8)	(N=2)
0 Unsuccessful	2%	0%	0%	0%	16%	0%	0%	0%
1	3	8	6	0	8	0	0	0
2	7	8	6	0	4	7	0	0
3	15	8	44	0	8	21	38	50
4	20	16	12	33	12	21	38	50
5	21	28	19	67	28	29	12	0
6 Successful	33	32	12	0	24	21	12	0
F. Pleasant/unpleasant	(N=61)	(N=25)	(N=16)	(N=3)	(N=25)	(N=14)	(N=8)	(N=2)
0 Unpleasant	3%	0%	0%	0%	0%	0%	0%	0%
1	5	4	0	0	4	0	12	0
2	2	0	12	0	8	0	0	0
3	11	12	19	0	8	7	0	0
4	15	16	19	0	12	14	25	0
5	20	20	25	67	28	29	25	0
6 Pleasant	44	48	25	33	40	50	38	100
G. Masculine/feminine	(N=60)	(N=25)	(N=16)	(N=3)	(N=25)	(N=14)	(N=8)	(N=2)
0 Feminine	40%	40%	25%	33%	36%	43%	50%	50%
1	18	16	12	33	28	29	0	0
2	12	8	31	33	12	7	12	50
3	12	20	19	0	8	0	12	0
4	13	4	12	0	8	7	25	0
5	3	0	0	0	4	7	0	0
6 Masculine	2	12	0	0	4	7	0	0

MOTHERS/Mother Surrogates' Personal Traits

H. Relaxed/up-tight

	WHM (N=61)	BHM (N=25)	WHTM (N=16)	BHTM (N=3)	WHF (N=25)	BHF (N=14)	WHTF (N=8)	BHTF (N=2)
0 Up-tight	11%	0%	19%	0%	20%	0%	12%	0%
1	3	8	12	0	12	0	0	0
2	13	8	6	0	20	7	12	0
3	20	28	19	0	4	29	38	0
4	15	16	31	33	24	29	25	100
5	20	20	6	67	16	14	12	0
6 Relaxed	18	20	6	0	4	21	0	0

I. Dominant/submissive

	WHM (N=61)	BHM (N=25)	WHTM (N=16)	BHTM (N=3)	WHF (N=24)	BHF (N=14)	WHTF (N=8)	BHTF (N=2)
0 Submissive	7%	4%	6%	0%	12%	14%	12%	0%
1	13	0	12	33	0	7	0	0
2	7	12	6	0	8	0	0	0
3	16	16	19	33	21	36	12	100
4	13	12	19	0	8	0	12	0
5	16	20	25	33	8	21	25	0
6 Dominant	28	36	12	0	42	21	38	0

J. Conforming/non-conforming

	WHM (N=61)	BHM (N=25)	WHTM (N=16)	BHTM (N=3)	WHF (N=25)	BHF (N=14)	WHTF (N=8)	BHTF (N=2)
0 Non-conforming	5%	16%	6%	0%	8%	7%	0%	0%
1	3	4	0	0	8	0	0	0
2	13	8	19	0	0	21	12	0
3	11	12	25	0	12	43	25	0
4	13	24	12	33	16	14	38	50
5	20	8	19	67	28	14	25	0
6 Conforming	34	28	19	0	28	0	0	50

K. Independent/dependent

	WHM (N=61)	BHM (N=25)	WHTM (N=16)	BHTM (N=3)	WHF (N=24)	BHF (N=14)	WHTF (N=8)	BHTF (N=2)
0 Dependent	5%	4%	12%	0%	8%	0%	12%	0%
1	10	0	12	33	0	7	0	0
2	8	0	19	33	0	0	12	50
3	10	16	25	0	25	29	25	0
4	25	16	12	33	17	14	38	50
5	13	12	12	0	4	7	12	0
6 Independent	30	52	6	0	46	43	50	0

MOTHERS/Mother Surrogates' Personal Traits

L. Healthy/sickly

	WHM (N=61)	BHM (N=25)	WHTM (N=16)	BHTM (N=3)	WHF (N=25)	BHF (N=14)	WHTF (N=8)	BHTF (N=2)
0 Sickly	2%	8%	12%	0%	16%	0%	0%	0%
1	5	4	0	0	4	14	0	0
2	5	8	0	0	8	7	0	0
3	8	20	12	0	4	14	25	0
4	10	12	19	33	12	7	12	0
5	16	16	31	33	12	36	12	50
6 Healthy	54	32	25	33	44	21	50	50

FATHERS/Father-Child Relationships

	WHM	BHM	WHTM	BHTM	WHF	BHF	WHTF	BHTF
During the time you were growing up, how afraid were you of your father?	(N=520)	(N=91)	(N=268)	(N=51)	(N=209)	(N=55)	(N=98)	(N=36)
Not at all	25%	41%	18%	59%	40%	45%	40%	44%
Very little	21	15	29	20	20	16	21	19
Somewhat	27	25	36	12	16	20	26	19
Very much	26	19	17	10	24	18	13	17
How much did your father act like a boyfriend or lover to you?	(N=0)	(N=0)	(N=0)	(N=0)	(N=206)	(N=57)	(N=96)	(N=36)
Not at all		[not asked of males]			70%	81%	75%	83%
Very little					11	9	15	14
Somewhat					11	5	9	3
Very much					8	5	1	0
Between the ages of 12 and 17, how much friction or bad feeling was there between you and your father?	(N=483)	(N=82)	(N=253)	(N=50)	(N=195)	(N=53)	(N=93)	(N=31)
None	16%	27%	18%	46%	26%	38%	31%	35%
Very little	26	15	29	14	17	15	25	19
Some	23	24	29	28	25	19	24	19
Much	36	34	24	12	32	28	20	26

22

FATHERS/Father-Child Relationships

As you think about the relationship you had with your father during the time you were growing up, I would like you to circle the number at each of these items which indicates best the way he behaved to you.

	WHM	BHM	WHTM	BHTM	WHF	BHF	WHTF	BHTF
A. Involved with me/detached from me	(N=510)	(N=90)	(N=265)	(N=50)	(N=200)	(N=54)	(N=96)	(N=32)
0 Detached from me	18%	27%	6%	2%	16%	19%	6%	6%
1	23	13	12	8	14	7	5	9
2	23	16	17	20	14	13	9	22
3	16	16	18	8	14	19	16	12
4	10	10	18	8	16	7	19	9
5	7	10	19	18	14	7	28	19
6 Involved with me	4	9	10	34	12	28	17	22
B. Not hostile toward me/hostile toward me	(N=509)	(N=90)	(N=265)	(N=50)	(N=201)	(N=55)	(N=96)	(N=32)
0 Hostile toward me	9%	9%	2%	2%	8%	4%	8%	9%
1	6	11	3	4	6	7	1	3
2	12	14	10	10	10	7	7	0
3	17	13	21	18	13	13	16	19
4	14	10	15	10	7	7	9	3
5	17	21	25	16	17	9	16	25
6 Not hostile toward me	25	21	23	40	38	53	43	41
C. Rejecting of me/accepting of me	(N=509)	(N=90)	(N=264)	(N=50)	(N=201)	(N=54)	(N=96)	(N=32)
0 Accepting of me	14%	23%	16%	38%	22%	35%	45%	41%
1	14	16	19	22	15	4	11	9
2	16	12	21	10	14	9	11	3
3	21	19	25	16	22	22	15	22
4	14	8	11	6	6	7	5	9
5	11	10	3	8	10	6	4	9
6 Rejecting of me	10	12	5	0	9	17	8	6

FATHERS/Father-Child Relationships

D. Non-controlling with me/controlling with me

	WHM (N=509)	BHM (N=90)	WHTM (N=265)	BHTM (N=51)	WHF (N=201)	BHF (N=55)	WHTF (N=96)	BHTF (N=36)
0 Controlling with me	11%	22%	8%	10%	11%	22%	25%	44%
1	13	9	14	6	13	13	12	3
2	14	10	18	18	12	5	14	6
3	20	19	25	24	16	18	20	22
4	9	8	11	18	10	13	8	9
5	17	13	16	20	16	9	8	6
6 Non-controlling with me	16	19	8	4	21	20	12	9

E. Overprotective of me/non-protective of me

	WHM (N=510)	BHM (N=90)	WHTM (N=265)	BHTM (N=50)	WHF (N=201)	BHF (N=55)	WHTF (N=96)	BHTF (N=32)
0 Non-protective with me	18%	31%	7%	6%	14%	13%	7%	19%
1	16	18	16	12	8	15	12	6
2	17	11	16	20	15	11	8	0
3	32	26	41	28	30	24	24	34
4	7	6	14	24	11	18	12	9
5	5	2	4	8	8	7	20	16
6 Overprotective of me	4	7	2	2	12	13	16	16

F. Fair toward me/Unfair toward me

	WHM (N=511)	BHM (N=90)	WHTM (N=265)	BHTM (N=50)	WHF (N=201)	BHF (N=55)	WHTF (N=96)	BHTF (N=32)
0 Unfair toward me	8%	12%	2	2%	11%	4%	6%	16%
1	6	3	6	2	7	7	3	6
2	14	13	11	18	6	7	4	6
3	25	22	25	12	23	18	20	19
4	10	11	11	8	7	7	11	12
5	15	14	27	18	18	9	20	6
6 Fair toward me	22	23	18	40	22	47	35	34

FATHERS/Father-Child Relationships

In addition to what we have just covered, how would you describe your relationship with your father, including your own feelings and reactions to him during the time you were growing up?

	WHM	BHM	WHTM	BHTM	WHF	BHF	WHTF	BHTF
	(N=502)	(N=90)	(N=263)	(N=50)	(N=202)	(N=56)	(N=97)	(N=32)
A. Closeness, involvement, close-binding								
Felt close to father	5%	12%	12%	6%	13%	14%	26%	28%
Felt distant from father	59	48	38	20	39	29	22	28
Closeness/distance varied	5	3	7	2	8	7	6	3
No mention of closeness/distance	32	37	44	72	40	50	46	41
	(N=493)	(N=84)	(N=261)	(N=50)	(N=193)	(N=56)	(N=94)	(N=30)
B. Affection								
Mentioned love, warmth, etc.	23%	27%	36%	38%	34%	32%	47%	63%
Mentioned dislike, hatred, etc.	29	14	12	14	13	20	3	10
Amount of affection varied	4	6	1	0	7	4	6	3
No mention of affection/dislike	44	52	51	48	46	45	44	23
	(N=504)	(N=90)	(N=262)	(N=50)	(N=199)	(N=56)	(N=97)	(N=32)
C. Regard, esteem								
Admired, respected father	18%	14%	31%	50%	20%	14%	26%	12%
Did not admire, respect father	12	10	5	4	6	4	1	0
Regard-esteem varied	1	3	2	0	3	7	4	0
No mention of regard-esteem	68	72	63	46	71	75	69	88
	(N=503)	(N=90)	(N=264)	(N=50)	(N=203)	(N=56)	(N=97)	(N=32)
D. Negative feelings								
Mentioned anger, hostility, etc.	32%	31%	20%	10%	31%	20%	18%	19%
Afraid of father	16	10	9	4	14	5	5	0
Negative feelings varied	2	3	0	0	2	5	3	3
No mention of negative feelings	50	56	71	86	53	70	74	78
	(N=507)	(N=90)	(N=264)	(N=50)	(N=203)	(N=56)	(N=97)	(N=32)
E. Similarity								
Much or some similarity	2%	1%	6%	4%	4%	4%	7%	0%
Little or no similarity	15	2	4	4	3	0	0	0
Similarity varied	1	1	1	0	0	2	0	0
No mention of similarity	82	96	89	92	93	95	93	100

FATHERS/Father-Child Relationships; Identification with Father

	WHM	BHM	WHTM	BHTM	WHF	BHF	WHTF	BHTF
F. Relationship as a whole	(N=503)	(N=90)	(N=261)	(N=49)	(N=201)	(N=56)	(N=95)	(N=32)
Generally or entirely positive	22%	33%	49%	65%	32%	45%	77%	69%
Neutral or varying	25	28	20	16	28	27	16	16
Generally or entirely negative	53	39	31	18	39	27	18	16
To what extent did you feel like or similar to your father?	(N=529)	(N=94)	(N=269)	(N=52)	(N=211)	(N=59)	(N=98)	(N=37)
Not at all	31%	24%	11%	8%	24%	22%	13%	30%
Very little	41	32	23	12	21	20	14	11
Somewhat	22	36	44	52	30	22	46	43
Very much	6	7	22	29	25	36	27	16
To whom did you think you were more similar?	(N=147)	(N=29)	(N=101)	(N=9)	(N=60)	(N=14)	(N=38)	(N=16)
Father	14%	24%	41%	33%	23%	14%	42%	19%
Mother	56	62	35	33	43	43	42	62
Don't know	30	14	25	33	33	43	16	19
To what extent did you want to be the kind of person your father was?	(N=526)	(N=95)	(N=270)	(N=52)	(N=212)	(N=59)	(N=98)	(N=36)
Not at all	38%	37%	19%	15%	33%	27%	11%	36%
Very little	27	26	20	17	18	32	21	14
Somewhat	24	33	36	35	28	25	41	33
Very much	11	4	25	33	20	15	27	17
Who did you want to be most like?	(N=198)	(N=29)	(N=121)	(N=18)	(N=73)	(N=15)	(N=54)	(N=16)
Father	22%	24%	31%	39%	25%	13%	22%	12%
Mother	34	48	17	22	25	13	39	31
Don't know	44	28	53	39	51	73	39	56

FATHERS/Identification with Father

How much would you say your mother wanted you to be the kind of person your father was?

	WHM	BHM	WHTM	BHTM	WHF	BHF	WHTF	BHTF
	(N=535)	(N=98)	(N=269)	(N=53)	(N=0)	(N=0)	(N=0)	(N=0)
						[not asked of females]		
In no way	23%	33%	15%	9%				
In very few ways	25	26	16	15				
In some ways	34	29	43	55				
In most ways	18	13	26	21				

FATHERS/Fathers' Personal Traits

Now I'd like you to describe, by circling the numbers below, the kind of person your father was during the time you were growing up. For example, if your father was extremely adequate you would circle 6. On the other hand, if your father was extremely inadequate you would circle 0.

	WHM	BHM	WHTM	BHTM	WHF	BHF	WHTF	BHTF
A. Adequate/Inadequate	(N=512)	(N=91)	(N=266)	(N=50)	(N=201)	(N=54)	(N=96)	(N=33)
0 Inadequate	8%	13%	3%	2%	6%	7%	6%	12%
1	9	11	6	4	9	7	1	0
2	15	14	9	8	13	6	4	3
3	18	14	14	4	12	15	8	12
4	14	14	13	14	14	13	9	6
5	19	20	30	18	20	11	26	18
6 Adequate	17	13	25	50	25	41	45	48
B. Strong/weak	(N=513)	(N=91)	(N=266)	(N=50)	(N=201)	(N=54)	(N=95)	(N=33)
0 Weak	4%	4%	1%	0%	5%	7%	3%	3%
1	8	14	5	2	9	6	2	3
2	14	7	10	6	12	7	4	9
3	13	15	8	4	13	7	7	12
4	14	9	14	8	11	9	12	3
5	21	19	30	18	20	22	18	15
6 Strong	26	32	33	62	28	41	54	55

28

FATHERS/Fathers' Personal Traits

	WHM (N=512)	BHM (N=91)	WHTM (N=265)	BHTM (N=50)	WHF (N=200)	BHF (N=53)	WHTF (N=95)	BHTF (N=33)
C. Active/passive								
0 Passive	4%	5%	1%	2%	2%	2%	3%	6%
1	5	4	3	0	7	2	1	0
2	9	12	11	6	8	8	1	6
3	14	9	9	10	12	9	6	21
4	13	15	18	12	10	6	15	12
5	23	24	27	20	26	19	27	15
6 Active	32	30	30	50	34	55	46	39
	(N=513)	(N=91)	(N=266)	(N=50)	(N=201)	(N=53)	(N=96)	(N=33)
D. Warm/cold								
0 Cold	10%	9%	5%	4%	9%	11%	6%	6%
1	11	16	9	2	9	6	3	3
2	18	14	12	8	13	13	5	6
3	26	24	18	20	17	19	19	30
4	14	8	26	24	12	9	14	12
5	12	15	18	24	19	11	16	9
6 Warm	9	13	12	18	20	30	38	33
	(N=513)	(N=91)	(N=266)	(N=50)	(N=201)	(N=54)	(N=96)	(N=33)
E. Successful/unsuccessful								
0 Unsuccessful	6%	12%	3%	2%	7%	4%	6%	6%
1	9	8	6	6	6	2	4	3
2	10	13	8	2	9	7	6	3
3	17	22	15	12	16	30	14	24
4	17	12	24	16	14	11	8	6
5	19	15	22	20	23	22	19	12
6 Successful	22	18	23	42	25	24	43	45
	(N=511)	(N=91)	(N=266)	(N=50)	(N=200)	(N=54)	(N=96)	(N=33)
F. Pleasant/unpleasant								
0 Unpleasant	5%	8%	2%	4%	4%	4%	3%	6%
1	7	4	6	0	3	7	2	0
2	11	13	9	6	10	9	6	9
3	23	23	19	16	16	15	16	15
4	16	15	21	26	18	17	17	21
5	20	20	26	22	24	11	23	15
6 Pleasant	18	16	19	26	24	37	33	33

29

FATHERS/Fathers' Personal Traits

		WHM (N=512)	BHM (N=91)	WHTM (N=266)	BHTM (N=50)	WHF (N=201)	BHF (N=53)	WHTF (N=96)	BHTF (N=33)
G.	Masculine/feminine								
	0 Feminine	0%	1%	0%	2%	0%	0%	0%	0%
	1	0	0	0	0	1	2	0	3
	2	2	1	1	2	2	2	1	6
	3	9	5	5	4	10	8	5	3
	4	14	15	12	8	14	6	7	3
	5	27	26	36	16	28	17	28	15
	6 Masculine	48	51	45	68	45	66	58	70
		(N=511)	(N=91)	(N=265)	(N=50)	(N=201)	(N=53)	(N=95)	(N=33)
H.	Relaxed/up-tight								
	0 Up-tight	11%	8%	5%	2%	12%	2%	5%	15%
	1	13	9	8	4	12	9	11	0
	2	14	9	18	12	14	4	13	6
	3	20	18	22	20	19	25	15	27
	4	17	16	21	18	17	19	21	9
	5	12	24	18	32	11	15	20	15
	6 Relaxed	11	16	7	12	14	26	16	27
		(N=510)	(N=91)	(N=265)	(N=50)	(N=201)	(N=54)	(N=96)	(N=33)
I.	Dominant/submissive								
	0 Submissive	4%	9%	3%	2%	4%	4%	0%	6%
	1	7	4	4	4	5	4	4	3
	2	12	13	9	6	13	13	5	6
	3	22	18	14	18	20	15	10	33
	4	19	16	20	28	16	11	24	18
	5	17	18	30	18	20	20	23	15
	6 Dominant	20	22	20	24	21	33	33	18
		(N=513)	(N=91)	(N=263)	(N=50)	(N=201)	(N=53)	(N=96)	(N=33)
J.	Conforming/non-conforming								
	0 Non-conforming	5%	12%	3%	2%	6%	2%	6%	9%
	1	6	7	6	8	7	9	10	6
	2	11	13	13	10	11	15	15	9
	3	17	26	25	16	17	23	18	45
	4	18	15	17	20	15	23	12	6
	5	24	16	24	26	22	17	24	15
	6 Conforming	20	10	12	18	21	11	15	9

30

FATHERS/Fathers' Personal Traits

	WHM	BHM	WHTM	BHTM	WHF	BHF	WHTF	BHTF
K. Independent/dependent	(N=512)	(N=91)	(N=265)	(N=50)	(N=201)	(N=54)	(N=96)	(N=33)
0 Dependent	3%	5%	2%	0%	4%	4%	0%	0%
1	7	5	5	4	6	4	2	0
2	8	9	10	8	8	2	5	6
3	15	9	11	8	12	7	8	15
4	14	12	22	12	14	15	11	12
5	28	19	28	10	25	20	27	15
6 Independent	26	41	22	58	30	48	46	52
L. Healthy/sickly	(N=512)	(N=91)	(N=266)	(N=50)	(N=201)	(N=54)	(N=96)	(N=33)
0 Sickly	1%	1%	2%	0%	2%	0%	1%	0%
1	2	7	2	2	1	2	4	0
2	4	2	5	2	4	6	1	0
3	9	9	11	6	7	4	8	15
4	10	8	14	8	8	4	7	3
5	27	23	35	20	26	31	17	24
6 Healthy	48	51	32	62	50	54	61	58
Who made most of the decisions about the children?	(N=535)	(N=95)	(N=271)	(N=51)	(N=205)	(N=58)	(N=99)	(N=38)
Father	13%	18%	23%	16%	13%	19%	24%	11%
Mother	69	71	53	65	64	57	44	61
Decisions made jointly	16	11	23	20	19	21	30	26
Neither parent made most decisions	1	1	1	0	4	3	1	3
Who made most of the decisions about the children?	(N=27)	(N=12)	(N=11)	(N=1)	(N=5)	(N=4)	(N=3)	(N=1)
Father surrogate	19%	17%	18%	0%	40%	25%	33%	0%
Mother surrogate	67	67	45	100	20	50	33	100
Decisions made jointly	7	8	36	0	40	25	33	0
Neither made most decisions	7	8	0	0	0	0	0	0

FATHERS/Fathers' Personal Traits

	WHM	BHM	WHTM	BHTM	WHF	BHF	WHTF	BHTF
If you had one word to describe your father during [the time you were growing up], what would it be?	(N=521)	(N=94)	(N=265)	(N=51)	(N=210)	(N=56)	(N=98)	(N=35)
Close, nurturant, involved	2%	4%	3%	6%	2%	0%	4%	0%
Warm, friendly	3	2	4	2	7	4	13	6
Exuberant, fun	0	1	1	0	0	2	1	0
Attractive	1	1	0	2	0	2	0	3
Steadfast	1	0	3	2	2	0	3	0
Happy	2	0	1	8	0	0	2	3
The greatest, the best	3	4	3	4	2	11	10	20
Competent	2	0	6	0	1	2	4	3
A decent human being	8	14	7	12	7	16	12	11
Tranquil, serene	0	3	1	0	1	0	2	0
Other positive word	2	1	3	4	2	2	3	6
Controlling, demanding	6	5	8	8	6	7	6	3
Cold, remote, uninvolved	17	6	9	8	15	7	4	3
Weak, passive, indecisive	7	6	6	4	6	5	3	0
Hostile	3	1	2	4	6	2	4	0
Incompetent	2	4	0	0	1	2	0	3
Irresponsible	2	2	1	0	3	4	1	3
Rigid	2	1	2	2	1	2	1	0
Unhappy	2	4	3	2	3	2	4	0
Messed up, unstable	2	3	3	4	4	4	2	0
Other negative word	11	18	6	2	11	12	4	9
Proper, prim, a gentleman	1	0	1	0	0	0	2	3
Abused victim	1	0	2	0	1	0	0	0
Glamorous, a movie star	0	0	0	0	0	2	1	0
Rebellious, nonconforming, forceful	4	3	6	6	4	0	3	6
Other ambiguous word	7	9	8	12	4	5	4	6
Neutral word (just plain Dad, young, etc.)	10	5	11	10	5	9	5	14

FATHERS/Father Surrogate

Now, I am going to ask you some questions about the male who in some sense substituted for your father. Who was he?

	WHM	BHM	WHTM	BHTM	WHF	BHF	WHTF	BHTF
	(N=83)	(N=31)	(N=30)	(N=6)	(N=42)	(N=16)	(N=10)	(N=8)
Stepfather	57%	55%	60%	67%	50%	31%	50%	88%
Foster or adoptive father	18	3	7	0	14	25	10	0
Grandfather	8	10	13	17	14	12	10	12
Uncle	6	26	10	0	10	25	20	0
Other male relative	7	3	7	17	7	6	0	0
Some other person	4	3	3	0	5	0	10	0

FATHERS/Father Surrogate-Child Relationships

	WHM	BHM	WHTM	BHTM	WHF	BHF	WHTF	BHTF
During the time that you were growing up, how afraid were you of your [father surrogate]?	(N=83)	(N=31)	(N=30)	(N=6)	(N=42)	(N=16)	(N=10)	(N=8)
Not at all	29%	52%	33%	67%	43%	38%	50%	62%
Very little	23	23	17	17	24	25	40	12
Somewhat	25	13	40	17	19	19	10	0
Very much	23	13	10	0	14	19	0	25
How much did your [father surrogate] act like a boyfriend or lover to you?	(N=0)	(N=0)	(N=0)	(N=0)	(N=42)	(N=16)	(N=10)	(N=8)
Not at all	[not asked of males]				67%	69%	70%	88%
Very little					5	6	10	0
Somewhat					7	19	20	12
Very much					21	6	0	0
Between the ages of 12 and 17, how much friction or bad feeling was there between you and your [father surrogate]?	(N=80)	(N=29)	(N=30)	(N=6)	(N=41)	(N=14)	(N=10)	(N=8)
None	19%	38%	23%	50%	24%	36%	30%	12%
Very little	18	14	40	50	22	0	40	12
Some	26	21	13	0	12	36	30	38
Much	38	28	23	0	41	29	0	38
During the time you were growing up, which did you talk most freely and easily with, your [father surrogate] or your [mother/mother surrogate]?	(N=82)	(N=30)	(N=30)	(N=6)	(N=41)	(N=16)	(N=10)	(N=8)
Father surrogate	11%	10%	27%	50%	32%	12%	20%	0%
Female	65	73	50	50	44	50	50	62
Both	11	7	13	0	5	6	10	10
Neither	13	10	10	0	20	31	20	38

FATHERS/Father Surrogate-Child Relationships

As you think about the relationship you had with your [father surrogate] during the time you were growing up, I would like you to circle the number of each of these items which indicates best the way he behaved to you.

A. Involved with me/detached from me

	WHM	BHM	WHTM	BHTM	WHF	BHF	WHTF	BHTF
	(N=83)	(N=31)	(N=30)	(N=6)	(N=42)	(N=16)	(N=10)	(N=8)
0 Detached from me	20%	10%	17%	0%	7%	6%	0%	25%
1	11	13	7	0	12	6	10	12
2	13	19	17	0	7	6	0	0
3	18	19	17	17	7	38	30	0
4	14	16	17	50	17	6	30	38
5	8	16	17	17	12	19	30	25
6 Involved with me	14	6	10	17	38	19	0	0

FATHERS/Father Surrogate- Child Relationships

B. Not hostile toward me/hostile toward me

	WHM (N=83)	BHM (N=31)	WHTM (N=30)	BHTM (N=6)	WHF (N=42)	BHF (N=16)	WHTF (N=10)	BHTF (N=8)
0 Hostile toward me	16%	0%	3%	0%	7%	6%	0%	0%
1	6	16	10	0	7	0	0	12
2	11	6	7	0	7	6	0	12
3	19	10	20	17	0	25	30	25
4	5	3	17	67	2	19	10	0
5	10	29	20	17	26	19	0	38
6 Not hostile toward me	34	35	23		50	25	60	12

C. Rejecting of me/accepting of me

	WHM (N=83)	BHM (N=31)	WHTM (N=30)	BHTM (N=6)	WHF (N=42)	BHF (N=16)	WHTF (N=10)	BHTF (N=8)
0 Accepting of me	28%	35%	23%	0%	4.0%	31%	70%	38%
1	11	6	23	50	17	12	10	0
2	11	13	27	0	7	0	10	12
3	17	6	3	17	10	25	10	12
4	7	10	17	17	5	19	0	25
5	12	19	3	17	12	6	0	0
6 Rejecting of me	14	10	3	0	10	6	0	12

D. Non-controlling with me/controlling with me

	WHM (N=83)	BHM (N=31)	WHTM (N=30)	BHTM (N=6)	WHF (N=42)	BHF (N=16)	WHTF (N=10)	BHTF (N=8)
0 Controlling with me	12%	6%	7%	0%	19%	6%	20%	25%
1	11	13	10	50	17	6	0	0
2	10	0	20	0	7	31	0	12
3	20	35	23	17	19	31	50	12
4	11	3	10	17	14	6	20	25
5	16	13	23	17	10	19	0	0
6 Non-controlling with me	20	29	7	0	14	0	10	25

E. Overprotective of me/non-protective of me

	WHM (N=83)	BHM (N=31)	WHTM (N=30)	BHTM (N=6)	WHF (N=42)	BHF (N=16)	WHTF (N=10)	BHTF (N=8)
0 Overprotective of me	27%	19%	20%	0%	2%	0%	0%	25%
1	12	13	13	17	12	12	0	0
2	18	16	10	33	7	6	0	12
3	28	35	37	50	43	25	70	38
4	6	10	13	0	19	31	20	12
5	5	6	3	0	5	19	10	0
6 Non-protective of me	5	0	3	0	12	6	0	12

FATHERS/Father Surrogate-Child Relationships

	WHM	BHM	WHTM	BHTM	WHF	BHF	WHTF	BHTF
F. Fair toward me/unfair toward me	(N=83)	(N=31)	(N=30)	(N=6)	(N=42)	(N=16)	(N=10)	(N=8)
0 Unfair toward me	14%	16%	10%	0%	14%	12%	0%	12%
1	10	6	7	0	2	6	0	0
2	8	6	3	0	7	12	10	0
3	18	3	10	0	10	19	20	38
4	12	16	13	50	5	19	10	12
5	11	23	23	17	19	6	0	0
6 Fair toward me	27	29	33	33	43	25	60	38

In addition to what we have just covered, how would you describe your relationship with your [father surrogate], including your own feelings and reactions to him, during the time you were growing up?

	WHM	BHM	WHTM	BHTM	WHF	BHF	WHTF	BHTF
A. Closeness, involvement, close-binding	(N=82)	(N=31)	(N=30)	(N=6)	(N=41)	(N=16)	(N=10)	(N=7)
Felt close to him	11%	13%	13%	33%	22%	12%	10%	14%
Felt distant from him	39	39	17	17	12	0	10	14
Closeness/distance varied	4	0	0	0	2	0	0	0
No mention of closeness/distance	46	48	70	50	63	88	80	71
B. Affection	(N=82)	(N=30)	(N=30)	(N=6)	(N=41)	(N=16)	(N=10)	(N=7)
Mentioned love, warmth, etc.	29%	47%	40%	67%	56%	50%	40%	57%
Mentioned dislike, hatred, etc.	38	27	17	0	29	12	10	14
Amount of affection varied	4	0	0	0	7	12	0	14
No mention of affection/dislike	29	27	43	33	7	25	50	14
C. Regard, esteem	(N=83)	(N=31)	(N=30)	(N=6)	(N=41)	(N=16)	(N=10)	(N=7)
Admired, respected him	14%	19%	27%	33%	24%	31%	10%	29%
Did not admire, respect him	19	3	10	0	10	6	0	0
Regard-esteem varied	2	0	0	0	2	6	10	0
No mention of regard-esteem	64	77	63	67	63	56	80	71

FATHERS/Father Surrogate-Child Relationships; Identification with Father Surrogate

	WHM	BHM	WHTM	BHTM	WHF	BHF	WHTF	BHTF
D. Negative feelings	(N=83)	(N=31)	(N=30)	(N=6)	(N=42)	(N=16)	(N=10)	(N=7)
Mentioned anger, hostility, etc.	29%	29%	3%	0%	26%	19%	10%	14%
Afraid of father surrogate	7	6	7	0	2	6	10	0
Negative feelings varied	1	0	0	0	7	6	0	0
No mention of negative feelings	63	65	90	100	64	69	80	86
E. Similarity	(N=83)	(N=31)	(N=30)	(N=6)	(N=42)	(N=16)	(N=10)	(N=7)
Much or some similarity	4%	6%	7%	0%	5%	0%	0%	0%
Little or no similarity	6	0	0	0	0	0	0	0
Feelings of similarity varied	1	0	0	0	0	0	0	0
No mention of similarity	89	94	93	100	95	100	100	100
F. Relationship as a whole	(N=83)	(N=30)	(N=30)	(N=6)	(N=42)	(N=16)	(N=10)	(N=7)
Generally or entirely positive	31%	47%	63%	83%	55%	50%	80%	57%
Neutral or varying	24	17	7	0	14	19	10	14
Generally or entirely negative	45	37	30	17	31	31	10	29
While you were growing up, to what extent did you feel like or similar to your [father surrogate]?	(N=83)	(N=31)	(N=30)	(N=6)	(N=42)	(N=16)	(N=10)	(N=8)
Not at all	43%	48%	20%	0%	50%	31%	40%	38%
Very little	27	26	27	50	12	25	50	12
Somewhat	24	19	37	33	24	38	10	38
Very much	6	6	17	17	14	6	0	12
To whom did you think you were more similar?	(N=27)	(N=11)	(N=12)	(N=2)	(N=14)	(N=7)	(N=2)	(N=3)
Father surrogate	30%	0%	50%	0%	21%	0%	0%	33%
Mother or mother surrogate	44	73	42	50	36	71	0	33
Don't know	26	27	8	50	43	29	100	33

FATHERS/Identification with Father Surrogate

	WHM	BHM	WHTM	BHTM	WHF	BHF	WHTF	BHTF
To what extent did you want to be the kind of person your [father surrogate] was?	(N=83)	(N=31)	(N=30)	(N=6)	(N=42)	(N=16)	(N=10)	(N=8)
Not at all	49%	42%	30%	0%	43%	38%	30%	62%
Very little	14	29	20	33	12	12	30	0
Somewhat	23	16	27	33	29	44	40	25
Very much	13	13	23	33	17	6	0	12
Who did you want to be the most like?	(N=23)	(N=13)	(N=13)	(N=5)	(N=21)	(N=9)	(N=1)	(N=2)
Father surrogate	30%	0%	38%	60%	19%	22%	100%	0%
Mother or mother surrogate	30	15	38	0	48	44	0	0
Don't know	39	85	23	40	33	33	0	100
How much would you say your [mother/mother surrogate] wanted you to be the kind of person your [father surrogate] was?	(N=80)	(N=31)	(N=30)	(N=6)	(N=0)	(N=0)	(N=0)	(N=0)
In no way	30%	32%	13%	0%	[not asked of females]			
In very few ways	22	23	27	0				
In some ways	22	23	23	67				
In most ways	25	23	37	33				
How much would you say your [mother surrogate] wanted you to be the kind of person your father was?	(N=24)	(N=9)	(N=11)	(N=1)	(N=0)	(N=0)	(N=0)	(N=0)
In no way	50%	11%	18%	0%	[not asked of females]			
In very few ways	12	44	9	0				
In some ways	25	33	64	100				
In most ways	12	11	9	0				

39

FATHERS/Father Surrogates' Personal Traits

Now, I'd like you to describe, by circling the numbers below, the kind of person your [father surrogate] was during the time you were growing up. For example, if he was extremely adequate, you would circle 6. On the other hand, if he was extremely inadequate, you would circle 0.

A. Adequate/inadequate

	WHM (N=83)	BHM (N=31)	WHTM (N=30)	BHTM (N=6)	WHF (N=42)	BHF (N=16)	WHTF (N=10)	BHTF (N=8)
0 Inadequate	11%	10%	13%	0%	12%	6%	0%	12%
1	7	10	7	0	7	6	0	0
2	12	13	10	17	10	19	20	0
3	16	19	7	0	12	12	0	50
4	13	13	13	33	10	19	20	0
5	20	16	27	33	21	12	10	0
6 Adequate	20	19	23	17	29	25	50	38

B. Strong/weak

	WHM (N=83)	BHM (N=31)	WHTM (N=30)	BHTM (N=6)	WHF (N=41)	BHF (N=16)	WHTF (N=10)	BHTF (N=8)
0 Weak	10%	3%	0%	0%	7%	0%	10%	0%
1	5	19	3	0	7	0	20	0
2	7	0	10	0	10	6	10	0
3	16	19	23	17	12	19	20	38
4	13	23	10	17	12	12	20	12
5	24	6	23	50	17	19	20	38
6 Strong	25	29	30	17	34	44	20	12

C. Active/passive

	WHM (N=83)	BHM (N=31)	WHTM (N=30)	BHTM (N=6)	WHF (N=42)	BHF (N=16)	WHTF (N=10)	BHTF (N=8)
0 Passive	5%	6%	7%	0%	0%	0%	0%	0%
1	1	6	0	0	7	0	10	0
2	6	6	7	17	17	19	0	0
3	13	19	23	33	10	0	10	38
4	14	26	23	17	12	12	0	12
5	30	19	17	33	14	31	30	25
6 Active	30	16	23	0	40	38	50	25

40

FATHERS/Father Surrogates' Personal Traits

	WHM (N=83)	BHM (N=31)	WHTM (N=31)	BHTM (N=6)	WHF (N=42)	BHF (N=16)	WHTF (N=10)	BHTF (N=8)
D. Warm/cold								
0 Cold	10%	6%	20%	0%	5%	6%	0%	12%
1	11	10	7	0	10	0	0	0
2	17	3	7	17	5	6	0	12
3	18	23	23	17	17	25	10	0
4	16	10	20	0	14	12	10	12
5	12	32	13	67	21	19	30	38
6 Warm	17	16	13	0	29	31	50	25
	(N=83)	(N=31)	(N=30)	(N=6)	(N=42)	(N=16)	(N=10)	(N=8)
E. Successful/unsuccessful								
0 Unsuccessful	10%	10%	13%	0%	5%	0%	0%	0%
1	7	10	7	0	7	6	0	0
2	8	19	7	17	2	0	0	38
3	14	23	23	0	21	25	30	12
4	14	19	20	33	21	19	30	0
5	23	6	17	50	17	19	20	12
6 Successful	23	13	13	0	26	31	20	38
	(N=83)	(N=31)	(N=30)	(N=6)	(N=42)	(N=16)	(N=10)	(N=8)
F. Pleasant/unpleasant								
0 Unpleasant	8%	10%	3%	0%	10%	6%	0%	12%
1	4	3	13	0	2	0	0	0
2	11	10	10	0	7	6	0	0
3	20	13	7	0	12	25	0	12
4	17	26	17	50	14	6	20	0
5	14	6	33	50	24	31	20	50
6 Pleasant	25	32	17	0	31	25	60	25
	(N=82)	(N=31)	(N=30)	(N=6)	(N=42)	(N=16)	(N=10)	(N=8)
G. Masculine/feminine								
0 Feminine	0%	0%	0%	0%	0%	0%	0%	0%
1	1	0	3	0	5	0	0	0
2	4	3	0	0	5	6	0	12
3	13	6	7	0	12	0	10	12
4	10	10	20	17	12	19	20	12
5	30	16	27	83	19	19	0	0
6 Masculine	41	65	43	0	48	56	70	62

FATHERS/Father Surrogates' Personal Traits

H. Relaxed/Up-tight

	WHM (N=82)	BHM (N=31)	WHTM (N=30)	BHTM (N=6)	WHF (N=41)	BHF (N=16)	WHTF (N=10)	BHTF (N=8)
0 Up-tight	6%	0%	10%	0%	20%	0%	0%	12%
1	7	10	10	0	5	6	0	0
2	13	6	23	0	3	25	10	38
3	17	16	3	17	22	19	10	12
4	23	26	20	17	10	6	20	12
5	18	26	17	50	22	**38**	10	25
6 Relaxed	15	16	17	17	20	19	50	38

I. Dominant/submissive

	WHM (N=83)	BHM (N=31)	WHTM (N=30)	BHTM (N=6)	WHF (N=42)	BHF (N=16)	WHTF (N=10)	BHTF (N=8)
0 Submissive	6%	0%	0%	0%	7%	0%	10%	0%
1	10	13	7	0	14	0	20	25
2	10	6	10	0	7	38	0	12
3	25	39	23	33	24	6	20	25
4	8	19	27	50	7	38	20	0
5	23	16	20	17	12	19	10	0
6 Dominant	18	6	13	0	29	19	20	38

J. Conforming/non-conforming

	WHM (N=82)	BHM (N=31)	WHTM (N=30)	BHTM (N=6)	WHF (N=42)	BHF (N=16)	WHTF (N=10)	BHTF (N=8)
0 Non-conforming	5%	0%	7%	0%	5%	19%	0%	12%
1	4	10	3	0	14	0	0	0
2	12	10	7	0	0	25	20	0
3	21	35	23	17	14	25	20	50
4	12	13	20	67	5	19	0	25
5	32	16	23	17	29	12	30	12
6 Conforming	15	16	17	0	33	0	30	0

K. Independent/dependent

	WHM (N=83)	BHM (N=31)	WHTM (N=30)	BHTM (N=6)	WHF (N=42)	BHF (N=16)	WHTF (N=10)	BHTF (N=8)
0 Dependent	4%	6%	3%	0%	5%	12%	0%	12%
1	7	10	7	0	10	0	10	12
2	5	6	10	0	2	6	0	12
3	13	19	17	0	14	0	20	25
4	27	10	23	33	24	12	10	0
5	20	16	17	50	24	31	30	0
6 Independent	24	32	23	17	21	38	30	38

FATHERS/Father Surrogates' Personal Traits

L. Healthy/sickly	WHM (N=83)	BHM (N=31)	WHTM (N=30)	BHTM (N=6)	WHF (N=42)	BHF (N=16)	WHTF (N=10)	BHTF (N=8)
0 Sickly	1%	0%	3%	0%	7%	0%	0%	0%
1	4	0	0	0	7	6	0	12
2	4	3	7	17	2	6	0	0
3	8	19	3	0	7	0	0	12
4	17	19	17	17	12	19	10	12
5	27	16	27	67	21	6	0	25
6 Healthy	40	42	43	0	43	62	90	38

Who made most of the decisions about the children?	(N=83)	(N=31)	(N=29)	(N=6)	(N=41)	(N=16)	(N=10)	(N=8)
Father surrogate	25%	3%	24%	17%	15%	6%	10%	0%
Mother or mother surrogate	63	87	66	67	71	88	60	75
Decisions made jointly	8	10	10	17	15	6	20	25
Neither made most decisions	4	0	0	0	0	0	10	0

43

MOTHER-FATHER RELATIONSHIPS/Family Intactness

	WHM	BHM	WHTM	BHTM	WHF	BHF	WHTF	BHTF
Did you live more or less continuously with both parents until you were 17?	(N=575)	(N=111)	(N=284)	(N=53)	(N=229)	(N=64)	(N=101)	(N=39)
Yes	66%	41%	76%	75%	62%	53%	75%	59%
No	34	59	24	25	38	47	25	41
Why didn't you live with both parents?	(N=192)	(N=65)	(N=69)	(N=13)	(N=86)	(N=30)	(N=25)	(N=16)
Parents divorced or separated	46%	48%	51%	69%	52%	57%	56%	56%
Father died	23	17	32	0	20	13	12	38
Mother died	14	8	10	15	13	3	16	0
Both parents died	2	5	0	8	3	3	8	0
Adoption, job circumstances, etc.	15	23	7	8	12	27	8	6
How old were you when [you no longer lived with both parents]?	(N=192)	(N=62)	(N=69)	(N=13)	(N=86)	(N=30)	(N=25)	(N=16)
Under 3	31%	39%	22%	8%	35%	40%	20%	25%
3-5	20	27	17	38	23	23	16	25
6-12	36	31	49	46	30	23	48	50
13-17	13	3	12	8	12	13	16	0
What effect would you say this had on you?								
A. Effect on relationship with mother	(N=186)	(N=65)	(N=66)	(N=13)	(N=79)	(N=30)	(N=25)	(N=16)
Felt closer, more dependent	7%	3%	0%	15%	1%	0%	0%	0%
Other positive effect	1	2	0	0	0	3	0	0
Felt more distant, angry at mother	4	6	9	7	9	3	32	0
Other negative effect	4	2	3	0	9	7	0	0
No particular effect	84	88	88	77	81	87	68	100
B. Effect on relationship with father	(N=179)	(N=65)	(N=65)	(N=13)	(N=80)	(N=30)	(N=25)	(N=16)
Felt closer, more dependent	2%	0%	2%	0%	0%	0%	4%	0%
Other positive effect	1	2	0	0	0	0	0	0
Felt more distant, angry at father	17	25	25	8	20	10	20	25
Other negative effect	5	2	2	8	5	3	4	0
No particular effect	76	72	72	85	75	87	72	75

MOTHER-FATHER RELATIONSHIPS/Family Intactness

	WHM	BHM	WHTM	BHTM	WHF	BHF	WHTF	BHTF
C. Effect on respondent*	(N=188)	(N=65)	(N=66)	(N=13)	(N=80)	(N=30)	(N=25)	(N=16)
Felt responsible for the breakup	2%	0%	2%	0%	4%	3%	0%	0%
Decided against ever marrying myself	2	0	2	0	1	0	4	0
Other negative effect	34	23	32	15	48	23	56	19
Mixed feelings	1	0	2	0	1	0	4	0
Contributed to my gender-role confusion	14	12	0	0	9	7	0	0
Positive effect	8	5	9	0	11	3	8	6
Some other effect	13	5	6	8	15	7	4	0
No particular effect	39	60	52	77	24	57	28	75
After [family breakup], with whom did you live most of the time until you were 17?	(N=193)	(N=65)	(N=69)	(N=13)	(N=86)	(N=30)	(N=25)	(N=16)
Mother, not remarried	37%	32%	43%	31%	35%	30%	20%	44%
Mother, remarried	21	26	25	31	21	17	16	44
Father, not remarried	7	3	3	0	7	10	28	0
Father, remarried	7	9	12	0	4	7	0	0
Other relative(s)	10	20	3	23	8	20	4	6
Adopted/foster family or institution	18	9	14	15	26	17	32	6

How old were you during the time you lived with [person(s) mentioned above]?

	WHM	BHM	WHTM	BHTM	WHF	BHF	WHTF	BHTF
A. Age when this arrangement began	(N=192)	(N=65)	(N=69)	(N=13)	(N=84)	(N=30)	(N=25)	(N=16)
Under 3	24%	32%	9%	0%	26%	23%	12%	19%
3-5	19	23	12	38	21	20	16	19
6-12	41	38	67	38	38	40	48	56
13-17	16	6	13	23	14	17	24	6
B. Age when this arrangement ended	(N=191)	(N=65)	(N=69)	(N=13)	(N=84)	(N=30)	(N=25)	(N=16)
Under 3	0%	0%	0%	0%	0%	0%	0%	0%
3-5	0	0	0	0	0	0	0	0
6-12	4	5	3	0	7	3	0	0
13-17	73	95	97	85	93	93	96	100
Over 17	23	0	0	16	0	3	4	0

*Respondents could give more than one answer to this question, so column percentages may add up to more than 100.

MOTHER-FATHER RELATIONSHIPS/Family Intactness; Marital Relationship

	WHM	BHM	WHTM	BHTM	WHF	BHF	WHTF	BHTF
Was there anyone else, like an older brother, sister, aunt, or uncle, with whom you lived until you were 17 whom you thought of as a [substitute mother/father]?	(N=139)	(N=45)	(N=43)	(N=9)	(N=59)	(N=23)	(N=18)	(N=9)
Yes	32%	47%	37%	33%	49%	57%	50%	22%
No	68	53	63	67	51	43	50	75
Who was that?	(N=44)	(N=21)	(N=16)	(N=3)	(N=29)	(N=13)	(N=9)	(N=2)
Male relative	7%	5%	31%	0%	0%	8%	11%	0%
Female relative	25	29	0	33	0	8	33	50
Male and female relatives	27	52	19	67	28	46	22	50
Brother	7	0	6	0	10	8	0	0
Sister	7	0	6	0	0	0	0	0
Brother and sister	0	0	0	0	3	0	0	0
Unrelated adult male	14	5	12	0	7	0	0	0
Unrelated adult female	7	5	12	0	10	0	0	0
Unrelated adult male and female	5	5	12	0	31	31	22	0
Some other person(s)	2	0	0	0	10	0	11	0
During the time you lived with them, how much affection do you think your mother had for your father?	(N=528)	(N=90)	(N=270)	(N=51)	(N=207)	(N=60)	(N=94)	(N=37)
None	4%	1%	1%	2%	9%	2%	3%	5%
Very little	12	13	8	2	22	17	9	14
Some	28	31	28	22	27	37	18	16
Much	56	54	63	75	42	45	70	65
During the time you lived with them, how much affection do you think your father had for your mother?	(N=526)	(N=90)	(N=267)	(N=51)	(N=209)	(N=58)	(N=94)	(N=35)
None	3%	4%	1%	2%	7%	5%	2%	3%
Very little	11	13	9	6	17	16	6	6
Some	29	37	31	24	30	40	19	26
Much	57	46	60	69	46	40	72	66

MOTHER-FATHER RELATIONSHIPS/Marital Relationship; Marital Dominance

	WHM	BHM	WHTM	BHTM	WHF	BHF	WHTF	BHTF
If your mother had had it to do over again, do you think she would have married your father?	(N=545)	(N=94)	(N=281)	(N=52)	(N=221)	(N=62)	(N=99)	(N=38)
No	25%	29%	18%	12%	30%	27%	16%	29%
Probably not	8	9	6	10	3	16	8	11
Probably	14	14	17	19	15	5	18	11
Yes	50	44	53	56	47	40	54	50
Don't know	3	5	5	4	5	11	4	0
If your father had had it to do over again, do you think he would have married your mother?	(N=542)	(N=94)	(N=279)	(N=52)	(N=219)	(N=60)	(N=99)	(N=37)
No	14%	18%	13%	12%	21%	18%	10%	16%
Probably not	6	5	8	6	8	10	5	3
Probably	15	18	18	23	14	12	20	14
Yes	61	49	52	56	50	50	62	62
Don't know	4	10	9	4	7	10	3	5
Generally speaking, while you were growing up did your father dominate your mother, or did your mother dominate your father?	(N=521)	(N=86)	(N=269)	(N=50)	(N=205)	(N=54)	(N=94)	(N=34)
Father dominated mother	29%	28%	49%	28%	32%	39%	47%	35%
Neither dominated the other	32	44	29	54	27	31	36	44
Mother dominated father	39	28	22	18	41	30	17	21
How much disagreement was there between your parents regarding decisions about the children?	(N=516)	(N=88)	(N=261)	(N=51)	(N=201)	(N=55)	(N=95)	(N=34)
None at all	17%	11%	10%	24%	27%	18%	18%	15%
Very little	43	47	45	59	30	29	54	41
Some	25	19	34	14	25	27	22	29
A great deal	15	23	11	4	17	25	6	15

47

MOTHER-FATHER RELATIONSHIPS/Marital Relationship

How much friction or bad feeling was there between your parents?	WHM (N=529)	BHM (N=90)	WHTM (N=269)	BHTM (N=52)	WHF (N=210)	BHF (N=57)	WHTF (N=95)	BHTF (N=38)
None at all	10%	7%	12%	19%	11%	9%	17%	13%
Very little	33	33	35	46	27	25	34	34
Some	30	39	32	27	23	28	25	29
A great deal	26	21	22	8	40	39	24	24

MOTHER-FATHER RELATIONSHIPS/Marital Relationship (Mother Surrogate and Father)

	WHM	BHM	WHTM	BHTM	WHF	BHF	WHTF	BHTF
During the time you lived with them, how much affection do you think your [mother surrogate] had for your father?	(N=22)	(N=8)	(N=10)	(N=1)	(N=5)	(N=3)	(N=3)	(N=0)
None	9%	25%	0%	0%	40%	0%	0%	
Very little	23	12	10	0	20	0	0	
Some	32	25	30	100	0	33	0	
Much	36	37	60	0	40	67	100	
During the time you lived with them, how much affection do you think your father had for your [mother surrogate]?	(N=22)	(N=8)	(N=10)	(N=1)	(N=5)	(N=3)	(N=3)	(N=0)
None	14%	12%	0%	0%	40%	0%	0%	
Very little	14	0	0	0	20	0	-0	
Some	50	62	40	0	0	67	0	
Much	23	25	60	100	40	33	100	
If your [mother surrogate] had had it to do over again, do you think she would have married your father?	(N=13)	(N=6)	(N=10)	(N=0)	(N=3)	(N=2)	(N=0)	(N=0)
No	23%	0%	10%		0%	0%		
Probably not	23	0	0		0	0		
Probably	8	17	20		33	50		
Yes	46	83	70		67	50		
Don't know	0	0	0		0	0		
If your father had had it to do over again, do you think he would have married your [mother surrogate]?	(N=13)	(N=6)	(N=10)	(N=0)	(N=3)	(N=2)	(N=0)	(N=0)
No	23%	17%	10%		0%	0%		
Probably not	15	0	10		0	0		
Probably	8	0	10		0	50		
Yes	46	83	70		100	50		
Don't know	8	0	0		0	0		

49

MOTHER-FATHER RELATIONSHIPS/Marital Relationship (Mother Surrogate and Father); Marital Dominance

	WHM	BHM	WHTM	BHTM	WHF	BHF	WHTF	BHTF
Generally speaking, while you were growing up did your father dominate your [mother surrogate], or did she dominate him?	(N=23)	(N=8)	(N=10)	(N=1)	(N=5)	(N=4)	(N=2)	(N=0)
Father dominated mother surrogate	35%	38%	30%	0%	20%	50%	50%	
Neither dominated the other	39	25	40	0	40	50	0	
Mother surrogate dominated father	26	38	30	100	40	0	50	
How much disagreement was there between them regarding decisions about the children?	(N=24)	(N=8)	(N=10)	(N=1)	(N=5)	(N=4)	(N=2)	(N=1)
None at all	33%	25%	10%	100%	40%	50%	50%	100%
Very little	29	38	30	0	0	50	50	0
Some	25	38	50	0	40	0	0	0
A great deal	12	0	10	0	20	0	0	0
How much friction or bad feeling was there between them?	(N=24)	(N=8)	(N=11)	(N=1)	(N=5)	(N=4)	(N=2)	(N=0)
None at all	33%	25%	0%	100%	20%	75%	50%	
Very little	12	25	55	0	40	0	0	
Some	29	38	27	0	20	0	50	
A great deal	25	12	18	0	20	25	0	

MOTHER-FATHER RELATIONSHIPS/Marital Relationship (Mother [Surrogate] and Father Surrogate)

	WHM	BHM	WHTM	BHTM	WHF	BHF	WHTF	BHTF
	(N=81)	(N=31)	(N=30)	(N=6)	(N=40)	(N=15)	(N=10)	(N=8)
During the time you lived with them, how much affection do you think your [mother/mother surrogate] had for your [father/mother surrogate]?								
None	0%	0%	0%	0%	5%	13%	10%	0%
Very little	15	13	10	0	10	7	0	0
Some	25	16	33	17	12	13	60	62
Much	60	71	57	83	72	67	30	38
	(N=81)	(N=31)	(N=30)	(N=6)	(N=40)	(N=15)	(N=10)	(N=8)
During the time you lived with them, how much affection do you think your [father surrogate] had for your [mother/mother surrogate]?								
None	0%	3%	0%	0%	2%	7%	0%	25%
Very little	14	6	3	0	8	13	0	12
Some	23	16	30	33	20	7	50	12
Much	63	74	67	67	70	73	50	50
	(N=76)	(N=29)	(N=23)	(N=6)	(N=33)	(N=15)	(N=10)	(N=8)
If your [mother/mother surrogate] had had it to do over again, do you think she would have married your [father surrogate]?								
No	20%	21%	17%	0%	9%	33%	10%	25%
Probably not	8	7	4	0	12	0	0	12
Probably	14	14	17	17	15	0	30	12
Yes	58	55	57	83	61	60	60	38
Don't know	0	3	4	0	3	7	0	12
	(N=76)	(N=29)	(N=23)	(N=6)	(N=33)	(N=15)	(N=10)	(N=8)
If your [father surrogate] had had it to do over again, do you think he would have married your [mother/mother surrogate]?								
No	18%	10%	4%	0%	18%	20%	20%	0%
Probably not	5	7	4	0	9	0	0	25
Probably	12	24	22	17	9	7	20	12
Yes	64	55	61	83	61	67	60	50
Don't know	0	3	9	0	3	7	0	12

51

MOTHER-FATHER RELATIONSHIPS/Marital Relationship (Mother [Surrogate] and Father Surrogate); Marital Dominance

	WHM	BHM	WHTM	BHTM	WHF	BHF	WHTF	BHTF
	(N=81)	(N=31)	(N=29)	(N=6)	(N=41)	(N=15)	(N=10)	(N=8)
Generally speaking, while you were growing up did your [father surrogate] dominate your [mother/mother surrogate], or did she dominate him?								
Male dominated female	35%	19%	31%	17%	15%	33%	20%	25%
Neither dominated the other	27	39	34	83	32	33	30	38
Female dominated male	38	42	34	0	54	33	50	38
How much disagreement was there between them regarding decisions about the children?	(N=81)	(N=31)	(N=29)	(N=6)	(N=41)	(N=16)	(N=10)	(N=8)
None at all	17%	23%	17%	0%	29%	19%	10%	12%
Very little	44	61	34	100	22	56	60	38
Some	23	10	24	0	22	6	20	12
A great deal	15	6	24	0	27	19	10	38
How much friction or bad feeling was there between them?	(N=81)	(N=31)	(N=29)	(N=6)	(N=41)	(N=16)	(N=10)	(N=8)
None at all	7%	10%	17%	33%	10%	19%	20%	0%
Very little	35	45	41	67	41	25	30	38
Some	30	29	24	0	24	38	30	12
A great deal	28	16	17	0	24	19	20	50

BROTHERS AND SISTERS/First Sibling

Now I'd like you to help list all of the children in your family (including yourself, stepbrothers and stepsisters) in the order of their birth.

	WHM	BHM	WHTM	BHTM	WHF	BHF	WHTF	BHTF
1A. Identity of first sibling	(N=575)	(N=111)	(N=284)	(N=49)	(N=229)	(N=64)	(N=101)	(N=39)
Natural	47%	41%	43%	59%	44%	52%	52%	62%
Step	7	13	6	2	8	17	4	5
Respondent	46	46	51	39	48	31	44	33
1B. Gender of first sibling	(N=575)	(N=111)	(N=284)	(N=53)	(N=229)	(N=64)	(N=101)	(N=39)
Male	75%	77%	81%	66%	31%	41%	28%	31%
Female	25	23	19	34	69	59	72	69
1C. Age of first sibling	(N=575)	(N=111)	(N=284)	(N=53)	(N=229)	(N=64)	(N=101)	(N=39)
Under 25	12%	23%	12%	15%	8%	9%	15%	21%
25-34	25	49	31	74	34	38	32	54
35-44	25	18	23	19	26	25	17	21
45-54	22	9	17	2	20	22	20	3
55 and older	16	2	17	0	13	6	17	0
1D. Did you ever engage in any sexual activity with him/her while growing up?	(N=478)	(N=96)	(N=232)	(N=47)	(N=183)	(N=58)	(N=88)	(N=37)
Yes	22%	17%	14%	15%	16%	17%	11%	5%
No	78	83	86	85	84	83	89	95
1E. How often did you engage in this activity with him/her?	(N=302)	(N=60)	(N=135)	(N=34)	(N=116)	(N=44)	(N=55)	(N=26)
Never	83%	95%	88%	85%	88%	80%	87%	96%
Rarely	11	3	8	9	7	11	13	4
Sometimes	4	2	2	6	5	7	0	0
Often	1	0	1	0	0	2	0	0

BROTHERS AND SISTERS/First Sibling

1F. How would you classify him/her on the Kinsey Scale?

	WHM	BHM	WHTM	BHTM	WHF	BHF	WHTF	BHTF
	(N=294)	(N=58)	(N=132)	(N=34)	(N=115)	(N=33)	(N=53)	(N=26)
0: Exclusively heterosexual	76%	86%	88%	100%	80%	84%	96%	92%
1: Mainly heterosexual with a small degree of homosexuality	19	9	10	0	13	7	4	8
2: Mainly heterosexual with a substantial degree of homosexuality	2	0	1	0	5	2	0	0
3: Equally heterosexual and homosexual	2	2	1	0	0	2	0	0
4: Mainly homosexual with a substantial degree of heterosexuality	1	0	0	0	0	2	0	0
5: Mainly homosexual with a small degree of heterosexuality	1	2	1	0	0	2	0	0
6: Exclusively homosexual	1	2	0	0	2	0	0	0

1G. During the time you were growing up, how close did you feel to him/her?

	WHM	BHM	WHTM	BHTM	WHF	BHF	WHTF	BHTF
	(N=300)	(N=60)	(N=131)	(N=34)	(N=115)	(N=44)	(N=56)	(N=26)
Not at all close	20%	20%	8%	3%	27%	20%	12%	12%
Not very close	27	23	27	15	26	11	27	12
Somewhat close	28	23	44	53	20	30	32	35
Very close	25	33	21	29	27	39	29	42

1H. During this same time, how much did you feel like or similar to him/her?

	WHM	BHM	WHTM	BHTM	WHF	BHF	WHTF	BHTF
	(N=300)	(N=60)	(N=131)	(N=34)	(N=115)	(N=44)	(N=55)	(N=26)
Not at all similar	50%	43%	30%	18%	53%	52%	29%	42%
Not very similar	21	13	34	32	22	14	24	23
Somewhat similar	22	28	31	35	20	27	38	27
Very similar	7	15	5	15	5	7	9	8

1I. How would you order your siblings in terms of their emotional closeness to you during the time you were growing up? [First sibling]

	WHM	BHM	WHTM	BHTM	WHF	BHF	WHTF	BHTF
	(N=294)	(N=59)	(N=132)	(N=33)	(N=116)	(N=44)	(N=55)	(N=26)
Closest to this sibling	20%	32%	21%	30%	15%	30%	18%	12%
Neither very close nor very distant	53	51	51	42	52	48	49	73
Least close to this sibling	2	7	3	0	2	5	0	4
Only one sibling (i.e., no order possible)	25	10	25	27	31	18	33	12

BROTHERS AND SISTERS/First Sibling; Second Sibling

	WHM	BHM	WHTM	BHTM		WHF	BHF	WHTF	BHTF
1J. Would you order them in terms of how similar you felt to each while growing up? [First sibling]	(N=293)	(N=60)	(N=132)	(N=33)		(N=112)	(N=44)	(N=55)	(N=26)
Most similar to this sibling	23%	27%	24%	24%		17%	30%	25%	12%
Neither very similar nor very dissimilar	49	55	48	48		48	50	42	72
Least similar to this sibling	2	8	2	0		3	2	0	4
Only one sibling (i.e., no order possible)	25	10	25	27		32	18	33	12
1K. Which would you say was your mother's favorite during the time you were growing up?	(N=477)	(N=93)	(N=233)	(N=45)		(N=179)	(N=58)	(N=90)	(N=37)
First sibling	30%	39%	38%	24%		40%	41%	24%	30%
Some other sibling	70	61	62	76		60	59	76	70
1L. Which would you say was your father's favorite?	(N=463)	(N=85)	(N=231)	(N=45)		(N=170)	(N=54)	(N=89)	(N=35)
First sibling	25%	26%	32%	27%		29%	19%	34%	14%
Some other sibling	75	74	68	73		71	81	66	86
2A. Identity of second sibling	(N=494)	(N=95)	(N=235)	(N=47)		(N=188)	(N=58)	(N=90)	(N=37)
Natural	60%	54%	63%	53%		56%	48%	56%	76%
Step	9	21	7	6		12	12	4	5
Respondent	32	25	31	40		31	40	40	19
2B. Gender of second sibling	(N=494)	(N=96)	(N=235)	(N=47)		(N=188)	(N=58)	(N=90)	(N=37)
Male	67%	67%	63%	60%		34%	28%	37%	43%
Female	33	33	37	40		66	72	63	57

55

BROTHERS AND SISTERS/Second Sibling

		WHM	BHM	WHTM	BHTM	WHF	BHF	WHTF	BHTF
		(N=492)	(N=96)	(N=235)	(N=47)	(N=188)	(N=58)	(N=90)	(N=37)
2C.	Age of second sibling								
	Under 25	23%	36%	22%	43%	23%	28%	28%	35%
	25-34	23	40	27	53	27	31	26	51
	35-44	25	17	18	4	20	24	21	14
	45-54	17	6	19	0	21	14	16	0
	55 and older	11	1	14	0	8	3	10	0
2D.	Did you ever engage in any sexual activity with him/her while you were growing up?	(N=478)	(N=96)	(N=234)	(N=47)	(N=185)	(N=58)	(N=89)	(N=37)
	Yes	24%	25%	14%	15%	18%	17%	12%	3%
	No	76	75	86	85	82	83	88	97
2E.	How often did you engage in this activity with him/her?	(N=326)	(N=72)	(N=162)	(N=28)	(N=124)	(N=35)	(N=53)	(N=30)
	Never	81%	78%	91%	89%	86%	91%	89%	97%
	Rarely	13	19	6	11	10	9	11	3
	Sometimes	4	0	2	0	2	0	0	0
	Often	1	3	1	0	2	0	0	0
2F.	How would you classify him/her on the Kinsey Scale?	(N=318)	(N=69)	(N=162)	(N=28)	(N=127)	(N=35)	(N=52)	(N=30)
	0: Exclusively heterosexual	75%	71%	91%	100%	79%	71%	87%	97%
	1: Mainly heterosexual with a small degree of homosexuality	17	17	6	0	10	20	12	3
	2: Mainly heterosexual with a substantial degree of homosexuality	2	3	1	0	4	6	2	0
	3: Equally homosexual and heterosexual	2	7	1	0	2	3	0	0
	4: Mainly homosexual with a substantial degree of heterosexuality	1	0	0	0	1	0	0	0
	5: Mainly homosexual with a small degree of heterosexuality	1	1	1	0	2	0	0	0
	6: Exclusively homosexual	.2	0	0	0	2	0	0	0

BROTHERS AND SISTERS/Second Sibling

	WHM	BHM	WHTM	BHTM	WHF	BHF	WHTF	BHTF
2G. During the time that you were growing up, how close did you feel to him/her?	(N=325)	(N=72)	(N=161)	(N=28)	(N=125)	(N=35)	(N=53)	(N=30)
Not at all close	17%	12%	6%	4%	21%	20%	9%	17%
Not very close	23	19	19	14	20	11	26	20
Somewhat close	29	38	46	39	26	29	30	13
Very close	31	31	29	43	33	40	34	50
2H. During this same time, how much did you feel like or similar to him/her?	(N=325)	(N=72)	(N=161)	(N=28)	(N=125)	(N=35)	(N=53)	(N=30)
Not at all similar	42%	42%	24%	21%	52%	54%	47%	50%
Not very similar	28	38	34	14	19	17	36	10
Somewhat similar	20	14	32	50	19	20	15	17
Very similar	10	7	10	14	10	9	2	23
2I. How would you order your siblings in terms of their emotional closeness to you during the time you were growing up? [Second sibling]	(N=239)	(N=58)	(N=110)	(N=22)	(N=95)	(N=30)	(N=38)	(N=29)
Closest to this sibling	39%	29%	49%	45%	38%	17%	39%	45%
Neither very close nor very distant	59	70	50	55	60	83	43	48
Least close to this sibling	1	2	0	0	2	0	8	7
2J. Would you order them in terms of how similar you felt to each while growing up? [Second sibling]	(N=238)	(N=58)	(N=110)	(N=22)	(N=90)	(N=29)	(N=39)	(N=29)
Most similar to this sibling	35%	29%	47%	36%	27%	21%	21%	31%
Neither very similar nor very dissimilar	63	69	53	64	70	72	71	68
Least similar to this sibling	2	2	0	0	2	7	8	0
2K. Which would you say was your mother's favorite during the time that you were growing up?	(N=478)	(N=93)	(N=233)	(N=45)	(N=179)	(N=58)	(N=89)	(N=37)
Second sibling	30%	27%	26%	20%	24%	24%	29%	16%
Some other sibling	70	73	74	80	76	76	71	84

BROTHERS AND SISTERS/Second Sibling; Third Sibling

	WHM	BHM	WHTM	BHTM	WHF	BHF	WHTF	BHTF
2L. Which would you say was your father's favorite?	(N=461)	(N=87)	(N=232)	(N=45)	(N=171)	(N=54)	(N=89)	(N=33)
Second sibling	34%	31%	25%	18%	33%	26%	34%	27%
Some other sibling	66	69	75	82	67	74	66	73
3A. Identity of third sibling	(N=337)	(N=76)	(N=152)	(N=33)	(N=122)	(N=46)	(N=58)	(N=33)
Natural	67%	59%	73%	61%	62%	65%	74%	64%
Step	11	24	10	9	11	20	7	9
Respondent	22	17	17	30	26	15	19	27
3B. Gender of third sibling	(N=337)	(N=76)	(N=153)	(N=33)	(N=123)	(N=46)	(N=58)	(N=33)
Male	60%	51%	54%	64%	41%	41%	36%	55%
Female	40	49	46	36	59	59	64	45
3C. Age of third sibling	(N=335)	(N=76)	(N=153)	(N=33)	(N=123)	(N=46)	(N=58)	(N=33)
Under 15	4%	5%	5%	12%	5%	4%	3%	6%
15-24	26	41	22	36	27	35	40	45
25-34	23	34	22	52	23	28	17	33
35-44	23	12	22	0	14	26	16	15
45 and older	25	8	29	0	32	7	24	0
3D. Did you ever engage in any sexual activity with him/her while growing up?	(N=327)	(N=76)	(N=152)	(N=33)	(N=121)	(N=46)	(N=57)	(N=33)
Yes	25%	17%	16%	12%	17%	11%	11%	3%
No	75	83	84	88	83	89	89	97

58

BROTHERS AND SISTERS/Third Sibling

	WHM	BHM	WHTM	BHTM		WHF	BHF	WHTF	BHTF
	(N=256)	(N=63)	(N=126)	(N=23)		(N=89)	(N=39)	(N=46)	(N=24)
3E. How often did you engage in this activity with him/her?									
Never	80%	86%	88%	91%		87%	95%	94%	100%
Rarely	16	13	10	0		10	5	4	0
Sometimes	3	0	2	9		1	0	0	0
Often	2	2	0	0		2	0	2	0
3F. How would you classify him/her on the Kinsey Scale?	(N=253)	(N=60)	(N=125)	(N=23)		(N=90)	(N=39)	(N=46)	(N=24)
0: Exclusively heterosexual	75%	85%	86%	100%		74%	74%	100%	83%
1: Mainly heterosexual with a small degree of homosexuality	15	10	11	0		14	15	0	12
2: Mainly heterosexual with a substantial degree of homosexuality	4	2	2	0		2	5	0	4
3: Equally heterosexual and homosexual	2	2	0	0		2	3	0	0
4: Mainly homosexual with a substantial degree of heterosexuality	0	0	1	0		2	3	0	0
5: Mainly homosexual with a small degree of heterosexuality	1	0	1	0		1	0	0	0
6: Exclusively homosexual	2	2	0	0		3	0	0	0
3G. During the time that you were growing up, how close did you feel to him/her?	(N=256)	(N=63)	(N=123)	(N=23)		(N=89)	(N=39)	(N=46)	(N=24)
Not at all close	14%	17%	14%	4%		25%	21%	7%	21%
Not very close	21	17	24	17		19	10	9	0
Somewhat close	30	33	34	43		26	28	41	38
Very close	34	32	28	35		30	41	43	42

59

BROTHERS AND SISTERS/Third Sibling

	WHM	BHM	WHTM	BHTM	WHF	BHF	WHTF	BHTF
3H. During this same time, how much did you feel like or similar to him/her?	(N=257)	(N=63)	(N=123)	(N=23)	(N=89)	(N=39)	(N=45)	(N=24)
Not at all similar	39%	59%	28%	13%	46%	51%	27%	38%
Not very similar	22	21	32	22	24	21	31	12
Somewhat similar	26	19	30	48	19	23	29	25
Very similar	12	2	11	17	11	5	13	25
3I. How would you order your siblings in terms of their emotional closeness to you during the time you were growing up? [Third sibling]	(N=252)	(N=62)	(N=120)	(N=21)	(N=85)	(N=36)	(N=44)	(N=24)
Closest to this sibling	35%	23%	31%	38%	26%	33%	41%	12%
Neither very close nor very distant	63	76	69	62	61	61	59	83
Least close to this sibling	2	2	0	0	2	6	0	4
3J. Would you order them in terms of how similar you felt to each while growing up? [Third sibling]	(N=249)	(N=62)	(N=120)	(N=21)	(N=80)	(N=35)	(N=45)	(N=24)
Most similar to this sibling	36%	11%	31%	52%	40%	23%	42%	25%
Neither very similar nor very dissimilar	62	87	69	48	59	77	58	71
Least similar to this sibling	2	2	0	0	1	0	0	4
3K. Which would you say was your mother's favorite during the time you were growing up?	(N=324)	(N=73)	(N=150)	(N=32)	(N=115)	(N=46)	(N=56)	(N=33)
Third sibling	22%	16%	17%	12%	23%	7%	27%	15%
Some other sibling	78	84	83	88	77	93	73	85
3L. Which would you say was your father's favorite?	(N=312)	(N=69)	(N=150)	(N=32)	(N=111)	(N=44)	(N=56)	(N=30)
Third sibling	24%	19%	15%	16%	28%	25%	18%	27%
Some other sibling	76	81	85	84	72	75	82	73

BROTHERS AND SISTERS/Fourth Sibling

	WHM	BHM	WHTM	BHTM	WHF	BHF	WHTF	BHTF
4A. Identity of fourth sibling	(N=213)	(N=64)	(N=97)	(N=18)	(N=63)	(N=37)	(N=33)	(N=29)
Natural	69%	61%	65%	65%	70%	59%	79%	66%
Step	16	30	8	18	17	19	9	14
Respondent	15	9	27	18	13	22	12	21
4B. Gender of fourth sibling	(N=213)	(N=64)	(N=97)	(N=18)	(N=63)	(N=37)	(N=34)	(N=29)
Male	54%	59%	65%	56%	49%	41%	35%	21%
Female	46	41	35	44	51	59	65	79
4C. Age of fourth sibling	(N=212)	(N=64)	(N=97)	(N=18)	(N=63)	(N=37)	(N=34)	(N=29)
Under 15	7%	12%	11%	11%	5%	8%	18%	10%
15-24	28	45	26	44	22	38	29	48
25-34	19	23	18	44	19	24	15	38
35-44	20	12	21	0	21	24	15	3
45 and older	26	6	25	0	33	5	24	0
4D. Did you ever engage in any sexual activity with him/her while growing up?	(N=207)	(N=64)	(N=97)	(N=18)	(N=62)	(N=37)	(N=34)	(N=23)
Yes	24%	16%	12%	11%	5%	8%	9%	7%
No	76	84	88	89	95	92	91	93
4 E. How often did you engage in this activity with him/her?	(N=177)	(N=58)	(N=71)	(N=15)	(N=54)	(N=29)	(N=30)	(N=23)
Never	85%	90%	90%	87%	96%	97%	97%	100%
Rarely	12	10	8	7	2	3	3	0
Sometimes	1	0	1	7	0	0	0	0
Often	2	0	0	0	2	0	0	0

61

BROTHERS AND SISTERS/Fourth Sibling

	WHM	BHM	WHTM	BHTM	WHF	BHF	WHTF	BHTF
4F. How would you classify him/her on the Kinsey Scale?	(N=173)	(N=56)	(N=70)	(N=14)	(N=53)	(N=29)	(N=31)	(N=23)
0: Exclusively heterosexual	76%	82%	90%	100%	75%	93%	93%	96%
1: Mainly heterosexual with a small degree of homosexuality	13	4	6	0	11	7	7	4
2: Mainly hetereosexual with a substantial degree of homosexuality	8	7	1	0	4	0	0	0
3: Equally heterosexual and homosexual	2	0	1	0	4	0	0	0
4: Mainly homosexual with a substantial degree of heterosexuality	1	4	0	0	0	0	0	0
5: Mainly homosexual with a small degree of heterosexuality	1	2	0	0	4	0	0	0
6: Exclusively homosexual	1	2	1	0	2	0	0	0
4G. During the time you were growing up, how close did you feel to him/her?	(N=174)	(N=57)	(N=70)	(N=15)	(N=54)	(N=29)	(N=29)	(N=23)
Not at all close	16%	14%	23%	20%	28%	28%	10%	22%
Not very close	20	21	24	27	13	7	14	9
Somewhat close	30	39	29	27	35	28	31	17
Very close	34	26	24	27	24	38	45	52
4H. During this same time, how much did you feel like or similar to him/her?	(N=175)	(N=57)	(N=70)	(N=15)	(N=54)	(N=29)	(N=28)	(N=23)
Not at all similar	46%	47%	46%	33%	63%	55%	32%	22%
Not very similar	21	26	24	27	17	14	11	13
Somewhat similar	23	19	23	33	11	21	32	48
Very similar	10	7	7	7	9	10	25	17
4I. How would you order your siblings in terms of their emotional closeness to you during the time you were growing up? [Fourth sibling]	(N=171)	(N=58)	(N=71)	(N=13)	(N=50)	(N=26)	(N=29)	(N=23)
Closest to this sibling	1%	0%	1%	0%	0%	0%	0%	0%
Neither very close nor very distant	97	98	99	100	96	96	100	100
Least close to this sibling	2	2	0	0	4	4	0	0

BROTHERS AND SISTERS/Fourth Sibling; Fifth Sibling

	WHM	BHM	WHTM	BHTM	WHF	BHF	WHTF	BHTF
4J. Would you order them in terms of how similar you felt to each while growing up? [Fourth sibling]	(N=167)	(N=58)	(N=71)	(N=13)	(N=47)	(N=25)	(N=29)	(N=23)
Most similar to this sibling	1%	0%	1%	0%	0%	0%	0%	0%
Neither very similar nor very dissimilar	97	98	98	100	98	100	100	100
Least similar to this sibling	2	2	1	0	2	0	0	0
4K. Which would you say was your mother's favorite during the time you were growing up?	(N=205)	(N=61)	(N=95)	(N=17)	(N=60)	(N=37)	(N=33)	(N=29)
Fourth sibling	15%	2%	14%	24%	15%	11%	21%	17%
Some other sibling	85	98	86	76	85	89	79	83
4L. Which would you say was your father's favorite?	(N=200)	(N=56)	(N=95)	(N=17)	(N=57)	(N=36)	(N=33)	(N=27)
Fourth sibling	18%	5%	23%	12%	9%	19%	18%	7%
Some other sibling	82	95	77	88	91	81	82	93
5A. Identity of fifth sibling	(N=136)	(N=48)	(N=60)	(N=9)	(N=36)	(N=26)	(N=23)	(N=22)
Natural	74%	54%	77%	78%	58%	77%	65%	77%
Step	15	29	10	11	19	23	13	14
Respondent	10	17	13	11	22	0	22	9
5B. Gender of fifth sibling	(N=136)	(N=48)	(N=60)	(N=9)	(N=36)	(N=26)	(N=23)	(N=22)
Male	58%	60%	50%	56%	31%	46%	30%	45%
Female	42	40	50	44	69	54	70	55
5C. Age of fifth sibling	(N=136)	(N=48)	(N=60)	(N=9)	(N=36)	(N=26)	(N=23)	(N=22)
Under 15	13%	25%	12%	11%	6%	15%	22%	14%
15-24	21	33	32	78	19	31	39	50
25-34	24	25	12	11	14	15	4	36
35-44	14	15	22	0	39	35	9	0
45 or older	28	2	23	0	22	4	26	0

63

BROTHERS AND SISTERS/Fifth Sibling

	WHM	BHM	WHTM	BHTM	WHF	BHF	WHTF	BHTF
	(N=135)	(N=48)	(N=60)	(N=9)	(N=35)	(N=26)	(N=23)	(N=21)
5D. Did you ever engage in any sexual activity with him/her while growing up?								
Yes	25%	12%	3%	11%	23%	8%	4%	0%
No	75	88	97	89	77	92	96	100
	(N=121)	(N=40)	(N=52)	(N=8)	(N=27)	(N=26)	(N=18)	(N=19)
5E. How often did you engage in this activity with him/her?								
Never	79%	95%	100%	88%	89%	92%	94%	100%
Rarely	17	2	0	12	7	4	6	0
Sometimes	2	2	0	0	0	4	0	0
Often	1	0	0	0	4	0	0	0
	(N=119)	(N=39)	(N=50)	(N=8)	(N=25)	(N=26)	(N=18)	(N=19)
5F. How would you classify him/her on the Kinsey Scale?								
0: Exclusively heterosexual	80%	92%	90%	100%	84%	96%	83%	95%
1: Mainly heterosexual with a small degree of homosexuality	13	5	8	0	4	4	17	5
2: Mainly heterosexual with a substantial degree of homosexuality	3	0	0	0	4	0	0	0
3: Equally heterosexual and homosexual	3	3	2	0	0	0	0	0
4: Mainly homosexual with a substantial degree of heterosexuality	0	0	0	0	0	0	0	0
5: Mainly homosexual with a small degree of heterosexuality	0	0	0	0	8	0	0	0
6: Exclusively homosexual	1	0	0	0	0	0	0	0
	(N=116)	(N=40)	(N=50)	(N=8)	(N=25)	(N=26)	(N=18)	(N=19)
5G. During the time you were growing up, how close did you feel to him/her?								
Not at all close	16%	15%	20%	0%	28%	35%	6%	37%
Not very close	19	32	22	25	28	4	17	11
Somewhat close	25	22	28	62	20	23	28	11
Very close	41	30	30	12	24	38	50	42

64

BROTHERS AND SISTERS/Fifth Sibling

	WHM	BHM	WHTM	BHTM	WHF	BHF	WHTF	BHTF
5H. During this same time, how much did you feel like or similar to him/her?	(N=116)	(N=40)	(N=50)	(N=8)	(N=25)	(N=26)	(N=17)	(N=19)
Not at all similar	41%	40%	40%	38%	64%	65%	35%	42%
Not very similar	23	30	26	38	20	12	12	11
Somewhat similar	22	20	22	25	8	12	35	32
Very similar	15	10	12	0	8	12	18	16
5I. How would you order your siblings in terms of their emotional,closeness to you during the time you were growing up? [Fifth sibling]	(N=116)	(N=40)	(N=51)	(N=7)	(N=25)	(N=24)	(N=18)	(N=20)
Closest to this sibling	16%	20%	10%	0%	24%	0%	11%	30%
Neither very close nor very distant	82	72	90	71	76	96	89	70
Least close to this sibling	3	8	0	29	0	4	0	0
5J. Would you order them in terms of how similar you felt to each while growing up? [Fifth sibling]	(N=113)	(N=39)	(N=51)	(N=7)	(N=24)	(N=23)	(N=18)	(N=20)
Most similar to this sibling	21%	13%	10%	0%	17%	0%	11%	25%
Neither very similar nor very dissimilar	77	85	90	71	79	96	83	75
Least similar to this sibling	2	3	0	29	4	4	6	0
5K. Which would you say was your mother's favorite during the time you were growing up?	(N=130)	(N=46)	(N=59)	(N=8)	(N=32)	(N=26)	(N=23)	(N=22)
Fifth sibling	9%	11%	10%	25%	16%	12%	9%	5%
Some other sibling	91	89	90	75	84	88	91	95
5L. Which would you say was your father's favorite?	(N=128)	(N=43)	(N=59)	(N=8)	(N=31)	(N=26)	(N=23)	(N=21)
Fifth sibling	15%	12%	10%	12%	13%	12%	9%	14%
Some other sibling	85	88	90	88	87	88	91	86

BROTHERS AND SISTERS/Sixth Sibling

		WHM	BHM	WHTM	BHTM	WHF	BHF	WHTF	BHTF
6A.	Identity of sixth sibling	(N=82)	(N=35)	(N=37)	(N=5)	(N=23)	(N=19)	(N=14)	(N=14)
	Natural	65%	63%	86%	60%	78%	58%	93%	71%
	Step	18	31	8	20	17	21	7	14
	Respondent	17	6	5	20	4	21	0	14
6B.	Gender of sixth sibling	(N=82)	(N=35)	(N=37)	(N=5)	(N=23)	(N=19)	(N=14)	(N=14)
	Male	65%	69%	57%	60%	48%	53%	71%	43%
	Female	35	31	43	40	52	47	29	57
6C.	Age of sixth sibling	(N=80)	(N=35)	(N=37)	(N=5)	(N=22)	(N=17)	(N=14)	(N=14)
	Under 15	11%	34%	14%	20%	5%	12%	21%	21%
	15-24	22	37	30	80	18	35	43	57
	25-34	24	14	16	0	9	29	0	21
	35-44	12	11	19	0	50	24	7	0
	45 or older	30	3	22	0	18	0	29	0
6D.	Did you ever engage in any sexual activity with him/her while growing up?	(N=79)	(N=35)	(N=37)	(N=5)	(N=20)	(N=19)	(N=14)	(N=14)
	Yes	24%	11%	3%	0%	10%	0%	7%	0%
	No	76	89	97	100	90	100	93	100
6E.	How often did you engage in this activity with him/her?	(N=65)	(N=33)	(N=35)	(N=4)	(N=19)	(N=15)	(N=14)	(N=12)
	Never	85%	91%	100%	100%	89%	100%	93%	100%
	Rarely	9	9	0	0	11	0	7	0
	Sometimes	3	0	0	0	0	0	0	0
	Often	3	0	0	0	0	0	0	0

BROTHERS AND SISTERS/Sixth Sibling

	WHM	BHM	WHTM	BHTM	WHF	BHF	WHTF	BHTF
6F. How would you classify him/her on the Kinsey Scale?	(N=60)	(N=32)	(N=32)	(N=4)	(N=17)	(N=15)	(N=14)	(N=12)
0: Exclusively heterosexual	85%	94%	97%	75%	76%	87%	93%	92%
1: Mainly heterosexual with a small degree of homosexuality	8	6	3	25	12	0	7	8
2: Mainly heterosexual with a substantial degree of homosexuality	2	0	0	0	6	0	0	0
3: Equally heterosexual and homosexual	3	0	0	0	0	7	0	0
4: Mainly homosexual with a substantial degree of heterosexuality	0	0	0	0	0	0	0	0
5: Mainly homosexual with a small degree of heterosexuality	2	0	0	0	6	0	0	0
6: Exclusively homosexual	0	0	0	0	0	7	0	0
6G. During the time you were growing up, how close did you feel to him/her?	(N=62)	(N=33)	(N=33)	(N=4)	(N=17)	(N=15)	(N=14)	(N=12)
Not at all close	15%	18%	15%	0%	17%	33%	7%	25%
Not very close	29	21	27	25	11	0	14	8
Somewhat close	24	39	21	25	22	27	50	17
Very close	32	21	0	50	50	40	29	50
6H. During this same time, how much did you feel like or similar to him/her?	(N=62)	(N=33)	(N=33)	(N=4)	(N=18)	(N=15)	(N=14)	(N=12)
Not at all similar	48%	36%	36%	75%	44%	67%	14%	42%
Not very similar	19	27	21	25	11	7	57	17
Somewhat similar	23	24	33	0	22	7	14	25
Very similar	10	12	9	0	22	20	14	17
6I. How would you order your siblings in terms of their emotional closeness to you during the time you were growing up? [Sixth sibling]	(N=59)	(N=32)	(N=34)	(N=3)	(N=19)	(N=14)	(N=14)	(N=12)
Closest to this sibling	14%	6%	6%	0%	42%	0%	7%	8%
Neither very close nor very distant	83	94	91	100	47	93	93	92
Least close to this sibling	3	0	3	0	11	7	0	0

BROTHERS AND SISTERS/Sixth Sibling; Seventh Sibling

	WHM	BHM	WHTM	BHTM	WHF	BHF	WHTF	BHTF
6J. Would you order them in terms of how similar you felt to each while growing up? [Sixth sibling]	(N=57)	(N=31)	(N=34)	(N=3)	(N=18)	(N=13)	(N=14)	(N=12)
Most similar to this sibling	7%	13%	9%	0%	44%	23%	7%	8%
Neither very similar nor very dissimilar	89	84	88	100	56	69	86	83
Least similar to this sibling	4	3	3	0	0	8	7	8
6K. Which would you say was your mother's favorite during the time you were growing up?	(N=76)	(N=34)	(N=36)	(N=4)	(N=20)	(N=19)	(N=14)	(N=14)
Sixth sibling	14%	3%	19%	0%	0%	16%	7%	0%
Some other sibling	86	97	81	100	100	84	93	100
6L. Which would you say was your father's favorite?	(N=73)	(N=33)	(N=36)	(N=4)	(N=21)	(N=19)	(N=14)	(N=14)
Sixth sibling	7%	12%	17%	0%	5%	16%	14%	7%
Some other sibling	93	88	83	100	95	84	86	93
7A. Identity of seventh sibling	(N=50)	(N=24)	(N=22)	(N=4)	(N=16)	(N=9)	(N=9)	(N=8)
Natural	72%	71%	91%	75%	69%	67%	78%	88%
Step	16	17	5	25	6	33	11	12
Respondent	12	12	5	0	25	0	11	0
7B. Gender of seventh sibling	(N=50)	(N=24)	(N=22)	(N=4)	(N=16)	(N=9)	(N=9)	(N=8)
Male	54%	50%	55%	100%	31%	67%	56%	88%
Female	46	50	45	0	69	33	44	12

68

BROTHERS AND SISTERS/Seventh Sibling

	WHM	BHM	WHTM	BHTM	WHF	BHF	WHTF	BHTF
	(N=48)	(N=24)	(N=22)	(N=4)	(N=16)	(N=9)	(N=9)	(N=8)
7C. Age of seventh sibling								
Under 15	6%	33%	23%	75%	0%	33%	11%	50%
15-24	23	29	18	25	12	22	44	25
25-34	27	17	18	0	6	33	0	25
35-44	17	17	18	0	56	11	22	0
45 or older	27	4	23	0	25	0	22	0
	(N=49)	(N=24)	(N=22)	(N=4)	(N=15)	(N=9)	(N=9)	(N=8)
7D. Did you ever engage in sexual activity with him/her while growing up?								
Yes	10%	21%	5%	0%	20%	0%	0%	0%
No	90	79	95	100	80	100	100	100
	(N=43)	(N=21)	(N=21)	(N=4)	(N=11)	(N=9)	(N=8)	(N=8)
7E. How often did you engage in this activity with him/her?								
Never	93%	90%	100%	100%	82%	100%	100%	100%
Rarely	7	10	0	0	9	0	0	0
Sometimes	0	0	0	0	9	0	0	0
Often	0	0	0	0	0	0	0	0
	(N=40)	(N=21)	(N=20)	(N=4)	(N=11)	(N=9)	(N=6)	(N=8)
7F. How would you classify him/her on the Kinsey Scale?								
0: Exclusively heterosexual	82%	95%	95%	100%	55%	100%	100%	100%
1: Mainly heterosexual with a small degree of homosexuality	12	5	5	0	27	0	0	0
2: Mainly heterosexual with a substantial degree of homosexuality	2	0	0	0	9	0	0	0
3: Equally heterosexual and homosexual	0	0	0	0	9	0	0	0
4: Mainly homosexual with a substantial degree of heterosexuality	0	0	0	0	0	0	0	0
5: Mainly homosexual with a small degree of heterosexuality	0	0	0	0	0	0	0	0
6: Exclusively homosexual	2	0	0	0	0	0	0	0

	WHM	BHM	WHTM	BHTM	WHF	BHF	WHTF	BHTF
	(N=43)	(N=21)	(N=20)	(N=4)	(N=11)	(N=9)	(N=7)	(N=8)
7G. During the time you were growing up, how close did you feel to him/her?								
Not at all close	21%	14%	20%	0%	36%	33%	14%	38%
Not very close	19	33	15	50	0	0	14	0
Somewhat close	35	24	45	25	27	22	29	12
Very close	26	29	20	25	36	44	43	50
	(N=43)	(N=21)	(N=20)	(N=4)	(N=11)	(N=9)	(N=7)	(N=8)
7H. During this same time, how much did you feel like or similar to him/her?								
Not at all similar	58%	33%	45%	50%	45%	67%	14%	62%
Not very similar	26	29	20	25	9	22	14	0
Somewhat similar	12	19	25	25	27	11	43	25
Very similar	5	19	10	0	18	0	29	12
	(N=41)	(N=21)	(N=21)	(N=3)	(N=11)	(N=8)	(N=8)	(N=8)
7I. How would you order your siblings in terms of their emotional closeness to you during the time you were growing up? [Seventh sibling]								
Closest to this sibling	10%	24%	10%	0%	18%	0%	0%	0%
Neither very close nor very distant	85	71	90	100	73	100	100	62
Least close to this sibling	5	5	0	0	9	0	0	38
	(N=39)	(N=20)	(N=21)	(N=3)	(N=10)	(N=7)	(N=8)	(N=8)
7J. Would you order them in terms of how similar you felt to each during the time you were growing up? [Seventh sibling]								
Most similar to this sibling	5%	25%	10%	0%	40%	14%	25%	0%
Neither very similar nor very dissimilar	92	70	90	100	40	57	75	88
Least similar to this sibling	3	5	0	0	20	29	0	12
	(N=48)	(N=24)	(N=21)	(N=3)	(N=15)	(N=9)	(N=9)	(N=8)
7K. Which would you say was your mother's favorite during the time you were growing up?								
Seventh sibling	15%	12%	5%	33%	7%	11%	0%	0%
Some other sibling	85	88	95	67	93	89	100	100

BROTHERS AND SISTERS/Seventh Sibling; Eighth Sibling

	WHM	BHM	WHTM	BHTM	WHF	BHF	WHTF	BHTF
7L. Which would you say was your father's favorite?	(N=47)	(N=23)	(N=21)	(N=3)	(N=16)	(N=9)	(N=9)	(N=8)
Seventh sibling	6%	9%	0%	67%	12%	0%	11%	0%
Some other sibling	94	91	100	33	88	100	89	100
8A. Identity of eighth sibling	(N=32)	(N=16)	(N=13)	(N=3)	(N=12)	(N=5)	(N=5)	(N=7)
Natural	59%	69%	85%	67%	67%	80%	100%	86%
Step	16	19	15	33	8	20	0	14
Respondent	25	12	0	0	25	0	0	0
8B. Gender of eighth sibling	(N=32)	(N=16)	(N=13)	(N=3)	(N=12)	(N=5)	(N=5)	(N=7)
Male	56%	50%	77%	33%	42%	60%	40%	57%
Female	44	50	23	67	58	40	60	43
8C. Age of eighth sibling	(N=31)	(N=14)	(N=13)	(N=3)	(N=12)	(N=5)	(N=5)	(N=7)
Under 15	10%	43%	46%	67%	0%	40%	60%	43%
15-24	23	29	8	33	0	40	0	57
25-34	23	7	15	0	42	20	0	0
35-44	16	21	8	0	33	0	20	0
45 or older	29	0	23	0	25	0	20	0
8D. Did you ever engage in any sexual activity with him/her while you were growing up?	(N=32)	(N=16)	(N=13)	(N=3)	(N=11)	(N=5)	(N=6)	(N=7)
Yes	16%	25%	8%	0%	27%	20%	0%	0%
No	84	75	92	100	73	80	100	100
8E. How often did you engage in this activity with him/her?	(N=24)	(N=14)	(N=13)	(N=3)	(N=8)	(N=5)	(N=5)	(N=7)
Never	100%	86%	100%	100%	88%	80%	100%	100%
Rarely	0	14	0	0	12	20	0	0
Sometimes	0	0	0	0	0	0	0	0
Often	0	0	0	0	0	0	0	0

71

BROTHERS AND SISTERS/Eighth Sibling

	WHM	BHM	WHTM	BHTM	WHF	BHF	WHTF	BHTF
8F. How would you classify him/her on the Kinsey Scale?	(N=22)	(N=14)	(N=12)	(N=3)	(N=7)	(N=5)	(N=5)	(N=7)
0: Exclusively heterosexual	86%	93%	83%	100%	71%	100%	100%	100%
1: Mainly heterosexual with a small degree of homosexuality	5	7	0	0	29	0	0	0
2: Mainly heterosexual with a substantial degree of homosexuality	5	0	8	0	0	0	0	0
3: Equally heterosexual and homosexual	5	0	0	0	0	0	0	0
4: Mainly homosexual with a substantial degree of heterosexuality	0	0	0	0	0	0	0	0
5: Mainly homosexual with a small degree of heterosexuality	0	0	8	0	0	0	0	0
6: Exclusively homosexual	0	0	0	0	0	0	0	0
8G. During the time you were growing up, how close did you feel to him/her?	(N=24)	(N=14)	(N=12)	(N=3)	(N=8)	(N=5)	(N=5)	(N=7)
Not at all close	21%	14%	25%	0%	62%	20%	0%	14%
Not very close	38	14	33	33	25	0	0	14
Somewhat close	21	43	33	33	0	20	60	14
Very close	21	29	8	33	12	60	40	57
8H. During this same time, how much did you feel like or similar to him/her?	(N=24)	(N=14)	(N=11)	(N=3)	(N=8)	(N=5)	(N=5)	(N=7)
Not at all similar	42%	43%	64%	67%	62%	60%	0%	43%
Not very similar	21	43	27	0	25	0	20	14
Somewhat similar	25	7	0	33	12	40	80	43
Very similar	12	7	9	0	0	0	0	0
8I. How would you order your siblings in terms of their emotional closeness to you during the time you were growing up? [Eighth sibling]	(N=22)	(N=14)	(N=13)	(N=2)	(N=8)	(N=4)	(N=5)	(N=7)
Closest to this sibling	9%	7%	15%	0%	12%	0%	20%	0%
Neither very close nor very distant	82	71	54	100	62	100	60	43
Least close to this sibling	9	21	31	0	25	0	20	57

72

BROTHERS AND SISTERS/Eighth Sibling

	WHM	BHM	WHTM	BHTM	WHF	BHF	WHTF	BHTF
8J. Would you order them in terms of how similar you felt to each while growing up? [Eighth sibling]	(N=21)	(N=14)	(N=13)	(N=2)	(N=7)	(N=3)	(N=5)	(N=7)
Most similar to this sibling	14%	21%	0%	0%	0%	0%	20%	0%
Neither very similar or very dissimilar	71	64	85	100	71	67	80	43
Least similar to this sibling	14	14	15	0	29	33	0	57
8K. Which would you say was your mother's favorite during the time you were growing up?	(N=31)	(N=16)	(N=12)	(N=2)	(N=11)	(N=5)	(N=5)	(N=7)
Eighth sibling	16%	12%	0%	50%	0%	0%	0%	29%
Some other sibling	84	88	100	50	100	100	100	71
8L. Which would you say was your father's favorite?	(N=31)	(N=15)	(N=12)	(N=2)	(N=12)	(N=5)	(N=5)	(N=7)
Eighth sibling	87%	100%	92%	100%	92%	80%	100%	86%
Some other sibling	13	0	8	0	8	20	0	14
Were there more than eight children in your family?	(N=575)	(N=111)	(N=284)	(N=53)	(N=229)	(N=64)	(N=101)	(N=39)
Yes	4%	6%	4%	0%	4%	2%	5%	13%
No	96	94	96	100	96	98	95	87

73

GENDER CONFORMITY/Play Activities

	WHM	BHM	WHTM	BHTM	WHF	BHF	WHTF	BHTF
[While you were in grade school,] to what extent did you enjoy specifically boys' activities (e.g., baseball, football)?	(N=575)	(N=111)	(N=284)	(N=53)	(N=229)	(N=64)	(N=101)	(N=39)
Not at all	36%	11%	2%	0%	8%	12%	21%	18%
Very little	32	26	9	4	7	22	23	10
Somewhat	21	32	19	13	14	9	29	18
Very much	11	32	70	83	71	56	28	54
To what extent did you enjoy activities which aren't particularly for boys or girls (e.g., drawing, music, reading)?	(N=575)	(N=111)	(N=284)	(N=53)	(N=229)	(N=64)	(N=101)	(N=39)
Not at all	3%	5%	10%	4%	5%	3%	4%	5%
Very little	7	8	24	13	10	5	5	5
Somewhat	22	28	33	43	14	20	23	21
Very much	68	59	34	40	72	72	68	69
To what extent did you enjoy specifically girls' activities (e.g., hopscotch, playing house, jacks)?	(N=575)	(N=111)	(N=284)	(N=53)	(N=229)	(N=64)	(N=101)	(N=39)
Not at all	25%	23%	59%	47%	38%	28%	5%	5%
Very little	28	22	30	43	29	23	13	3
Somewhat	29	29	11	8	19	28	28	23
Very much	17	27	1	2	14	20	54	69
Did you ever dress in [opposite-sex] clothes and pretend to be a [child of the opposite sex] other than at Halloween or for school plays?	(N=574)	(N=111)	(N=284)	(N=53)	(N=229)	(N=64)	(N=100)	(N=39)
Yes	32%	36%	10%	8%	49%	28%	7%	5%
No	63	64	90	92	51	72	93	95

Now, I'd like you to describe the kind of person you were during the time you were growing up (until age 17). [For example, if you were extremely strong you would circle 6. On the other hand, if you were extremely weak you would circle 0.]

	WHM	BHM	WHTM	BHTM	WHF	BHF	WHTF	BHTF
	(N=573)	(N=110)	(N=284)	(N=53)	(N=229)	(N=64)	(N=101)	(N=39)
A. Strong/weak								
0 Weak	4%	0%	1%	2%	3%	6%	1%	0%
1	8	5	0	0	4	0	2	3
2	20	6	9	8	9	8	6	5
3	23	16	20	6	15	9	18	23
4	21	24	28	19	19	16	23	5
5	14	25	30	32	27	22	25	10
6 Strong	11	24	11	34	22	39	26	54
B. Active/passive								
	(N=573)	(N=110)	(N=284)	(N=53)	(N=229)	(N=64)	(N=101)	(N=39)
0 Passive	3%	3%	0%	0%	3%	6%	1%	0%
1	5	6	1	2	3	0	3	5
2	13	5	7	2	6	6	10	5
3	17	6	7	8	8	9	9	8
4	14	12	17	9	12	14	11	15
5	19	23	40	28	27	23	24	18
6 Active	27	45	29	51	41	41	43	49
C. Masculine/feminine								
	(N=573)	(N=110)	(N=284)	(N=53)	(N=229)	(N=64)	(N=101)	(N=39)
0 Feminine	2%	4%	0%	0%	6%	11%	32%	51%
1	8	3	0	0	5	11	19	21
2	18	11	1	0	7	6	23	13
3	30	30	7	6	21	22	17	13
4	25	15	24	13	26	22	8	0
5	13	25	42	26	22	17	2	0
6 Masculine	5	13	25	55	14	11	0	3

GENDER CONFORMITY/Gender Traits; Parents' Prenatal Wishes

	WHM	BHM	WHTM	BHTM	WHF	BHF	WHTF	BHTF
D. Dominant/submissive	(N=573)	(N=110)	(N=284)	(N=53)	(N=227)	(N=64)	(N=101)	(N=39)
0 Submissive	8%	7%	1%	2%	7%	8%	4%	8%
1	12	7	2	0	5	6	13	10
2	23	12	10	6	12	11	13	8
3	26	30	38	45	21	17	27	26
4	14	19	25	23	22	12	23	23
5	11	13	18	17	16	36	15	13
6 Dominant	6	12	6	8	17	9	6	13
E. Independent/dependent	(N=574)	(N=110)	(N=282)	(N=53)	(N=228)	(N=64)	(N=101)	(N=39)
0 Dependent	6%	1%	1%	2%	5%	8%	4%	3%
1	9	4	3	2	5	3	9	8
2	11	6	7	0	4	0	6	0
3	15	8	16	21	12	12	18	23
4	15	18	24	28	12	5	15	15
5	22	29	31	21	29	27	21	8
6 Independent	22	34	18	26	32	45	28	44
Before you were born, did either or both of your parents want you to be of the opposite sex?	(N=552)	(N=111)	(N=283)	(N=53)	(N=222)	(N=64)	(N=100)	(N=39)
Both parents did	4%	1%	2%	0%	9%	0%	4%	8%
Father did	1	0	0	0	17	17	11	3
Mother did	14	17	6	2	4	3	1	5
Neither parent did	55	43	61	32	51	34	66	56
Don't know	27	39	30	66	19	45	18	28

76

OUTSIDE THE FAMILY CIRCLE/Relationships with Peers (Grade School)

	WHM	BHM	WHTM	BHTM	WHF	BHF	WHTF	BHTF
I wonder if you could tell me a little bit about your grade school years (grades 1-8). Was there any time during this period that you had an especially close friend of the same sex?	(N=575)	(N=111)	(N=284)	(N=53)	(N=229)	(N=64)	(N=101)	(N=39)
Yes	73%	81%	81%	94%	70%	73%	84%	74%
No	27	19	19	6	30	27	16	26
Was there any time during this period that you had an especially close friend of the opposite sex?	(N=575)	(N=111)	(N=284)	(N=53)	(N=229)	(N=64)	(N=101)	(N=39)
Yes	54%	64%	46%	81%	44%	47%	37%	23%
No	46	36	54	19	56	53	63	77
During these years, what proportion of your friends your own age were boys?	(N=573)	(N=111)	(N=284)	(N=53)	(N=228)	(N=64)	(N=101)	(N=39)
None	1%	1%	0%	2%	10%	8%	7%	3%
Only a few	8	5	0	2	18	27	30	33
Less than half	10	8	1	9	11	8	26	18
About half	22	31	7	23	29	17	27	28
More than half	15	14	19	34	9	16	7	3
Most	35	38	57	30	21	19	4	13
All	9	5	15	0	2	7	0	3
During these years, to what extent were you a loner?	(N=575)	(N=111)	(N=284)	(N=53)	(N=229)	(N=64)	(N=101)	(N=39)
Not at all	8%	12%	15%	28%	17%	17%	17%	31%
Very little	22	27	35	30	17	20	39	23
Somewhat	33	29	33	32	34	36	34	28
Very much	38	32	17	9	31	27	11	18

OUTSIDE THE FAMILY CIRCLE/Relationships with Peers (Grade School)

	WHM	BHM	WHTM	BHTM	WHF	BHF	WHTF	BHTF
	(N=575)	(N=111)	(N=284)	(N=53)	(N=229)	(N=64)	(N=101)	(N=39)
How often did you feel left out?								
Never	8%	16%	14%	36%	17%	16%	16%	23%
Rarely	25	33	32	34	23	23	28	36
Sometimes	33	38	41	23	28	38	33	26
Often	34	13	13	8	31	23	24	15
After regular school hours, how much of your leisure time was spent with kids your own age?	(N=575)	(N=111)	(N=284)	(N=53)	(N=229)	(N=64)	(N=101)	(N=39)
None	3%	8%	1%	2%	3%	9%	5%	3%
Very little	27	23	9	11	23	27	11	28
Some	30	25	31	38	27	41	34	36
Much	39	43	60	49	47	23	50	33
During this time, was there a group of all [same-sex children] with whom you palled around?	(N=575)	(N=111)	(N=284)	(N=53)	(N=229)	(N=64)	(N=101)	(N=39)
Yes	55%	61%	76%	85%	41%	44%	75%	64%
No	45	39	24	15	59	56	25	36
Would you say that you had more, as many as, or fewer friends during those years than other kids your age?	(N=575)	(N=111)	(N=284)	(N=53)	(N=229)	(N=64)	(N=101)	(N=39)
Fewer	42%	30%	20%	8%	37%	36%	22%	26%
As many as	49	42	66	72	51	53	66	67
More	9	28	14	21	12	11	12	8
How popular were you with kids your own age?	(N=575)	(N=111)	(N=284)	(N=52)	(N=229)	(N=64)	(N=101)	(N=39)
Not popular at all	6%	3%	1%	0%	7%	8%	3%	0%
Not very popular	23	14	15	6	23	17	13	15
Somewhat popular	52	46	64	54	51	36	55	51
Very popular	19	37	20	40	20	39	29	33

78

OUTSIDE THE FAMILY CIRCLE/Feeling Different (Grade School); Relationships with Peers (High School)

	WHM	BHM	WHTM	BHTM	WHF	BHF	WHTF	BHTF
During grade school, to what extent do you think you were different from the other [same-sex children] your age?	(N=573)	(N=111)	(N=283)	(N=53)	(N=229)	(N=64)	(N=101)	(N=39)
Not at all	12%	23%	21%	55%	17%	23%	17%	28%
Very little	16	14	40	15	11	12	29	28
Somewhat	43	39	27	17	32	36	40	31
Very much	30	23	12	13	41	28	15	13
In what ways do you think you were different?*	(N=417)	(N=69)	(N=111)	(N=16)	(N=165)	(N=41)	(N=55)	(N=17)
Amount of interest in sports	48%	26%	21%	0%	21%	10%	2%	0%
Homosexual interests and/or lack of heterosexual ones	18	20	1	6	15	22	2	0
Other gender-role reasons	23	12	1	0	35	27	9	18
Physical appearance or characteristics	17	9	19	25	18	34	29	12
Shy, ill at ease with peers	4	1	2	12	7	5	9	0
Felt more grown-up than peers	6	12	14	0	10	2	16	12
Traits or interests not related to gender	72	65	90	94	66	78	60	88
Some other reason	15	13	19	19	21	10	29	6
I wonder if you could tell me a little bit about your high school years (grades 9-12). Was there any time during this period that you had an especially close friend of the same sex?	(N=575)	(N=111)	(N=284)	(N=53)	(N=229)	(N=64)	(N=100)	(N=39)
Yes	85%	88%	80%	96%	87%	83%	90%	85%
No	15	12	20	4	13	17	10	15
Was there any time during this period that you had an especially close friend of the opposite sex?	(N=575)	(N=111)	(N=284)	(N=53)	(N=229)	(N=64)	(N=101)	(N=39)
Yes	63%	74%	70%	98%	50%	56%	70%	69%
No	37	26	30	2	50	44	30	31

*Respondents could give more than one answer to this question, so column percentages may add up to more than 100.

OUTSIDE THE FAMILY CIRCLE/Relationships with Peers (High School)

	WHM	BHM	WHTM	BHTM	WHF	BHF	WHTF	BHTF
	(N=575)	(N=111)	(N=284)	(N=53)	(N=229)	(N=64)	(N=101)	(N=39)
During those years, what proportion of your friends your own age were boys?								
None	1%	0%	0%	0%	15%	14%	6%	0%
Only a few	5	7	0	4	33	23	19	21
Less than half	7	9	1	13	17	20	33	18
About half	29	23	25	47	24	20	35	46
More than half	20	24	32	26	6	9	4	5
Most	30	30	36	9	4	11	4	10
All	9	6	5	0	0	2	0	0
	(N=575)	(N=111)	(N=284)	(N=53)	(N=229)	(N=64)	(N=101)	(N=39)
During those years, to what extent were you a loner?								
Not at all	8%	22%	17%	26%	15%	25%	23%	23%
Very little	22	23	31	36	18	31	32	33
Some	40	34	42	30	35	19	34	33
Very much	30	21	11	8	32	25	12	10
	(N=575)	(N=111)	(N=284)	(N=53)	(N=229)	(N=64)	(N=101)	(N=39)
How often did you feel left out?								
Never	10%	31%	15%	47%	19%	29%	18%	31%
Rarely	28	33	42	28	24	23	31	31
Sometimes	37	32	36	19	31	38	37	31
Often	25	5	7	6	27	11	15	8
	(N=574)	(N=111)	(N=284)	(N=53)	(N=229)	(N=64)	(N=101)	(N=39)
How much of your leisure time was spent with kids your own age?								
None	4%	10%	2%	4%	7%	12%	3%	3%
Very little	27	29	10	11	24	30	18	28
Some	32	31	33	40	28	30	35	36
Much	38	31	55	45	41	28	45	33

80

	WHM	BHM	WHTM	BHTM	WHF	BHF	WHTF	BHTF
During this time, was there a group of all [same-sex peers] with whom you palled around?	(N=575)	(N=111)	(N=284)	(N=53)	(N=229)	(N=64)	(N=101)	(N=39)
Yes	52%	63%	75%	79%	69%	56%	75%	49%
No	48	37	25	21	31	44	25	51
Would you say that you had more, as many as, or fewer friends during those years than other kids your age?	(N=575)	(N=111)	(N=284)	(N=53)	(N=229)	(N=64)	(N=101)	(N=39)
Fewer	40%	25%	13%	9%	34%	19%	19%	23%
As many as	45	46	68	60	48	64	69	69
More	15	29	19	30	17	17	12	8
How popular were you with kids your own age?	(N=575)	(N=111)	(N=284)	(N=53)	(N=227)	(N=64)	(N=100)	(N=39)
Not popular at all	5%	0%	0%	0%	7%	11%	2%	3%
Not very popular	20	12	10	6	26	5	9	10
Somewhat popular	53	42	66	43	46	26	66	56
Very popular	22	46	25	51	22	59	23	31
During this time period, to what extent do you think you were different from the other [same-sex peers] your age?	(N=571)	(N=111)	(N=284)	(N=53)	(N=227)	(N=63)	(N=101)	(N=39)
Not at all	4%	20%	18%	49%	9%	22%	14%	33%
Very little	9	21	37	28	10	13	29	28
Somewhat	47	33	32	11	38	30	34	33
Very much	39	26	13	11	43	35	24	5
In what ways do you think you were different?*	(N=495)	(N=66)	(N=128)	(N=12)	(N=185)	(N=42)	(N=58)	(N=15)
Amount of interest in sports	34%	21%	13%	0%	11%	5%	2%	0%
Homosexual interests and/or lack of heterosexual ones	57	58	2	0	51	48	7	7
Other gender-role reasons	12	8	1	0	12	10	0	0
Physical appearance or characteristics	8	2	9	8	10	19	19	13
Shy, ill at ease with peers	3	0	6	8	5	2	7	7
Felt more grown-up than peers	4	11	8	17	10	24	5	0
Traits or interests not related to gender	59	52	99	75	65	62	76	73
Some other reason	11	11	23	33	17	14	38	33

*Respondents could give more than one answer to this question, so column percentages may add up to more than 100.

81

OUTSIDE THE FAMILY CIRCLE/Feeling Different

	WHM	BHM	WHTM	BHTM	WHF	BHF	WHTF	BHTF
During the time that you were growing up, did you ever feel that you were sexually different?	(N=0)	(N=0)	(N=284)	(N=53)	(N=0)	(N=0)	(N=101)	(N=39)
Yes	[not asked of homosexuals]		12%	4%	[not asked of homosexuals]		10%	3%
No			88	96			90	97
In what way did you feel sexually different?*	(N=0)	(N=0)	(N=32)	(N=2)	(N=0)	(N=0)	(N=10)	(N=1)
Homosexual interests or behaviors	[not asked of homosexuals]		22%	0%	[not asked of homosexuals]		10%	0%
Lack of heterosexual interests or relationships			9	0			10	0
Dislike or fear of heterosexual sex			16	50			20	0
Some other way			66	50			70	100
How old were you when you felt that way?	(N=0)	(N=0)	(N=33)	(N=2)	(N=0)	(N=0)	(N=10)	(N=1)
Under 12	[not asked of homosexuals]		12%	0%	[not asked of homosexuals]		20%	100%
12-14			45	50			50	0
15-16			27	50			30	0
17-18			12	0			0	0
Over 18			3	0			0	0
How old were you when you first began to think of yourself as sexually different?	(N=572)	(N=110)	(N=0)	(N=0)	(N=219)	(N=63)	(N=0)	(N=0)
Under 12	20%	25%	[not asked of heterosexuals]		20%	29%	[not asked of heterosexuals]	
12-14	33	27			23	21		
15-16	19	13			20	10		
17-18	12	21			10	13		
Over 18	15	13			25	25		
Always felt sexually different	0	0			1	0		
Never felt sexually different	1	1			1	2		

*Respondents could give more than one answer to this question, so column percentages may add up to more than 100.

OUTSIDE THE FAMILY CIRCLE/Labeling

	WHM	BHM	WHTM	BHTM	WHF	BHF	WHTF	BHTF
[While you were growing up], had anyone ever suggested that you were sexually different or homosexual?	(N=571)	(N=111)	(N=284)	(N=53)	(N=229)	(N=64)	(N=101)	(N=39)
Yes	53%	64%	6%	6%	36%	44%	6%	5%
No	47	36	94	94	64	56	94	95
In what way did someone suggest that you were sexually different?	(N=0)	(N=0)	(N=17)	(N=3)	(N=0)	(N=0)	(N=6)	(N=2)
Homosexual label	[not asked of homosexuals]	[not asked of homosexuals]	76%	67%	[not asked of homosexuals]		100%	0%
Other label			24	33			0	100
How old were you when someone suggested that you were sexually different?	(N=438)	(N=83)	(N=17)	(N=2)	(N=216)	(N=62)	(N=6)	(N=2)
Under 12	12%	29%	0%	33%	4%	8%	0%	50%
12-14	21	25	53	67	9	8	0	0
15-16	17	14	12	0	19	21	0	0
17-18	20	17	12	0	21	17	0	0
Over 18	31	14	24	0	48	47	100	50
What was your reaction?	(N=433)	(N=82)	(N=17)	(N=2)	(N=144)	(N=52)	(N=6)	(N=2)
Positive (pleasure, relief, etc.)	9%	6%	12%	0%	13%	12%	0%	0%
Hurt feelings, disbelief	4	5	6	0	8	8	0	0
Negative (anger, worry, etc.)	57	66	47	50	53	46	83	50
Very negative (guilt, panic, etc.)	4	1	0	0	2	4	0	0
Mixed feelings	3	1	0	0	6	4	0	0
Some other reaction	3	1	0	0	4	2	17	0
No particular reaction	21	20	35	50	15	25	0	50
How old were you when you labeled the difference you felt "homosexual"?	(N=569)	(N=110)	(N=0)	(N=0)	(N=224)	(N=61)	(N=0)	(N=0)
Under 12	4%	13%	[not asked of heterosexuals]	[not asked of heterosexuals]	4%	5%	[not asked of heterosexuals]	[not asked of heterosexuals]
12-14	15	14			12	8		
15-16	16	15			13	11		
17-18	22	25			15	25		
Over 18	43	33			55	51		

83

OUTSIDE THE FAMILY CIRCLE/Dating Experiences

	WHM	BHM	WHTM	BHTM	WHF	BHF	WHTF	BHTF
While you were of high school age, did you date [opposite-sex peers] regularly, more than a few times but not regularly, just a few times, or did you never date?	(N=575)	(N=110)	(N=284)	(N=53)	(N=229)	(N=64)	(N=100)	(N=39)
Never	13%	11%	11%	2%	14%	17%	8%	13%
Just a few times	34	48	22	19	36	44	32	28
More than a few times, but not regularly	17	15	26	17	23	16	25	18
Regularly	36	26	41	62	27	23	35	41
How did you feel about dating? [Type of feelings reported]	(N=541)	(N=109)	(N=273)	(N=52)	(N=211)	(N=63)	(N=96)	(N=38)
Generally negative	37%	33%	13%	6%	31%	32%	10%	5%
Mixed feelings	10	11	7	4	11	8	7	5
Neutral feelings	9	14	7	4	7	19	8	3
Generally positive	44	42	73	87	52	41	74	87
[Specific reactions to dating]*	(N=574)	(N=110)	(N=280)	(N=53)	(N=224)	(N=64)	(N=97)	(N=38)
Enjoyed social aspects only	29%	10%	19%	21%	22%	22%	13%	68%
Enjoyed sexual aspects only	3	1	7	8	2	0	1	0
Enjoyed both aspects	16	25	34	47	16	14	49	8
It was the thing to do (to be accepted)	28	37	9	19	21	19	11	11
Wanted to appear heterosexual	4	5	0	0	3	3	0	0
Lack of heterosexual interests	19	15	1	0	17	17	3	3
Ill at ease with the opposite sex	24	13	19	8	14	6	14	3
Disliked sexual aspects of dating	9	5	1	0	8	8	0	3
Disliked dating altogether	5	5	3	6	4	2	5	0
Other positive comment	7	6	4	9	9	9	0	5
Other negative comment	11	16	17	11	19	24	17	5

*Respondents could give more than one answer to this question, so column percentages may add up to more than 100.

OUTSIDE THE FAMILY CIRCLE/Dating Experiences

	WHM	BHM	WHTM	BHTM	WHF	BHF	WHTF	BHTF
When you were of high school age, to what extent did your mother [mother surrogate] encourage or discourage dating?	(N=564)	(N=110)	(N=281)	(N=53)	(N=219)	(N=63)	(N=97)	(N=39)
Discouraged very much	4%	4%	3%	2%	11%	11%	10%	15%
Discouraged somewhat	8	3	9	4	9	16	8	10
Neither encouraged nor discouraged	49	59	59	43	42	40	60	62
Encouraged somewhat	26	24	23	40	24	19	16	10
Encouraged very much	12	11	6	11	15	14	5	3
How much did your father [father surrogate] encourage you to date?	(N=533)	(N=95)	(N=268)	(N=52)	(N=202)	(N=57)	(N=96)	(N=34)
Discouraged very much	2%	0%	1%	2%	11%	12%	11%	21%
Discouraged somewhat	3	2	5	2	10	19	11	9
Neither encouraged nor discouraged	66	69	68	42	55	49	61	53
Encouraged somewhat	21	13	19	38	19	18	14	18
Encouraged very much	8	16	7	15	4	2	2	0
Do you think you had less opportunity to become involved with the opposite sex than other [same-sex peers] in your age group?	(N=575)	(N=111)	(N=284)	(N=53)	(N=229)	(N=64)	(N=101)	(N=39)
Yes	19%	15%	13%	6%	23%	19%	32%	33%
No	81	85	87	94	77	81	68	67
[Circle the number that best describes you during the time you were growing up:] Good-looking/ugly.	(N=574)	(N=110)	(N=284)	(N=53)	(N=229)	(N=64)	(N=101)	(N=39)
0 Ugly	3%	6%	1%	4%	6%	6%	4%	8%
1	6	4	4	0	4	8	4	3
2	11	7	8	4	12	8	11	8
3	30	23	28	13	34	33	36	18
4	23	25	34	36	24	17	33	13
5	17	26	20	32	15	11	5	26
6 Good-looking	10	9	6	11	4	17	8	26

85

	WHM	BHM	WHTM	BHTM	WHF	BHF	WHTF	BHTF

Now, I'd like you to describe the kind of person you were during the time you were growing up (until age 17). [For example, if you were extremely adequate you would circle 6. On the other hand, if you were extremely inadequate you would circle 0.]

A. Adequate/inadequate

	WHM	BHM	WHTM	BHTM	WHF	BHF	WHTF	BHTF
	(N=573)	(N=110)	(N=284)	(N=53)	(N=227)	(N=64)	(N=101)	(N=39)
0 Inadequate	4%	2%	1%	2%	7%	11%	5%	3%
1	10	3	1	0	.7	3	1	8
2	15	5	13	4	16	9	12	3
3	23	17	19	15	19	17	16	18
4	21	23	33	13	19	19	19	15
5	17	31	25	25	18	19	26	15
6 Adequate	10	20	8	42	15	22	22	38

B. Relaxed/up-tight

	WHM	BHM	WHTM	BHTM	WHF	BHF	WHTF	BHTF
	(N=573)	(N=109)	(N=283)	(N=53)	(N=229)	(N=64)	(N=100)	(N=39)
0 Up-tight	10%	3%	2%	4%	12%	14%	7%	8%
1	14	10	6	4	18	12	9	0
2	21	10	16	6	20	12	19	8
3	22	17	25	18	21	20	26	44
4	16	23	21	15	14	12	14	3
5	12	20	18	32	9	16	16	26
6 Relaxed	5	17	11	23	7	12	9	13

During this period in your life [adolescence], how did you feel about things generally? Were you very happy, pretty happy, not too happy, or were you very unhappy?

	WHM	BHM	WHTM	BHTM	WHF	BHF	WHTF	BHTF
	(N=575)	(N=111)	(N=284)	(N=53)	(N=229)	(N=64)	(N=101)	(N=39)
Very unhappy	13%	5%	5%	4%	19%	11%	8%	5%
Not too happy	29	28	26	11	35	33	24	15
Pretty happy	39	54	50	43	36	39	52	59
Very happy	18	14	20	42	10	17	16	21

86

OUTSIDE THE FAMILY CIRCLE/Happiness and Self-Esteem

If you had one word to describe yourself during the time you were growing up, what would it be?

	WHM (N=569)	BHM (N=110)	WHTM (N=281)	BHTM (N=53)	WHF (N=229)	BHF (N=64)	WHTF (N=99)	BHTF (N=39)
Close, nurturant, involved	0%	1%	0%	2%	0%	2%	0%	0%
Warm, friendly	2	5	1	6	1	0	4	5
Exuberant, fun	0	1	1	2	1	0	0	0
Attractive	0	2	0	2	0	0	0	0
Steadfast	0	1	1	0	0	0	0	0
Happy	4	3	7	9	4	2	8	3
The greatest, the best	0	2	0	4	0	3	1	3
Competent	2	3	2	6	1	2	0	0
A decent human being	3	6	1	8	2	6	9	10
Tranquil, serene	1	0	0	4	0	0	0	0
Other positive word	2	3	1	2	0	3	3	0
Controlling, demanding	1	1	1	1	0	0	0	0
Cold, remote, uninvolved	8	2	4	0	5	5	3	13
Weak, passive, indecisive	7	4	5	4	5	6	7	10
Hostile	1	0	1	0	2	5	2	0
Incompetent	15	16	9	4	14	11	2	5
Irresponsible	1	0	2	2	1	0	0	0
Rigid	0	1	1	0	3	2	1	3
Unhappy	12	4	5	4	13	11	8	0
Messed up, unstable	9	8	7	6	7	8	9	8
Other negative word	10	9	7	2	7	16	8	8
Proper, prim, a lady/gentleman	1	0	0	0	0	0	0	8
Abused victim	0	0	2	0	2	0	3	0
Glamorous, a movie star	0	0	0	0	0	0	0	3
Rebellious, nonconforming, forceful	4	8	11	4	11	3	7	10
Other ambiguous word	9	13	11	13	13	9	7	3
Neutral word (an ordinary person, young, etc.)	8	8	19	19	5	8	17	18

87

OUTSIDE THE FAMILY CIRCLE/Homosexual Associations

	WHM	BHM	WHTM	BHTM
	(N=575)	(N=111)	(N=0)	(N=0)
What proportion of your associates did you think were homosexual at that time [when you were of high school age]?				
None of them	34%	22%	[not asked of heterosexuals]	
Only a few	47	55		
About half	7	13		
Most of them	2	2		
All of them	1	1		
Don't know	8	8		
	(N=574)	(N=111)	(N=0)	(N=0)
At what age would you say you became part of a homosexual clique or crowd?				
During grade school (under age 14)	0%	2%	[not asked of heterosexuals]	
14-15	3	5		
16-18	16	23		
Over 18	71	58		
Never	13	13		

	WHF	BHF	WHTF	BHTF
	(N=228)	(N=64)	(N=0)	(N=0)
What proportion of your associates did you think were homosexual at that time [when you were of high school age]?				
None of them	43%	41%	[not asked of heterosexuals]	
Only a few	35	38		
About half	4	9		
Most of them	1	2		
All of them	1	0		
Don't know	14	11		
	(N=229)	(N=64)	(N=0)	(N=0)
At what age would you say you became part of a homosexual clique or crowd?				
During grade school (under age 14)	1%	2%	[not asked of heterosexuals]	
14-15	3	0		
16-18	14	19		
Over 18	68	64		
Never	14	16		

CHILDHOOD AND ADOLESCENT SEXUALITY/Sexual Orientation(s)

You have already classified yourself on the Kinsey Scale in terms of the present time; now, starting at age 12, how would you have classified yourself on the Kinsey Scale in terms of your sexual feelings? During this age period, how would you classify yourself in terms of your sexual behavior?

	WHM	BHM	WHTM	BHTM	WHF	BHF	WHTF	BHTF
1A. Age first Kinsey stage began	(N=573)	(N=111)	(N=284)	(N=53)	(N=229)	(N=64)	(N=101)	(N=39)
12	100%	100%	100%	100%	100%	100%	100%	100%
Over 12	0	0	0	0	0	0	0	0
1B. Age first Kinsey stage ended	(N=573)	(N=111)	(N=284)	(N=53)	(N=229)	(N=64)	(N=101)	(N=39)
12	2%	3%	1%	2%	3%	5%	0%	0%
13	6	7	4	4	10	6	6	3
14	9	13	5	2	10	12	6	0
15	12	20	6	0	10	11	2	0
16	9	8	2	0	12	19	1	0
17	12	8	4	4	12	9	1	0
18	9	7	4	2	9	3	2	5
Over 18	41	34	75	87	34	34	82	92
1C. Feelings rating for first Kinsey stage	(N=556)	(N=109)	(N=282)	(N=53)	(N=216)	(N=61)	(N=97)	(N=39)
0: Exclusively heterosexual	12%	14%	74%	91%	26%	39%	84%	95%
1: Mainly heterosexual with a small degree of homosexuality	12	15	20	6	10	11	11	3
2: Mainly heterosexual with a substantial degree of homosexuality	8	10	2	2	8	8	2	3
3: Equally heterosexual and homosexual	14	17	3	0	13	11	2	0
4: Mainly homosexual with a substantial degree of heterosexuality	10	17	0	0	9	5	0	0
5: Mainly homosexual with a small degree of heterosexuality	15	7	0	2	16	11	1	0
6: Exclusively homosexual	31	20	0	0	18	13	0	0

CHILDHOOD AND ADOLESCENT SEXUALITY/Sexual Orientation(s)

	WHM	BHM	WHTM	BHTM	WHF	BHF	WHTF	BHTF
1D. Behaviors rating for first Kinsey stage	(N=526)	(N=108)	(N=273)	(N=53)	(N=195)	(N=53)	(N=96)	(N=39)
0: Exclusively heterosexual	16%	17%	84%	94%	54%	55%	95%	97%
1: Mainly heterosexual with a small degree of homosexuality	16	14	12	2	10	8	4	0
2: Mainly heterosexual with a substantial degree of homosexuality	4	15	2	0	6	6	0	3
3: Equally heterosexual and homosexual	9	14	0	2	6	6	0	0
4: Mainly homosexual with a substantial degree of heterosexuality	7	9	1	0	5	2	0	0
5: Mainly homosexual with a small degree of heterosexuality	14	15	1	2	6	15	0	0
6: Exclusively homosexual	34	17	0	0	12	9	1	0
2A. Age second Kinsey stage began	(N=467)	(N=89)	(N=91)	(N=6)	(N=213)	(N=60)	(N=18)	(N=2)
13	3%	3%	3%	33%	3%	5%	0%	0%
14	7	9	11	17	11	7	33	50
15	12	16	16	17	11	13	33	0
16	15	25	19	0	12	12	11	0
17	10	10	7	0	12	20	6	0
18	15	10	12	33	13	10	6	0
Over 18	39	27	32	0	38	33	11	50
2B. Age second Kinsey stage ended	(N=467)	(N=89)	(N=91)	(N=7)	(N=213)	(N=60)	(N=18)	(N=2)
13	1%	0%	0%	0%	0%	2%	0%	0%
14	0	1	0	14	2	2	0	0
15	3	3	0	14	4	2	0	0
16	5	4	4	0	4	2	11	0
17	7	12	3	14	12	12	0	0
18	10	20	5	0	8	17	11	0
Over 18	74	58	87	57	69	65	78	100

CHILDHOOD AND ADOLESCENT SEXUALITY/Sexual Orientation(s)

	WHM	BHM	WHTM	BHTM	WHF	BHF	WHTF	BHTF
	(N=467)	(N=89)	(N=91)	(N=7)	(N=209)	(N=59)	(N=18)	(N=2)
2C. Feelings rating for second Kinsey stage								
0: Exclusively heterosexual	1%	2%	46%	71%	7%	8%	72%	0%
1: Mainly heterosexual with a small degree of homosexuality	10	13	33	14	12	10	22	100
2: Mainly heterosexual with a substantial degree of homosexuality	9	9	15	0	7	7	0	0
3: Equally heterosexual and homosexual	14	13	3	14	14	10	0	0
4: Mainly homosexual with a substantial degree of heterosexuality	16	20	0	0	15	17	6	0
5: Mainly homosexual with a small degree of heterosexuality	25	25	1	0	23	17	0	0
6: Exclusively homosexual	25	17	1	0	22	31	0	0
	(N=460)	(N=88)	(N=91)	(N=7)	(N=206)	(N=58)	(N=17)	(N=2)
2D. Behaviors rating for second Kinsey stage								
0: Exclusively heterosexual	8%	19%	74%	14%	32%	19%	94%	0%
1: Mainly heterosexual with a small degree of homosexuality	12	12	15	71	8	10	0	100
2: Mainly heterosexual with a substantial degree of homosexuality	10	7	7	14	5	3	0	0
3: Equally heterosexual and homosexual	8	14	0	0	15	10	0	0
4: Mainly homosexual with a substantial degree of heterosexuality	11	17	1	0	9	12	6	0
5: Mainly homosexual with a small degree of heterosexuality	18	19	1	0	14	14	0	0
6: Exclusively homosexual	32	25	2	0	17	31	0	0
	(N=344)	(N=55)	(N=28)	(N=4)	(N=181)	(N=44)	(N=3)	(N=0)
3A. Age third Kinsey stage began								
14	1%	0%	0%	0%	1%	2%	0%	
15	1	2	0	25	2	2	0	
16	3	5	0	25	4	2	0	
17	7	7	14	0	5	2	67	
18	10	20	11	25	14	18	0	
Over 18	78	65	75	25	73	73	33	

CHILDHOOD AND ADOLESCENT SEXUALITY/Sexual Orientation(s)

3B. Age third Kinsey stage ended

	WHM (N=344)	BHM (N=55)	WHTM (N=28)	BHTM (N=4)	WHF (N=181)	BHF (N=44)	WHTF (N=3)	BHTF (N=0)
14	0%	0%	0%	0%	0%	0%	0%	
15	1	0	0	0	0	2	0	
16	0	0	0	25	3	2	0	
17	1	2	0	0	2	0	0	
18	4	11	7	0	3	2	0	
Over 18	94	87	93	75	92	93	100	

3C. Feelings rating for third Kinsey stage

	WHM (N=344)	BHM (N=55)	WHTM (N=28)	BHTM (N=4)	WHF (N=180)	BHF (N=43)	WHTF (N=3)	BHTF (N=0)
0: Exclusively heterosexual	0%	0%	11%	75%	6%	5%	100%	
1: Mainly heterosexual with a small degree of homosexuality	4	4	57	0	5	9	0	
2: Mainly heterosexual with a substantial degree of homosexuality	8	7	21	25	9	7	0	
3: Equally heterosexual and homosexual	11	7	0	0	12	21	0	
4: Mainly homosexual with a substantial degree of heterosexuality	15	11	11	0	12	9	0	
5: Mainly homosexual with a small degree of heterosexuality	31	38	0	0	23	14	0	
6: Exclusively homosexual	30	33	0	0	33	35	0	

3D. Behaviors rating for third Kinsey stage

	WHM (N=340)	BHM (N=55)	WHTM (N=28)	BHTM (N=4)	WHF (N=178)	BHF (N=43)	WHTF (N=3)	BHTF (N=0)
0: Exclusively heterosexual	4%	5%	50%	100%	21%	16%	100%	
1: Mainly heterosexual with a small degree of homosexuality	7	2	39	0	7	7	0	
2: Mainly heterosexual with a substantial degree of homosexuality	8	4	0	0	7	9	0	
3: Equally heterosexual and homosexual	12	5	0	0	15	16	0	
4: Mainly homosexual with a substantial degree of heterosexuality	7	5	4	0	3	7	0	
5: Mainly homosexual with a small degree of heterosexuality	20	27	0	0	12	14	0	
6: Exclusively homosexual	41	51	7	0	34	30	0	

CHILDHOOD AND ADOLESCENT SEXUALITY/Sexual Orientation(s)

	WHM (N=195)	BHM (N=18)	WHTM (N=12)	BHTM (N=2)	WHF (N=120)	BHF (N=24)	WHTF (N=1)	BHTF (N=0)
4A. Age fourth Kinsey stage began								
15	1%	0%	0%	0%	0%	0%	0%	
16	1	0	0	0	0	4	0	
17	1	0	0	50	5	4	0	
18	3	6	0	0	2	0	0	
Over 18	95	94	100	50	92	92	100	
4B. Age fourth Kinsey stage ended	(N=195)	(N=18)	(N=12)	(N=2)	(N=120)	(N=24)	(N=1)	(N=0)
15	0%	0%	0%	0%	0%	0%	0%	
16	1	0	0	0	0	0	0	
17	1	0	0	0	1	4	0	
18	1	0	0	0	5	0	0	
Over 18	97	100	100	100	94	96	100	
4C. Feelings rating for fourth Kinsey stage	(N=195)	(N=18)	(N=12)	(N=2)	(N=120)	(N=24)	(N=1)	(N=0)
0: Exclusively heterosexual	1%	0%	58%	0%	3%	0%	0%	
1: Mainly heterosexual with a small degree of homosexuality	2	0	25	100	4	4	100	
2: Mainly heterosexual with a substantial degree of homosexuality	3	11	0	0	7	8	0	
3: Equally heterosexual and homosexual	9	11	17	0	8	12	0	
4: Mainly homosexual with a substantial degree of heterosexuality	17	22	0	0	16	8	0	
5: Mainly homosexual with a small degree of homosexuality	32	28	0	0	28	21	0	
6: Exclusively homosexual	36	28	0	0	33	46	0	

93

CHILDHOOD AND ADOLESCENT SEXUALITY/Sexual Orientation(s)

	WHM	BHM	WHTM	BHTM	WHF	BHF	WHTF	BHTF
	(N=193)	(N=18)	(N=12)	(N=2)	(N=118)	(N=23)	(N=1)	(N=0)
4D. Behaviors rating for fourth Kinsey stage								
0: Exclusively heterosexual	5%	0%	83%	50%	19%	4%	100%	
1: Mainly heterosexual with a small degree of homosexuality	3	6	0	0	3	9	0	
2: Mainly heterosexual with a substantial degree of homosexuality	5	6	8	50	6	17	0	
3: Equally heterosexual and homosexual	7	11	0	0	3	4	0	
4: Mainly homosexual with a substantial degree of heterosexuality	13	17	0	0	7	4	0	
5: Mainly homosexual with a small degree of heterosexuality	25	17	0	0	29	22	0	
6: Exclusively homosexual	41	44	8	0	33	39	0	

	WHM	BHM	WHTM	BHTM	WHF	BHF	WHTF	BHTF
	(N=87)	(N=5)	(N=4)	(N=1)	(N=74)	(N=14)	(N=0)	(N=0)
5A. Age fifth Kinsey stage began								
16	0%	0%	0%	0%	0%	0%		
17	1	0	0	0	0	0		
18	2	0	0	0	1	7		
Over 18	97	100	100	100	99	93		

	WHM	BHM	WHTM	BHTM	WHF	BHF	WHTF	BHTF
	(N=87)	(N=5)	(N=4)	(N=1)	(N=74)	(N=14)	(N=0)	(N=0)
5B. Age fifth Kinsey stage ended								
16	0%	0%	0%	0%	0%	0%		
17	0	0	0	0	0	0		
18	0	0	0	0	0	0		
Over 18	100	100	100	100	100	100		

CHILDHOOD AND ADOLESCENT SEXUALITY/Sexual Orientation(s)

5C. Feelings rating for fifth Kinsey stage

	WHM	BHM	WHTM	BHTM	WHF	BHF	WHTF	BHTF
	(N=86)	(N=5)	(N=4)	(N=1)	(N=74)	(N=14)	(N=0)	(N=0)
0: Exclusively heterosexual	0%	0%	25%	0%	4%	7%		
1: Mainly heterosexual with a small degree of homosexuality	2	0	75	100	0	7		
2: Mainly heterosexual with a substantial degree of homosexuality	6	0	0	0	3	7		
3: Equally heterosexual and homosexual	5	0	0	0	8	21		
4: Mainly homosexual with a substantial degree of heterosexuality	15	60	0	0	11	7		
5: Mainly homosexual with a small degree of heterosexuality	36	20	0	0	34	7		
6: Exclusively homosexual	36	20	0	0	41	43		

5D. Behaviors rating for fifth Kinsey stage

	WHM	BHM	WHTM	BHTM	WHF	BHF	WHTF	BHTF
	(N=85)	(N=5)	(N=4)	(N=1)	(N=74)	(N=14)	(N=0)	(N=0)
0: Exclusively heterosexual	4%	0%	75%	0%	11%	14%		
1: Mainly heterosexual with a small degree of homosexuality	6	0	25	100	1	0		
2: Mainly heterosexual with a substantial degree of homosexuality	8	0	0	0	8	14		
3: Equally heterosexual and homosexual	4	0	0	0	11	7		
4: Mainly homosexual with a substantial degree of heterosexuality	6	40	0	0	7	7		
5: Mainly homosexual with a small degree of heterosexuality	25	0	0	0	15	29		
6: Exclusively homosexual	48	60	0	0	47	29		

How old were you when you first felt sexually aroused by a male?

	(N=575)	(N=111)	(N=284)	(N=53)	(N=229)	(N=64)	(N=101)	(N=39)
Under 5	3%	1%	0%	0%	0%	2%	1%	0%
5-6	8	6	0	0	2	2	1	0
7-8	8	11	2	0	3	2	1	0
9-11	19	14	3	2	3	14	7	3
12	16	15	5	0	6	5	5	3
13	13	11	1	4	6	9	14	8
14	9	13	2	0	9	14	8	8
15	9	6	1	2	9	11	16	28
16	4	10	1	2	12	9	16	21
17-18	6	8	4	6	15	8	24	23
Over 18	5	5	4	2	15	5	6	8
Never aroused by a male	0	0	76	83	21	20	2	0

How old were you when you first felt sexually aroused by a female?

	(N=575)	(N=111)	(N=283)	(N=53)	(N=229)	(N=64)	(N=100)	(N=39)
Under 5	0%	0%	2%	4%	1%	3%	0%	0%
5-6	4	5	7	4	3	2	1	0
7-8	3	6	8	17	3	8	0	0
9-11	8	14	18	36	9	16	1	3
12	7	12	18	11	4	9	0	0
13	8	10	13	11	7	2	1	0
14	12	10	14	6	10	9	1	0
15	6	8	7	11	8	2	1	0
16	6	5	6	0	10	8	1	0
17-18	8	9	6	0	14	16	0	0
Over 18	10	5	2	0	30	27	1	3
Never aroused by a female	28	16	1	0	0	0	93	95

	WHM	BHM	WHTM	BHTM	WHF	BHF	WHTF	BHTF
Now, prior to the time you had your first [ejaculation/period], I wonder if you can recall any experience with a member of the opposite sex which you or others thought of as being sexual?	(N=573)	(N=111)	(N=284)	(N=52)	(N=228)	(N=64)	(N=101)	(N=39)
Yes	56%	50%	63%	81%	68%	59%	47%	23%
No	44	50	37	19	32	41	53	77
How frequent were these experiences with the opposite sex?	(N=321)	(N=56)	(N=166)	(N=44)	(N=152)	(N=37)	(N=47)	(N=9)
Happened only once	30%	16%	17%	2%	28%	32%	32%	56%
2-5 experiences	36	38	43	20	28	27	43	22
6-10 experiences	14	14	16	16	11	8	9	0
11-20 experiences	9	16	14	14	16	8	2	0
More than 20 experiences	12	16	9	48	18	24	15	22
What did your first such experience consist of?								
1A. Age of respondent	(N=313)	(N=54)	(N=173)	(N=42)	(N=149)	(N=37)	(N=47)	(N=9)
Under 5	8%	2%	3%	7%	8%	8%	13%	11%
5-6	30	19	23	24	27	14	21	11
7-8	27	20	25	31	30	41	28	33
9-11	27	43	36	31	31	30	32	0
12 or older	9	17	12	7	5	8	6	44
1B. Age of partner	(N=317)	(N=55)	(N=165)	(N=41)	(N=151)	(N=37)	(N=47)	(N=9)
Under 5	8%	2%	3%	7%	3%	8%	6%	0%
5-6	24	18	22	27	13	8	15	0
7-8	21	18	19	12	17	16	21	11
9-11	24	31	28	34	15	22	15	0
12-15	11	24	17	12	11	14	15	56
16-39	3	4	2	0	11	19	19	11
40 or older	0	0	0	0	9	3	6	0
Child, age not given	9	4	9	7	14	5	0	22
Adult, age not given	0	0	0	0	5	5	2	0

97

CHILDHOOD AND ADOLESCENT SEXUALITY/First Prepubertal Heterosexual Encounter

	WHM	BHM	WHTM	BHTM	WHF	BHF	WHTF	BHTF
	(N=268)	(N=49)	(N=130)	(N=44)	(N=141)	(N=31)	(N=44)	(N=8)
1C. Identity of partner								
Sibling	10%	6%	5%	8%	6%	10%	14%	12%
Parent	1	0	0	0	6	0	0	0
Other relative	8	8	7	3	9	10	11	0
Friend or acquaintance	55	67	58	64	48	74	32	88
Stranger	1	0	0	0	5	0	7	0
Group	24	18	29	25	25	6	36	0
Other	0	0	0	0	0	0	0	0
1D. If partner was a group, members of the group	(N=63)	(N=7)	(N=34)	(N=9)	(N=33)	(N=2)	(N=15)	(N=0)
Siblings	2%	0%	3%	0%	3%	0%	7%	
Parents	0	0	0	0	0	0	0	
Other relatives	5	0	0	0	0	0	0	
Friends or acquaintances	81	100	85	89	91	50	73	
Strangers	0	0	3	0	0	50	0	
Some combination of these	13	0	9	11	6	0	20	
1E. First sexual activity described	(N=304)	(N=55)	(N=174)	(N=39)	(N=155)	(N=38)	(N=45)	(N=9)
Proposition, without subsequent activity	1%	0%	1%	0%	1%	0%	2%	0%
Looking at bodies, watching masturbation	35	9	32	26	30	16	29	0
Kissing or necking	7	13	18	5	10	16	27	33
Non-genital physical contact	9	18	9	13	11	24	4	0
Manual-genital contact, genital apposition	13	16	6	36	21	18	9	44
Oral-genital contact	2	4	1	0	3	0	0	0
Oral-anal or anal-genital contact	0	0	0	0	0	0	0	0
Sexual intercourse	5	4	1	5	1	11	0	22
Rape or attempted rape	0	0	0	0	3	3	4	0
Other activity not involving contact	7	4	10	0	6	3	11	0
Other activity involving physical contact	21	33	22	15	14	11	13	0
1F. Who performed first sexual activity	(N=298)	(N=52)	(N=169)	(N=41)	(N=153)	(N=52)	(N=44)	(N=9)
Respondent	21%	12%	25%	17%	16%	13%	18%	0%
Partner(s)	8	6	3	0	29	24	27	22
Both	70	83	72	83	55	63	55	78

98

CHILDHOOD AND ADOLESCENT SEXUALITY/First Prepubertal Heterosexual Encounter

		WHM	BHM	WHTM	BHTM	WHF	BHF	WHTF	BHTF
1G.	Second sexual activity described	(N=85)	(N=15)	(N=54)	(N=11)	(N=47)	(N=16)	(N=12)	(N=1)
	Proposition, without subsequent activity	2%	0%	0%	0%	0%	0%	0%	0%
	Looking at bodies, watching masturbation	7	7	2	0	13	0	0	0
	Kissing or necking	5	0	7	0	6	0	8	0
	Non-genital physical contact	13	40	44	0	9	19	8	0
	Manual-genital contact, genital apposition	22	20	19	45	21	44	33	0
	Oral-genital contact	1	0	2	0	2	0	8	0
	Oral-anal or anal-genital contact	0	0	0	0	0	0	0	0
	Sexual intercourse	9	27	2	36	6	6	8	0
	Rape or attempted rape	0	0	0	0	0	0	0	0
	Other activity not involving contact	4	0	2	0	6	6	0	0
	Other activity involving physical contact	36	7	22	18	36	25	33	100
1H.	Who performed second sexual activity	(N=82)	(N=14)	(N=49)	(N=11)	(N=47)	(N=16)	(N=11)	(N=1)
	Respondent	16%	14%	33%	9%	15%	6%	0%	0%
	Partner(s)	12	0	2	0	21	12	36	0
	Both	72	86	65	91	64	81	64	100
1I.	Respondent's reaction to the experience	(N=252)	(N=48)	(N=151)	(N=33)	(N=132)	(N=34)	(N=42)	(N=7)
	Positive feelings	51%	56%	66%	88%	33%	47%	36%	29%
	Enjoyed it but felt guilty	6	8	3	0	2	6	5	0
	Mixed feelings	5	8	5	0	8	3	2	0
	Negative feelings	11	10	9	3	36	32	24	29
	Some other reaction	5	4	11	9	8	6	10	14
	No particular reaction	22	21	6	0	12	6	24	29
1J.	Were any adults aware of this experience?	(N=317)	(N=54)	(N=180)	(N=42)	(N=153)	(N=37)	(N=46)	(N=9)
	No	64%	70%	67%	64%	68%	70%	63%	89%
	Not sure	2	0	5	0	5	5	2	0
	Yes	34	30	28	36	27	24	35	11

CHILDHOOD AND ADOLESCENT SEXUALITY/First Prepubertal Heterosexual Encounter

	WHM	BHM	WHTM	BHTM	WHF	BHF	WHTF	BHTF
1K. Who was the [first] adult who was aware of the experience?	(N=97)	(N=12)	(N=30)	(N=13)	(N=37)	(N=8)	(N=15)	(N=0)
Respondent's mother	29%	33%	47%	23%	62%	25%	53%	
Respondent's father	9	17	0	23	8	25	0	
Both parents	14	17	23	8	14	24	27	
Other adult relative(s)	9	8	10	31	3	12	13	
Partner's parent(s)	28	17	20	0	8	0	7	
Some other person	10	8	0	15	5	12	0	
1L. Emotional reaction of [first] aware adult	(N=79)	(N=13)	(N=39)	(N=14)	(N=41)	(N=7)	(N=13)	(N=1)
Very negative (shocked, horrified)	44%	38%	21%	14%	37%	86%	38%	100%
Mildly negative	32	46	36	64	29	0	8	0
Indifferent	10	8	31	14	12	0	8	0
Accepting, supportive, amused	11	8	13	7	15	0	31	0
Some other reaction	3	0	0	0	7	14	15	0
1M. First thing the [first] aware adult did	(N=94)	(N=14)	(N=48)	(N=15)	(N=41)	(N=7)	(N=13)	(N=1)
Scolded or punished	65%	57%	54%	73%	44%	57%	38%	100%
Just stopped the activity	20	29	8	13	17	14	15	0
Supportive or accepting response	6	7	4	13	5	0	23	0
Some other response	2	0	4	0	12	29	15	0
Said or did nothing	6	7	29	0	22	0	8	0
1N. Second thing the [first] aware adult did	(N=21)	(N=2)	(N=6)	(N=3)	(N=9)	(N=2)	(N=3)	(N=0)
Scolded or punished	5%	0%	0%	0%	0%	50%	0%	
Just stopped the activity	90	100	100	100	78	50	67	
Supportive or accepting response	0	0	0	0	11	0	0	
Some other response	5	0	0	0	11	0	33	
10. Were any other adults aware of the experience?	(N=315)	(N=54)	(N=179)	(N=42)	(N=152)	(N=38)	(N=47)	(N=0)
No	90%	94%	96%	88%	91%	92%	91%	
Yes	10	6	4	12	9	8	9	

CHILDHOOD AND ADOLESCENT SEXUALITY/First Prepubertal Heterosexual Encounter

	WHM	BHM	WHTM	BHTM		WHF	BHF	WHTF	BHTF
1P. Who was the second adult who was aware of the experience?	(N=33)	(N=3)	(N=8)	(N=5)		(N=13)	(N=3)	(N=4)	(N=0)
Respondent's mother	30%	33%	12%	0%		0%	33%	0%	
Respondent's father	24	0	38	20		23	33	25	
Both parents	15	67	12	20		8	0	0	
Other adult relative(s)	3	0	0	40		15	0	50	
Partner's parent(s)	18	0	25	20		38	33	25	
Some other person	9	0	12	0		15	0	0	
1Q. Emotional reaction of second aware adult	(N=22)	(N=3)	(N=8)	(N=4)		(N=13)	(N=1)	(N=4)	(N=0)
Very negative (shocked, horrified)	32%	67%	25%	25%		38%	100%	25%	
Mildly negative	50	0	0	25		15	0	25	
Indifferent	5	33	38	0		8	0	0	
Accepting, supportive, amused	14	0	25	50		15	0	25	
Some other reaction	0	0	12	0		23	0	25	
1R. First thing the second aware adult did	(N=26)	(N=3)	(N=7)	(N=4)		(N=10)	(N=3)	(N=3)	(N=0)
Scolded or punished	69%	67%	14%	50%		30%	33%	33%	
Just stopped the activity	12	0	14	0		20	33	33	
Supportive or accepting response	4	0	29	50		10	0	0	
Some other response	0	0	0	0		40	0	33	
Said or did nothing	15	33	43	0		0	33	0	
1S. Second thing the second aware adult did	(N=3)	(N=0)	(N=0)	(N=0)		(N=1)	(N=0)	(N=2)	(N=0)
Scolded or punished	0%					0%		0%	
Just stopped the activity	67					100		50	
Supportive or accepting response	0					0		0	
Some other response	33					0		50	
1T. Were any other adults aware of the experience?	(N=316)	(N=54)	(N=180)	(N=41)		(N=152)	(N=38)	(N=47)	(N=9)
No	99%	100%	100%	100%		98%	95%	100%	100%
Yes	1	0	0	0		2	5	0	0

IOI

CHILDHOOD AND ADOLESCENT SEXUALITY/First Prepubertal Heterosexual Encounter

	WHM	BHM	WHTM	BHTM	WHF	BHF	WHTF	BHTF
1U. Who was the third adult who was aware of the experience?	(N=4)	(N=0)	(N=0)	(N=0)	(N=3)	(N=2)	(N=0)	(N=0)
Respondent's mother	50%				0%	0%		
Respondent's father	0				33	0		
Both parents	25				0	0		
Other adult relative(s)	0				33	0		
Partner's parent(s)	25				0	50		
Some other person	0				33	50		
1V. Emotional reaction of third aware adult	(N=3)	(N=0)	(N=0)	(N=1)	(N=3)	(N=1)	(N=0)	(N=0)
Very negative (shocked, horrified)	33%			0%	0%	100%		
Mildly negative	0			100	0	0		
Indifferent	67			0	0	0		
Accepting, supportive, amused	0			0	67	0		
Some other reaction	0			0	33	0		
1W. First thing the third aware adult did	(N=3)	(N=0)	(N=0)	(N=1)	(N=3)	(N=1)	(N=0)	(N=0)
Scolded or punished	33%			100%	0%	100%		
Just stopped the activity	0			0	0	0		
Supportive or accepting response	0			0	0	0		
Some other response	0			0	67	0		
Said or did nothing	67			0	33	0		
1X. Second thing the third aware adult did	(N=0)	(N=0)	(N=0)	(N=0)	(N=0)	(N=0)	(N=0)	(N=0)
Scolded or punished								
Just stopped the activity								
Supportive or accepting response								
Some other response								
1Y. Did anyone observe the experience?	(N=308)	(N=50)	(N=156)	(N=41)	(N=147)	(N=35)	(N=41)	(N=9)
No; just respondent and partner were present	67%	76%	63%	76%	67%	77%	54%	78%
Yes; a group experience and/or one or more spectators	33	24	37	24	33	23	46	22

CHILDHOOD AND ADOLESCENT SEXUALITY/Second Prepubertal Heterosexual Encounter

Did you have any other experiences with the opposite sex? What did the second such experience consist of?

	WHM	BHM	WHTM	BHTM	WHF	BHF	WHTF	BHTF
2A. Age of respondent	(N=70)	(N=5)	(N=41)	(N=16)	(N=66)	(N=7)	(N=15)	(N=0)
Under 5	1%	0%	2%	6%	3%	0%	7%	
5-6	14	20	12	12	12	0	13	
7-8	26	0	34	12	26	29	27	
9-11	50	60	29	44	50	57	47	
12 or older	9	20	22	25	9	14	7	
2B. Age of partner	(N=68)	(N=6)	(N=40)	(N=17)	(N=70)	(N=7)	(N=15)	(N=0)
Under 5	1%	0%	5%	6%	0%	0%	7%	
5-6	13	0	15	12	6	0	0	
7-8	22	17	20	6	7	14	0	
9-11	35	33	22	35	29	57	20	
12-15	13	33	10	18	9	0	27	
16-39	0	0	10	6	16	29	20	
40 or older	1	0	0	0	13	0	13	
Child, age not given	13	17	12	18	14	0	13	
Adult, age not given	0	0	5	0	7	0	0	
2C. Identity of partner	(N=60)	(N=6)	(N=37)	(N=14)	(N=67)	(N=7)	(N=14)	(N=0)
Sibling	8%	17%	5%	7%	7%	0%	14%	
Parent	0	0	0	0	12	0	0	
Other relative	7	17	5	0	4	14	14	
Friend or acquaintance	53	33	54	57	45	29	21	
Stranger	0	0	5	7	4	0	14	
Group	30	33	30	29	27	57	36	
Other	2	0	0	0	0	0	0	
2D. If partner was a group, members of the group	(N=17)	(N=2)	(N=11)	(N=4)	(N=17)	(N=4)	(N=5)	(N=0)
Siblings	6%	0%	0%	0%	6%	0%	20%	
Parents	0	0	0	0	0	0	0	
Other relatives	6	0	9	0	6	0	0	
Friends or acquaintances	59	100	82	100	65	75	80	
Strangers	0	0	0	0	0	0	0	
Some combination of these	29	0	9	0	24	25	0	

CHILDHOOD AND ADOLESCENT SEXUALITY/Second Prepubertal Heterosexual Encounter

2E. First sexual activity described

	WHM (N=71)	BHM (N=6)	WHTM (N=44)	BHTM (N=17)	WHF (N=71)	BHF (N=7)	WHTF (N=15)	BHTF (N=0)
Proposition, without subsequent activity	1%	0%	0%	0%	3%	0%	7%	
Looking at bodies, watching masturbation	35	0	23	6	27	14	20	
Kissing or necking	6	0	20	12	13	29	13	
Non-genital physical contact	13	0	9	12	7	0	13	
Manual-genital contact, genital apposition	14	33	7	24	23	29	7	
Oral-genital contact	1	0	0	0	4	0	0	
Oral-anal or anal-genital contact	0	0	0	0	0	0	0	
Sexual intercourse	6	0	5	24	10	29	0	
Rape or attempted rape	1	0	0	0	1	0	7	
Other activity not involving contact	10	0	16	0	6	0	20	
Other activity involving physical contact	13	67	20	24	7	0	13	

2F. Who performed first sexual activity

	WHM (N=69)	BHM (N=6)	WHTM (N=40)	BHTM (N=16)	WHF (N=70)	BHF (N=7)	WHTF (N=15)	BHTF (N=0)
Respondent	22%	33%	25%	12%	16%	14%	20%	
Partner(s)	4	17	2	0	30	0	47	
Both	74	50	72	88	54	86	33	

2G. Second sexual activity described

	WHM (N=28)	BHM (N=1)	WHTM (N=9)	BHTM (N=5)	WHF (N=21)	BHF (N=1)	WHTF (N=4)	BHTF (N=0)
Proposition, without subsequent activity	0%	0%	0%	0%	5%	0%	0%	
Looking at bodies, watching masturbation	4	0	0	0	14	0	0	
Kissing or necking	4	0	0	0	5	0	0	
Non-genital physical contact	29	0	44	20	29	0	0	
Manual-genital contact, genital apposition	29	0	33	60	24	0	75	
Oral-genital contact	11	0	0	0	0	0	0	
Oral-anal or anal-genital contact	0	0	0	0	0	0	0	
Sexual intercourse	4	100	0	20	0	0	0	
Rape or attempted rape	0	0	0	0	0	0	0	
Other activity not involving contact	4	0	0	0	5	0	25	
Other activity involving physical contact	18	0	22	0	19	100	0	

2H. Who performed second sexual activity

	WHM (N=25)	BHM (N=1)	WHTM (N=7)	BHTM (N=5)	WHF (N=21)	BHF (N=1)	WHTF (N=4)	BHTF (N=0)
Respondent	16%	0%	0%	20%	14%	0%	0%	
Partner(s)	4	0	0	0	33	0	75	
Both	80	100	100	80	52	100	25	

CHILDHOOD AND ADOLESCENT SEXUALITY/Second Prepubertal Heterosexual Encounter

	WHM	BHM	WHTM	BHTM	WHF	BHF	WHTF	BHTF
2I. Respondent's reaction to the experience	(N=56)	(N=6)	(N=34)	(N=17)	(N=60)	(N=5)	(N=14)	(N=0)
Positive feelings	62%	83%	71%	94%	38%	60%	50%	
Enjoyed it but felt guilty	7	0	3	0	7	0	0	
Mixed feelings	4	17	9	0	2	0	0	
Negative feelings	9	0	3	6	38	0	29	
Some other reaction	2	0	12	0	5	20	14	
No particular reaction	16	0	3	0	10	20	7	
2J. Were any adults aware of this experience?	(N=74)	(N=6)	(N=43)	(N=16)	(N=71)	(N=7)	(N=15)	(N=0)
No	73%	67%	56%	62%	63%	57%	73%	
Not sure	5	17	23	19	7	14	0	
Yes	22	17	21	19	30	29	27	
2K. Who was the [first] adult who was aware of the experience?	(N=11)	(N=0)	(N=6)	(N=2)	(N=20)	(N=1)	(N=4)	(N=0)
Respondent's mother	27%		50%	100%	55%	0%	50%	
Respondent's father	0		0	0	0	0	25	
Both parents	27		50	0	10	0	25	
Other adult relative(s)	36		0	0	10	0	0	
Partner's parent(s)	9		0	0	10	100	0	
Some other person	0		0	0	15	0	0	
2L. Emotional reaction of [first] aware adult	(N=11)	(N=1)	(N=8)	(N=2)	(N=19)	(N=2)	(N=3)	(N=0)
Very negative (shocked, horrified)	18%	0%	38%	0%	47%	50%	33%	
Mildly negative	27	100	38	100	26	0	0	
Indifferent	27	0	12	0	0	50	33	
Accepting, supportive, amused	28	0	0	0	21	0	33	
Some other reaction	0	0	12	0	5	0	0	
2M. First thing the [first] aware adult did	(N=14)	(N=1)	(N=7)	(N=3)	(N=18)	(N=2)	(N=2)	(N=0)
Scolded or punished	43%	100%	57%	67%	50%	50%	0%	
Just stopped the activity	21	0	14	0	11	0	0	
Supportive or accepting response	21	0	0	33	22	0	50	
Some other response	7	0	14	0	11	0	0	
Said or did nothing	7	0	14	0	6	50	50	

	WHM	BHM	WHTM	BHTM	WHF	BHF	WHTF	BHTF
2N. Second thing the [first] aware adult did	(N=3)	(N=0)	(N=2)	(N=0)	(N=6)	(N=0)	(N=0)	(N=0)
Scolded or punished	0%		0%		17%			
Just stopped the activity	100		50		33			
Supportive or accepting response	0		50		0			
Some other response	0		0		50			
20. Were any other adults aware of the experience?	(N=73)	(N=6)	(N=42)	(N=16)	(N=71)	(N=7)	(N=15)	(N=0)
No	93%	100%	97%	100%	92%	100%	100%	
Yes	7	0	3	0	8	0	0	
2P. Who was the second adult who was aware of the experience?	(N=5)	(N=0)	(N=1)	(N=0)	(N=6)	(N=0)	(N=0)	(N=0)
Respondent's mother	20%		0%		17%			
Respondent's father	20		100		0			
Both parents	40		0		0			
Other adult relative(s)	0		0		17			
Partner's parent(s)	20		0		33			
Some other person	0		0		33			
2Q. Emotional reaction of second aware adult	(N=4)	(N=0)	(N=1)	(N=0)	(N=5)	(N=0)	(N=0)	(N=0)
Very negative (shocked, horrified)	25%		0%		20%			
Mildly negative	50		100		60			
Indifferent	0		0		0			
Accepting, supportive, amused	0		0		20			
Some other reaction	25		0		0			
2R. First thing the second aware adult did	(N=5)	(N=0)	(N=0)	(N=0)	(N=2)	(N=0)	(N=0)	(N=0)
Scolded or punished	60%				50%			
Just stopped the activity	20				0			
Supportive or accepting response	0				0			
Some other response	0				50			
Said or did nothing	20				0			

106

	WHM	BHM	WHTM	BHTM	WHF	BHF	WHTF	BHTF
2S. Second thing the second aware adult did	(N=1)	(N=0)	(N=0)	(N=0)	(N=0)	(N=0)	(N=0)	(N=0)
Scolded or punished	0%							
Just stopped the activity	100							
Supportive or accepting response	0							
Some other response	0							
2T. Were any other adults aware of the experience?	(N=73)	(N=6)	(N=43)	(N=16)	(N=71)	(N=7)	(N=15)	(N=0)
No	99%	100%	100%	100%	100%	100%	100%	
Yes	1	0	0	0	0	0	0	
2U. Who was the third adult who was aware of the experience?	(N=1)	(N=0)	(N=0)	(N=0)	(N=0)	(N=0)	(N=0)	(N=0)
Respondent's mother	0%							
Respondent's father	0							
Both parents	0							
Other adult relative(s)	0							
Partner's parent(s)	100							
Some other person	0							
2V. Emotional reaction of third aware adult	(N=1)	(N=0)	(N=0)	(N=0)	(N=0)	(N=0)	(N=0)	(N=0)
Very negative (shocked, horrified)	0%							
Mildly negative	100							
Indifferent	0							
Accepting, supportive, amused	0							
Some other reaction	0							
2W. First thing the third aware adult did	(N=1)	(N=0)	(N=0)	(N=0)	(N=0)	(N=0)	(N=0)	(N=0)
Scolded or punished	100%							
Just stopped the activity	0							
Supportive or accepting response	0							
Some other response	0							
Said or did nothing	0							

CHILDHOOD AND ADOLESCENT SEXUALITY/Second and Third Prepubertal Heterosexual Encounters

	WHM	BHM	WHTM	BHTM	WHF	BHF	WHTF	BHTF
2X. Second thing the third aware adult did	(N=0)	(N=0)	(N=0)	(N=0)	(N=0)	(N=0)	(N=0)	(N=0)
Scolded or punished								
Just stopped the activity								
Supportive or accepting response								
Some other response								
2Y. Did anyone observe the experience?	(N=67)	(N=6)	(N=36)	(N=12)	(N=69)	(N=7)	(N=14)	(N=0)
No; just respondent and partner were present	57%	67%	56%	58%	71%	43%	64%	
Yes; a group experience and/or one or more spectators	43	33	44	42	29	57	36	

Did you have any other experiences with the opposite sex? What did the third such experience consist of?

	WHM	BHM	WHTM	BHTM	WHF	BHF	WHTF	BHTF
3A. Age of respondent	(N=20)	(N=2)	(N=9)	(N=5)	(N=35)	(N=2)	(N=4)	(N=0)
Under 5	5%	0%	0%	0%	0%	0%	0%	
5-6	5	0	11	0	9	0	0	
7-8	10	0	22	20	17	50	50	
9-11	60	50	22	60	54	50	50	
12 or older	20	50	44	20	20	0	0	
3B. Age of partner	(N=22)	(N=2)	(N=8)	(N=6)	(N=38)	(N=2)	(N=4)	(N=0)
Under 5	0%	0%	0%	0%	0%	0%	0%	
5-6	9	0	12	0	3	0	0	
7-8	9	0	0	17	3	50	0	
9-11	55	100	0	50	18	0	50	
12-15	14	0	25	0	5	0	0	
16-39	5	0	12	0	18	0	25	
40 or older	0	0	12	0	24	50	0	
Child, age not given	18	0	38	17	15	0	0	
Adult, age not given	0	0	0	17	11	0	25	

CHILDHOOD AND ADOLESCENT SEXUALITY/Third Prepubertal Heterosexual Encounter

	WHM	BHM	WHTM	BHTM	WHF	BHF	WHTF	BHTF
	(N=20)	(N=2)	(N=7)	(N=5)	(N=36)	(N=1)	(N=4)	(N=0)
3C. Identity of partner								
Sibling	0%	0%	0%	0%	8%	0%	0%	
Parent	0	0	14	0	14	0	0	
Other relative	10	0	0	0	8	0	25	
Friend or acquaintance	65	50	71	80	33	100	50	
Stranger	5	0	0	0	22	0	0	
Group	20	50	14	20	14	0	25	
Other	0	0	0	0	0	0	0	
	(N=4)	(N=1)	(N=1)	(N=0)	(N=5)	(N=0)	(N=1)	(N=0)
3D. If partner was a group, members of the group								
Siblings	0%	0%	0%		0%		0%	
Parents	0	0	0		0		0	
Other relatives	25	0	0		0		0	
Friends or acquaintances	50	100	100		80		100	
Strangers	25	0	0		0		0	
Some combination of these	0	0	0		20		0	
	(N=23)	(N=2)	(N=11)	(N=5)	(N=36)	(N=2)	(N=4)	(N=0)
3E. First sexual activity described								
Proposition, without subsequent activity	4%	0%	0%	0%	6%	0%	0%	
Looking at bodies, watching masturbation	26	0	18	0	25	0	50	
Kissing or necking	9	50	27	20	11	0	25	
Non-genital physical contact	17	0	9	20	11	0	0	
Manual-genital contact, genital apposition	17	0	9	40	6	0	25	
Oral-genital contact	4	0	0	0	3	0	0	
Oral-anal or anal-genital contact	4	0	0	0	3	0	0	
Sexual intercourse	4	0	9	20	6	0	0	
Rape or attempted rape	0	0	0	0	3	0	0	
Other activity not involving contact	4	0	9	0	9	0	0	
Other activity involving physical contact	9	50	18	0	19	100	0	
	(N=22)	(N=2)	(N=10)	(N=5)	(N=36)	(N=2)	(N=4)	(N=0)
3F. Who performed first sexual activity								
Respondent	32%	0%	40%	0%	14%	0%	50%	
Partner(s)	5	0	0	20	42	50	0	
Both	64	100	60	80	44	50	50	

CHILDHOOD AND ADOLESCENT SEXUALITY/Third Prepubertal Heterosexual Encounter

	WHM	BHM	WHTM	BHTM	WHF	BHF	WHTF	BHTF
3G. Second sexual activity described	(N=9)	(N=1)	(N=1)	(N=0)	(N=9)	(N=0)	(N=0)	(N=0)
Proposition, without subsequent activity	0%	0%	0%		11%			
Looking at bodies, watching masturbation	11	0	0		0			
Kissing or necking	0	0	0		0			
Non-genital physical contact	11	100	100		11			
Manual-genital contact, genital apposition	44	0	0		44			
Oral-genital contact	22	0	0		0			
Sexual intercourse	11	0	0		22			
Rape or attempted rape	0	0	0		0			
Other activity not involving contact	0	0	0		0			
Other activity involving physical contact	0	0	0		11			
3H. Who performed second sexual activity	(N=9)	(N=1)	(N=1)	(N=0)	(N=10)	(N=0)	(N=0)	(N=0)
Respondent	11%	0%	0%		20%			
Partner(s)	11	0	0		30			
Both	78	100	100		50			
3I. Respondent's reaction to the experience	(N=18)	(N=2)	(N=8)	(N=5)	(N=33)	(N=1)	(N=4)	(N=0)
Positive feelings	83%	100%	88%	80%	33%	0%	75%	
Enjoyed it but felt guilty	0	0	0	0	12	0	0	
Mixed feelings	0	0	0	0	0	0	0	
Negative feelings	11	0	0	20	45	0	25	
Some other reaction	0	0	12	0	3	0	0	
No particular reaction	6	0	0	0	6	100	0	
3J. Were any adults aware of this experience?	(N=22)	(N=2)	(N=11)	(N=6)	(N=37)	(N=2)	(N=4)	(N=0)
No	68%	50%	73%	50%	62%	50%	75%	
Not sure	18	50	9	17	11	0	0	
Yes	14	0	18	33	27	50	25	

CHILDHOOD AND ADOLESCENT SEXUALITY/Third Prepubertal Heterosexual Encounter

	WHM	BHM	WHTM	BHTM	WHF	BHF	WHTF	BHTF
3K. Who was the [first] adult who was aware of the experience?	(N=2)	(N=0)	(N=1)	(N=2)	(N=11)	(N=0)	(N=1)	(N=0)
Respondent's mother	50%		0%	0%	45%		100%	
Respondent's father	0		0	50	9		0	
Both parents	50		0	0	18		0	
Other adult relative(s)	0		0	0	9		0	
Partner's parent(s)	0		0	50	0		0	
Some other person	0		100	0	18		0	
3L. Emotional reaction of [first] aware adult	(N=2)	(N=0)	(N=2)	(N=1)	(N=10)	(N=1)	(N=0)	(N=0)
Very negative (shocked, horrified)	50%		0%	0%	40%	0%		
Mildly negative	0		0	100	10	0		
Indifferent	50		0	0	20	0		
Accepting, supportive, amused	0		0	0	20	0		
Some other reaction	0		100	0	10	100		
3M. First thing the [first] aware adult did	(N=2)	(N=0)	(N=1)	(N=2)	(N=11)	(N=1)	(N=1)	(N=0)
Scolded or punished	0%		0%	0%	36%	0%	0%	
Just stopped the activity	0		0	100	9	0	0	
Supportive or accepting response	0		0	0	18	0	100	
Some other response	50		100	0	18	100	0	
Said or did nothing	50		0	0	18	0	0	
3N. Second thing the [first] aware adult did	(N=0)	(N=0)	(N=0)	(N=0)	(N=0)	(N=0)	(N=0)	(N=0)
Scolded or punished								
Just stopped the activity								
Supportive or accepting response								
Some other response								
30. Were any other adults aware of the experience?	(N=22)	(N=2)	(N=10)	(N=6)	(N=37)	(N=2)	(N=4)	(N=0)
No	100%	100%	100%	83%	92%	100%	75%	
Yes	0	0	0	17	8	0	25	

III

	WHM	BHM	WHTM	BHTM	WHF	BHF	WHTF	BHTF
3P. Who was the second adult who was aware of the experience?	(N=0)	(N=0)	(N=0)	(N=1)	(N=3)	(N=0)	(N=1)	(N=0)
Respondent's mother				100%	33%		0%	
Respondent's father				0	0		0	
Both parents				0	0		0	
Other adult relative(s)				0	0		0	
Partner's parent(s)				0	0		100	
Some other person				0	67		0	
3Q. Emotional reaction of second aware adult	(N=0)	(N=0)	(N=1)	(N=1)	(N=3)	(N=0)	(N=1)	(N=0)
Very negative (shocked, horrified)			100%	0%	0%		0%	
Mildly negative			0	100	67		0	
Indifferent			0	0	33		100	
Accepting, supportive, amused			0	0	0		0	
Some other reaction			0	0	0		0	
3R. First thing the second aware adult did	(N=0)	(N=0)	(N=0)	(N=1)	(N=2)	(N=0)	(N=1)	(N=0)
Scolded or punished				100%	0%		0%	
Just stopped the activity				0	0		0	
Supportive or accepting response				0	0		100	
Some other response				0	50		0	
Said or did nothing				0	50		0	
3S. Second thing the second aware adult did	(N=0)	(N=0)	(N=0)	(N=0)	(N=0)	(N=0)	(N=0)	(N=0)
Scolded or punished								
Just stopped the activity								
Supportive or accepting response								
Some other response								
3T. Were any other adults aware of the experience?	(N=22)	(N=2)	(N=11)	(N=6)	(N=37)	(N=3)	(N=4)	(N=0)
No	100%	100%	100%	100%	100%	100%	100%	
Yes	0	0	0	0	0	0	0	

112

CHILDHOOD AND ADOLESCENT SEXUALITY/Third Prepubertal Heterosexual Encounter

	WHM (N=19)	BHM (N=2)	WHTM (N=9)	BHTM (N=6)		WHF (N=36)	BHF (N=1)	WHTF (N=4)	BHTF (N=0)
3U. Did anyone observe the experience?									
No; just respondent and partner were present	79%	50%	78%	83%		75%	100%	25%	
Yes; a group experience and/or one or more spectators	21	50	22	17		25	0	75	

CHILDHOOD AND ADOLESCENT SEXUALITY/Fourth Prepubertal Heterosexual Encounter

Did you have any other experiences with the opposite sex? What did the fourth such experience consist of?

	WHM	BHM	WHTM	BHTM	WHF	BHF	WHTF	BHTF
4A. Age of respondent	(N=7)	(N=1)	(N=1)	(N=2)	(N=12)	(N=1)	(N=2)	(N=0)
Under 5	14%	0%	0%	0%	0%	0%	0%	
5-6	0	0	0	0	8	0	0	
7-8	14	0	0	0	8	0	0	
9-11	57	100	100	50	67	100	100	
12 or older	14	0	0	50	17	0	0	
4B. Age of partner	(N=8)	(N=1)	(N=0)	(N=3)	(N=15)	(N=1)	(N=2)	(N=0)
Under 5	0%	0%		0%	0%	0%	0%	
5-6	12	0		0	7	0	0	
7-8	12	100		0	7	100	50	
9-11	25	0		33	20	0	0	
12-15	25	0		33	13	0	50	
16-39	0	0		0	20	0	0	
40 or older	0	0		0	13	0	0	
Child, age not given	25	0		33	7	0	0	
Adult, age not given	0	0		0	13	0	0	
4C. Identity of partner	(N=8)	(N=1)	(N=0)	(N=2)	(N=14)	(N=1)	(N=2)	(N=0)
Sibling	12%	0%		0%	7%	0%	0%	
Parent	0	0		0	21	0	0	
Other relative	0	0		0	0	100	0	
Friend or acquaintance	75	0		100	50	0	50	
Stranger	0	0		0	7	0	0	
Group	12	100		0	14	0	50	
Other	0	0		0	0	0	0	
4D. If partner was a group, members of the group	(N=1)	(N=1)	(N=0)	(N=0)	(N=2)	(N=0)	(N=1)	(N=0)
Siblings	0%	0%			0%		0%	
Parents	0	0			0		0	
Other relatives	0	100			0		0	
Friends or acquaintances	0	0			50		100	
Strangers	0				50		0	

CHILDHOOD AND ADOLESCENT SEXUALITY/Fourth Prepubertal Heterosexual Encounter

4E. First sexual activity described

	WHM	BHM	WHTM	BHTM	WHF	BHF	WHTF	BHTF
	(N=8)	(N=1)	(N=1)	(N=3)	(N=14)	(N=1)	(N=2)	(N=0)
Proposition, without subsequent activity	0%	0%	0%	0%	29%	0%	0%	
Looking at bodies, watching masturbation	25	0	0	0	14	0	0	
Kissing or necking	0	0	100	0	7	0	0	
Non-genital physical contact	25	0	0	0	7	0	50	
Manual-genital contact, genital apposition	25	0	0	67	14	0	0	
Oral-genital contact	12	0	0	0	7	0	0	
Oral-anal or anal-genital contact	0	0	0	0	0	100	0	
Sexual intercourse	0	0	0	33	7	0	0	
Rape or attempted rape	0	0	0	0	0	0	0	
Other activity not involving contact	12	0	0	0	0	0	50	
Other activity involving physical contact	0	100	0	0	14	0	0	

4F. Who performed first sexual activity

	WHM	BHM	WHTM	BHTM	WHF	BHF	WHTF	BHTF
	(N=7)	(N=1)	(N=0)	(N=3)	(N=14)	(N=1)	(N=2)	(N=0)
Respondent	14%	0%		33%	14%	0%	0%	
Partner(s)	0	0		0	64	0	50	
Both	86	100		67	21	100	50	

4G. Second sexual activity described

	WHM	BHM	WHTM	BHTM	WHF	BHF	WHTF	BHTF
	(N=2)	(N=0)	(N=1)	(N=1)	(N=4)	(N=0)	(N=0)	(N=0)
Proposition, without subsequent activity	0%		0%	0%	0%			
Looking at bodies, watching masturbation	50		0	0	0			
Kissing or necking	0		0	0	0			
Non-genital physical contact	0		100	0	25			
Manual-genital contact, genital apposition	0		0	0	25			
Oral-genital contact	0		0	0	0			
Oral-anal or anal-genital contact	0		0	0	0			
Sexual intercourse	50		0	100	25			
Rape or attempted rape	0		0	0	0			
Other activity not involving contact	0		0	0	25			
Other activity involving physical contact	0		0	0	0			

4H. Who performed second sexual activity

	WHM	BHM	WHTM	BHTM	WHF	BHF	WHTF	BHTF
	(N=2)	(N=0)	(N=0)	(N=1)	(N=4)	(N=0)	(N=0)	(N=0)
Respondent	50%			0%	25%			
Partner(s)	0			0	25			
Both	50			100	50			

CHILDHOOD AND ADOLESCENT SEXUALITY/Fourth Prepubertal Heterosexual Encounter

	WHM	BHM	WHTM	BHTM	WHF	BHF	WHTF	BHTF
4I. Respondent's reaction to the experience	(N=7)	(N=1)	(N=1)	(N=3)	(N=13)	(N=1)	(N=2)	(N=0)
Positive feelings	57%	100%	100%	100%	31%	0%	50%	
Enjoyed it but felt guilty	14	0	0	0	15	0	0	
Mixed feelings	14	0	0	0	15	0	0	
Negative feelings	0	0	0	0	38	100	50	
Some other reaction	0	0	0	0	0	0	0	
No particular reaction	14	0	0	0	0	0	0	
4J. Were any adults aware of this experience?	(N=8)	(N=1)	(N=1)	(N=3)	(N=14)	(N=1)	(N=2)	(N=0)
No	50%	0%	100%	67%	64%	100%	100%	
Not sure	12	100	0	0	21	0	0	
Yes	38	0	0	33	14	0	0	
4K. Who was the [first] adult who was aware of the experience?	(N=2)	(N=0)	(N=0)	(N=1)	(N=2)	(N=0)	(N=0)	(N=0)
Respondent's mother	0%			0%	100%			
Respondent's father	0			0	0			
Both parents	50			0	0			
Other adult relative(s)	0			0	0			
Partner's parent(s)	50			100	0			
Some other person	0			0	0			
4L. Emotional reaction of [first] aware adult	(N=2)	(N=0)	(N=0)	(N=0)	(N=2)	(N=0)	(N=0)	(N=0)
Very negative (shocked, horrified)	50%				0%			
Mildly negative	0				0			
Indifferent	50				50			
Accepting, supportive, amused	0				0			
Some other reaction	0				50			
4M. First thing the [first] aware adult did	(N=2)	(N=0)	(N=0)	(N=1)	(N=2)	(N=0)	(N=0)	(N=0)
Scolded or punished	50%			100%	50%			
Just stopped the activity	0			0	0			
Supportive or accepting response	0			0	0			
Some other response	50			0	0			
Said or did nothing	0			0	50			

CHILDHOOD AND ADOLESCENT SEXUALITY/Fourth Prepubertal Heterosexual Encounter; Prepubertal Homosexual Frequency

	WHM	BHM	WHTM	BHTM	WHF	BHF	WHTF	BHTF
4N. Second thing the [second] aware adult did	(N=0)	(N=0)	(N=0)	(N=0)	(N=0)	(N=0)	(N=0)	(N=0)
Scolded or punished								
Just stopped the activity								
Supportive or accepting response								
Some other response								
4O. Were any other adults aware of the experience?	(N=7)	(N=1)	(N=1)	(N=3)	(N=14)	(N=1)	(N=2)	(N=0)
No	100%	100%	100%	100%	100%	100%	100%	
Yes	0	0	0	0	0	0	0	
4P. Did anyone observe the experience?	(N=6)	(N=1)	(N=1)	(N=3)	(N=14)	(N=1)	(N=2)	(N=0)
No; just respondent and partner were present	67%	0%	100%	100%	79%	0%	0%	
Yes; a group experience and/or one or more spectators	33	100	0	0	21	100	100	
Prior to the time you had your first [ejaculation/period], can you recall any experiences with a member of the same sex which you or others thought of as being sexual?	(N=574)	(N=111)	(N=284)	(N=53)	(N=229)	(N=63)	(N=101)	(N=39)
Yes	69%	61%	26%	19%	42%	52%	34%	8%
No	31	39	74	81	58	48	66	92
How frequent were these experiences with a member of the same sex?	(N=397)	(N=66)	(N=70)	(N=10)	(N=95)	(N=33)	(N=34)	(N=3)
Happened only once	18%	14%	34%	30%	27%	15%	0%	100%
2-5 experiences	26	18	41	20	28	39	79	0
6-10 experiences	14	12	7	20	14	3	15	0
11-20 experiences	12	20	6	30	7	15	0	0
More than 20 experiences	29	36	11	0	23	27	6	0

CHILDHOOD AND ADOLESCENT SEXUALITY/First Prepubertal Homosexual Encounter

	WHM	BHM	WHTM	BHTM	WHF	BHF	WHTF	BHTF
What did your first such experience consist of?								
1A. Age of respondent	(N=386)	(N=64)	(N=73)	(N=11)	(N=94)	(N=33)	(N=35)	(N=3)
Under 5	7%	5%	5%	27%	7%	3%	0%	0%
5-6	23	22	15	27	16	12	17	67
7-8	25	20	23	27	21	27	37	0
9-11	33	38	34	18	43	48	31	33
12 or older	11	16	22	0	13	9	14	0
1B. Age of partner	(N=388)	(N=62)	(N=71)	(N=11)	(N=96)	(N=33)	(N=35)	(N=3)
Under 5	4%	3%	4%	0%	1%	0%	3%	0%
5-6	14	13	11	36	11	9	11	0
7-8	16	19	17	9	15	18	29	0
9-11	22	19	18	9	29	42	34	33
12-15	22	19	25	9	22	12	20	0
16-39	11	19	4	0	7	6	3	0
40 or older	1	2	6	0	0	0	0	0
Child, age not given	8	3	13	36	10	0	0	67
Adult, age not given	3	2	1	0	4	3	0	0
1C. Identity of partner	(N=344)	(N=53)	(N=64)	(N=9)	(N=90)	(N=31)	(N=33)	(N=2)
Sibling	7%	4%	14%	11%	9%	13%	3%	0%
Parent	0	2	2	0	2	0	0	0
Other relative	11	8	3	11	8	13	9	0
Friend or acquaintance	51	62	39	11	64	68	48	0
Stranger	5	0	6	0	0	3	3	100
Group	25	25	36	67	17	3	36	0
Other	1	0	0	0	0	0	0	0
1D. If partner was a group, members of the group	(N=78)	(N=13)	(N=21)	(N=5)	(N=15)	(N=1)	(N=12)	(N=0)
Siblings	1%	0%	5%	0%	0%	0%	0%	
Parents	0	0	0	0	0	0	0	
Other relatives	4	8	0	0	0	0	8	
Friends or acquaintances	86	92	90	80	80	100	75	
Strangers	0	0	0	0	0	0	0	
Some combination of these							17	

CHILDHOOD AND ADOLESCENT SEXUALITY/First Prepubertal Homosexual Encounter

	WHM	BHM	WHTM	BHTM	WHF	BHF	WHTF	BHTF
1E. First sexual activity described	(N=381)	(N=62)	(N=75)	(N=11)	(N=96)	(N=33)	(N=34)	(N=3)
Proposition, without subsequent activity	1%	0%	1%	0%	1%	0%	0%	0%
Looking at bodies, watching masturbation	20	10	29	9	17	9	24	0
Non-genital physical contact	11	16	7	9	15	30	24	67
Kissing or necking	2	11	1	0	22	30	6	0
Manual-genital contact, genital apposition	33	23	25	0	19	15	12	0
Oral-genital contact	11	15	12	0	2	0	0	0
Oral-anal or anal-genital contact	3	11	0	0	0	0	0	0
Rape or attempted rape	1	2	0	0	0	0	0	0
Other activity not involving contact	5	6	9	45	9	0	12	33
Other activity involving physical contact	13	6	15	36	16	15	24	0
1F. Who performed first sexual activity	(N=372)	(N=60)	(N=75)	(N=11)	(N=95)	(N=33)	(N=34)	(N=3)
Respondent	17%	13%	9%	0%	16%	15%	6%	0%
Partner(s)	16	15	15	9	8	12	9	67
Both	67	72	76	91	76	73	85	33
1G. Second sexual activity described	(N=126)	(N=17)	(N=16)	(N=2)	(N=30)	(N=12)	(N=11)	(N=1)
Proposition, without subsequent activity	1%	0%	0%	0%	0%	0%	0%	0%
Looking at bodies, watching masturbation	5	0	6	0	3	0	0	0
Non-genital physical contact	13	12	38	0	43	42	18	0
Kissing or necking	1	0	0	0	10	0	0	0
Manual-genital contact, genital apposition	29	53	12	0	27	58	73	100
Oral-genital contact	26	24	12	50	3	0	0	0
Oral-anal or anal-genital contact	13	6	6	0	0	0	0	0
Rape or attempted rape	1	0	0	0	0	0	0	0
Other activity not involving contact	2	0	0	0	0	0	0	0
Other activity involving physical contact	9	6	25	50	13	0	9	0
1H. Who performed second sexual activity	(N=118)	(N=17)	(N=14)	(N=2)	(N=30)	(N=12)	(N=11)	(N=1)
Respondent	17%	18%	14%	0%	7%	8%	0%	0%
Partner(s)	17	12	14	0	7	8	18	0
Both	66	71	71	100	87	83	82	100

CHILDHOOD AND ADOLESCENT SEXUALITY/First Prepubertal Homosexual Encounter

	WHM	BHM	WHTM	BHTM	WHF	BHF	WHTF	BHTF
1I. Respondent's reaction to the experience	(N=323)	(N=54)	(N=64)	(N=9)	(N=85)	(N=30)	(N=31)	(N=3)
Positive feelings	63%	63%	39%	56%	71%	77%	29%	33%
Enjoyed it but felt guilty	7	2	8	0	8	3	10	0
Mixed feelings	4	6	5	0	4	7	0	0
Negative feelings	11	15	34	11	8	10	39	33
Some other reaction	2	2	8	0	2	3	0	0
No particular reaction	12	13	6	33	7	0	23	33
1J. Were any adults aware of this experience?	(N=389)	(N=43)	(N=74)	(N=11)	(N=95)	(N=33)	(N=35)	(N=3)
No	80%	89%	72%	91%	82%	91%	91%	100%
Not sure	1	0	7	9	0	0	3	0
Yes	18	11	22	0	18	9	6	0
1K. Who was the [first] adult who was aware of the experience?	(N=61)	(N=7)	(N=12)	(N=0)	(N=13)	(N=2)	(N=2)	(N=0)
Respondent's mother	31%	57%	33%		31%	50%	50%	
Respondent's father	13	14	0		8	0	0	
Both parents	18	0	25		15	50	0	
Other adult relative(s)	5	14	8		8	0	0	
Partner's parent(s)	21	0	25		23	0	0	
Some other person	11	14	8		15	0	50	
1L. Emotional reaction of [first] aware adult	(N=58)	(N=7)	(N=13)	(N=0)	(N=15)	(N=3)	(N=2)	(N=0)
Very negative (shocked, horrified)	38%	43%	54%		33%	33%	100%	
Mildly negative	28	43	8		47	67	0	
Indifferent	24	14	15		13	0	0	
Accepting, supportive, amused	3	0	23		7	0	0	
Some other reaction	7	0	0		0	0	0	

CHILDHOOD AND ADOLESCENT SEXUALITY/First Prepubertal Homosexual Encounter

	WHM	BHM	WHTM	BHTM	WHF	BHF	WHTF	BHTF
1M. First thing the [first] aware adult did	(N=65)	(N=6)	(N=14)	(N=0)	(N=16)	(N=3)	(N=2)	(N=0)
Scolded or punished	46%	50%	57%		50%	67%	100%	
Just stopped the activity	15	17	14		25	33	0	
Supportive or accepting response	3	0	7		6	0	0	
Some other response	8	17	0		6	0	0	
Said or did nothing	28	17	21		12	0	0	
1N. Second thing the [first] aware adult did	(N=9)	(N=0)	(N=1)	(N=0)	(N=4)	(N=0)	(N=0)	(N=0)
Scolded or punished	11%		0%		0%			
Just stopped the activity	67		100		100			
Supportive or accepting response	11		0		0			
Some other response	11		0		0			
1O. Were any other adults aware of the experience?	(N=386)	(N=60)	(N=71)	(N=11)	(N=96)	(N=33)	(N=34)	(N=3)
No	97%	97%	99%	100%	96%	97%	100%	100%
Yes	3	3	1	0	4	3	0	0
1P. Who was the second adult who was aware of the experience?	(N=12)	(N=2)	(N=1)	(N=0)	(N=4)	(N=1)	(N=0)	(N=0)
Respondent's mother	33%	0%	0%		0%	0%		
Respondent's father	25	50	0		0	0		
Both parents	17	0	100		25	0		
Other adult relative(s)	0	0	0		25	0		
Partner's parent(s)	25	0	0		25	100		
Some other person	0	50	0		25	0		
1Q. Emotional reaction of second aware adult	(N=8)	(N=2)	(N=2)	(N=0)	(N=3)	(N=1)	(N=0)	(N=0)
Very negative (shocked, horrified)	38%	0%	0%		67%	0%		
Mildly negative	38	100	0		33	100		
Indifferent	0	0	50		0	0		
Accepting, supportive, amused	12	0	50		0	0		
Some other reaction	12	0	0		0	0		

CHILDHOOD AND ADOLESCENT SEXUALITY/First Prepubertal Homosexual Encounter

	WHM	BHM	WHTM	BHTM	WHF	BHF	WHTF	BHTF
1R. First thing the second aware adult did	(N=12)	(N=1)	(N=2)	(N=0)	(N=1)	(N=1)	(N=0)	(N=0)
Scolded or punished	50%	100%	0%		100%	0%		
Just stopped the activity	17	0	0		0	100		
Supportive or accepting response	8	0	50		0	0		
Some other response	8	0	0		0	0		
Said or did nothing	17	0	50		0	0		
1S. Second thing the second aware adult did	(N=2)	(N=0)	(N=0)	(N=0)	(N=1)	(N=0)	(N=0)	(N=0)
Scolded or punished	0%				0%			
Just stopped the activity	50				100			
Supportive or accepting response	50				0			
Some other response	0				0			
1T. Were any other adults aware of the experience?	(N=388)	(N=60)	(N=72)	(N=11)	(N=96)	(N=33)	(N=34)	(N=3)
No	100%	100%	100%	100%	99%	100%	100%	100%
Yes	0	0	0	0	1	0	0	0
1U. Who was the third adult who was aware of the experience?	(N=0)	(N=0)	(N=0)	(N=0)	(N=1)	(N=0)	(N=0)	(N=0)
Respondent's mother					0%			
Respondent's father					0			
Both parents					0			
Other adult relative(s)					0			
Partner's parent(s)					0			
Some other person					100			
1V. Emotional reaction of third aware adult	(N=0)	(N=0)	(N=0)	(N=0)	(N=0)	(N=0)	(N=0)	(N=0)
Very negative (shocked, horrified)								
Mildly negative								
Indifferent								
Accepting, supportive, amused								
Some other reaction								

CHILDHOOD AND ADOLESCENT SEXUALITY/First Prepubertal Homosexual Encounter

	WHM	BHM	WHTM	BHTM	WHF	BHF	WHTF	BHTF
1W. First thing the third aware adult did	(N=0)	(N=0)	(N=0)	(N=0)	(N=1)	(N=0)	(N=0)	(N=0)
Scolded or punished					0%			
Just stopped the activity					0			
Supportive or accepting response					0			
Some other response					0			
Said or did nothing					100			
1X. Second thing the third aware adult did	(N=0)	(N=0)	(N=0)	(N=0)	(N=0)	(N=0)	(N=0)	(N=0)
Scolded or punished								
Just stopped the activity								
Supportive or accepting response								
Some other response								
1Y. Did anyone observe the experience?	(N=375)	(N=62)	(N=67)	(N=10)	(N=94)	(N=32)	(N=33)	(N=2)
No; just respondent and partner were present	75%	79%	57%	40%	78%	88%	58%	100%
Yes; a group experience and/or one or more spectators	25	21	43	60	22	12	42	0

123

CHILDHOOD AND ADOLESCENT SEXUALITY/Second Prepubertal Homosexual Encounter

	WHM	BHM	WHTM	BHTM	WHF	BHF	WHTF	BHTF

Did you have any other experiences with a member of the same sex? What did your second such experience consist of?

2A. Age of respondent

	WHM	BHM	WHTM	BHTM	WHF	BHF	WHTF	BHTF
	(N=112)	(N=18)	(N=10)	(N=2)	(N=24)	(N=7)	(N=2)	(N=0)
Under 5	1%	6%	10%	0%	8%	0%	0%	
5-6	10	11	10	0	8	14	0	
7-8	29	22	20	0	12	29	0	
9-11	38	44	40	0	46	43	50	
12 or older	22	17	20	100	25	14	50	

2B. Age of partner

	WHM	BHM	WHTM	BHTM	WHF	BHF	WHTF	BHTF
	(N=132)	(N=17)	(N=10)	(N=1)	(N=26)	(N=6)	(N=2)	(N=0)
Under 5	0%	0%	10%	0%	0%	0%	0%	
5-6	5	0	0	0	4	0	0	
7-8	11	29	20	0	15	0	0	
9-11	25	12	30	0	27	17	0	
12-15	23	35	30	0	15	17	100	
16-39	8	18	10	100	8	17	0	
40 or older	3	0	0	0	0	0	0	
Child, age not given	20	6	0	0	19	17	0	
Adult, age not given	7	0	0	0	12	33	0	

CHILDHOOD AND ADOLESCENT SEXUALITY/Second Prepubertal Homosexual Encounter

	WHM	BHM	WHTM	BHTM	WHF	BHF	WHTF	BHTF
2C. Identity of partner	(N=120)	(N=15)	(N=7)	(N=2)	(N=25)	(N=6)	(N=2)	(N=0)
Sibling	3%	13%	14%	0%	4%	0%	50%	
Parent	0	0	0	0	0	0	0	
Other relative	8	13	0	0	4	0	50	
Friend or acquaintance	44	53	43	50	76	67	0	
Stranger	4	0	0	50	0	0	0	
Group	39	20	43	0	16	33	0	
Other	1	0	0	0	0	0	0	
2D. If partner was a group, members of the group	(N=38)	(N=2)	(N=3)	(N=0)	(N=4)	(N=2)	(N=0)	(N=0)
Siblings	3%	0%	0%		0%	0%		
Parents	0	0	0		0	0		
Other relatives	3	50	0		0	0		
Friends or acquaintances	82	50	100		50	50		
Strangers	0	0	0		0	50		
Some combination of these	13	0	0		50	0		
2E. First sexual activity described	(N=133)	(N=18)	(N=10)	(N=2)	(N=27)	(N=6)	(N=2)	(N=0)
Proposition, without subsequent activity	1%	6%	0%	0%	0%	0%	0%	
Looking at bodies, watching masturbation	14	11	20	50	33	0	0	
Non-genital physical contact	10	28	0	50	11	33	0	
Kissing or necking	0	0	0	0	22	17	0	
Manual-genital contact, genital apposition	41	17	0	0	19	17	0	
Oral-genital contact	14	22	30	0	4	0	0	
Oral-anal or anal-genital contact	3	17	10	0	0	0	0	
Rape or attempted rape	0	0	10	0	0	0	0	
Other activity not involving contact	4	0	20	0	4	33	100	
Other activity involving physical contact	14	0	10	0	7	0	0	
2F. Who performed first sexual activity	(N=124)	(N=17)	(N=9)	(N=2)	(N=26)	(N=6)	(N=2)	(N=0)
Respondent	18%	12%	33%	100%	27%	33%	0%	
Partner(s)	14	12	22	0	4	0	0	
Both	69	76	44	0	69	67	100	

CHILDHOOD AND ADOLESCENT SEXUALITY/Second Prepubertal Homosexual Encounter

	WHM	BHM	WHTM	BHTM	WHF	BHF	WHTF	BHTF
	(N=34)	(N=4)	(N=2)	(N=1)	(N=8)	(N=2)	(N=1)	(N=0)
2G. Second sexual activity described								
Proposition, without subsequent activity	0%	0%	0%	0%	0%	0%	0%	
Looking at bodies, watching masturbation	3	0	0	0	25	0	0	
Non-genital physical contact	21	0	50	0	12	50	100	
Kissing or necking	0	25	0	0	0	0	0	
Manual-genital contact, genital apposition	21	50	0	100	38	50	0	
Oral-genital contact	32	25	0	0	12	0	0	
Oral-anal or anal-genital contact	15	25	50	0	0	0	0	
Rape or attempted rape	0	0	0	0	0	0	0	
Other activity not involving contact	3	0	0	0	0	0	0	
Other activity involving physical contact	6	0	0	0	12	0	0	

	WHM	BHM	WHTM	BHTM	WHF	BHF	WHTF	BHTF
	(N=29)	(N=4)	(N=2)	(N=1)	(N=8)	(N=2)	(N=1)	(N=0)
2H. Who performed second sexual activity								
Respondent	10%	25%	0%	0%	12%	0%	0%	
Partner(s)	21	0	0	100	0	0	0	
Both	69	75	100	0	88	100	100	

	WHM	BHM	WHTM	BHTM	WHF	BHF	WHTF	BHTF
	(N=105)	(N=16)	(N=9)	(N=1)	(N=22)	(N=6)	(N=2)	(N=0)
2I. Respondent's reaction to the experience								
Positive feelings	74%	62%	44%	0%	73%	83%	100%	
Enjoyed it but felt guilty	5	0	0	0	9	0	0	
Mixed feelings	4	0	0	0	0	0	0	
Negative feelings	8	31	22	100	14	17	0	
Some other reaction	2	0	11	0	5	0	0	
No particular reaction	8	6	22	0	0	0	0	

	WHM	BHM	WHTM	BHTM	WHF	BHF	WHTF	BHTF
	(N=137)	(N=18)	(N=10)	(N=2)	(N=27)	(N=7)	(N=2)	(N=0)
2J. Were any adults aware of this experience?								
No	82%	89%	90%	100%	78%	71%	100%	
Not sure	2	6	10	0	0	14	0	
Yes	15	6	0	0	22	14	0	

CHILDHOOD AND ADOLESCENT SEXUALITY/Second Prepubertal Homosexual Encounter

	WHM	BHM	WHTM	BHTM	WHF	BHF	WHTF	BHTF
2K. Who was the [first] adult who was aware of the experience?	(N=18)	(N=1)	(N=0)	(N=0)	(N=5)	(N=1)	(N=0)	(N=0)
Respondent's mother	39%	100%			40%	0%		
Respondent's father	6	0			20	0		
Both parents	6	0			0	0		
Other adult relative(s)	6	0			0	0		
Partner's parent(s)	39	0			40	0		
Some other person	6	0			0	100		
2L. Emotional reaction of [first] aware adult	(N=18)	(N=1)	(N=0)	(N=0)	(N=5)	(N=1)	(N=0)	(N=0)
Very negative (shocked, horrified)	22%	0%			0%	100%		
Mildly negative	39	0			40	0		
Indifferent	28	100			20	0		
Accepting, supportive, amused	6	0			40	0		
Some other reaction	6	0			0	0		
2M. First thing the [first] aware adult did	(N=21)	(N=1)	(N=0)	(N=0)	(N=5)	(N=1)	(N=0)	(N=0)
Scolded or punished	48%	0%			20%	0%		
Just stopped the activity	19	0			20	100		
Supportive or accepting response	10	0			20	0		
Some other response	0	0			20	0		
Said or did nothing	24	100			20	0		
2N. Second thing the [first] aware adult did	(N=3)	(N=0)	(N=0)	(N=0)	(N=1)	(N=0)	(N=0)	(N=0)
Scolded or punished	0%				100%			
Just stopped the activity	100				0			
Supportive or accepting response	0				0			
Some other response	0				0			
20. Were any other adults aware of the experience?	(N=136)	(N=18)	(N=10)	(N=2)	(N=27)	(N=7)	(N=2)	(N=0)
No	98%	94%	100%	100%	96%	86%	100%	
Yes	2	6	0	0	4	14	0	

CHILDHOOD AND ADOLESCENT SEXUALITY/Second Prepubertal Homosexual Encounter

	WHM	BHM	WHTM	BHTM	WHF	BHF	WHTF	BHTF
2P. Who was the second adult who was aware of the experience?	(N=3)	(N=1)	(N=0)	(N=0)	(N=1)	(N=1)	(N=0)	(N=0)
Respondent's mother	0%	0%			0%	0%		
Respondent's father	0	100			0	0		
Both parents	33	0			0	100		
Other adult relative(s)	0	0			0	0		
Partner's parent(s)	33	0			0	0		
Some other person	33	0			100	0		
2Q. Emotional reaction of second aware adult	(N=2)	(N=1)	(N=0)	(N=0)	(N=0)	(N=1)	(N=0)	(N=0)
Very negative (shocked, horrified)	0%	0%				0%		
Mildly negative	100	100				100		
Indifferent	0	0				0		
Accepting, supportive, amused	0	0				0		
Some other reaction	0	0				0		
2R. First thing the second aware adult did	(N=3)	(N=0)	(N=0)	(N=0)	(N=0)	(N=1)	(N=0)	(N=0)
Scolded or punished	33%					0%		
Just stopped the activity	33					100		
Supportive or accepting response	0					0		
Some other response	0					0		
Said or did nothing	33					0		
2S. Second thing the second aware adult did	(N=0)	(N=0)	(N=0)	(N=0)	(N=0)	(N=0)	(N=0)	(N=0)
Scolded or punished								
Just stopped the activity								
Supportive or accepting response								
Some other response								
2T. Were any other adults aware of the experience?	(N=137)	(N=18)	(N=10)	(N=2)	(N=27)	(N=7)	(N=2)	(N=0)
No	99%	100%	100%	100%	100%	86%	100%	
Yes	1	0	0	0	0	14	0	

CHILDHOOD AND ADOLESCENT SEXUALITY/Second Prepubertal Homosexual Encounter

	WHM	BHM	WHTM	BHTM	WHF	BHF	WHTF	BHTF
2U. Who was the third adult who was aware of the experience?	(N=1)	(N=0)	(N=0)	(N=0)	(N=0)	(N=1)	(N=0)	(N=0)
Respondent's mother	100%					0%		
Respondent's father	0					0		
Both parents	0					0		
Other adult relative(s)	0					0		
Partner's parent(s)	0					100		
Some other person	0					0		
2V. Emotional reaction of third aware adult	(N=0)	(N=0)	(N=0)	(N=0)	(N=0)	(N=1)	(N=0)	(N=0)
Very negative (shocked, horrified)						0%		
Mildly negative						100		
Indifferent						0		
Accepting, supportive, amused						0		
Some other reaction								
2W. First thing the third aware adult did	(N=0)	(N=0)	(N=0)	(N=0)	(N=0)	(N=1)	(N=0)	(N=0)
Scolded or punished						0%		
Just stopped the activity						100		
Supportive or accepting response						0		
Some other response						0		
Said or did nothing						0		
2X. Second thing the second aware adult did	(N=0)	(N=0)	(N=0)	(N=0)	(N=0)	(N=0)	(N=0)	(N=0)
Scolded or punished								
Just stopped the activity								
Supportive or accepting response								
Some other response								
2Y. Did anyone observe the experience?	(N=128)	(N=16)	(N=8)	(N=2)	(N=25)	(N=5)	(N=2)	(N=0)
No; just respondent and partner were present	60%	81%	50%	50%	84%	80%	100%	
Yes; a group experience and/or one or more spectators	40	19	50	50	16	20	0	

CHILDHOOD AND ADOLESCENT SEXUALITY/Third Prepubertal Homosexual Encounter

Did you have any other experiences with a member of the same sex? What did the third such experience consist of?

		WHM	BHM	WHTM	BHTM	WHF	BHF	WHTF	BHTF
3A.	Age of respondent	(N=32)	(N=5)	(N=0)	(N=1)	(N=5)	(N=0)	(N=0)	(N=0)
	Under 5	0%	0%		0%	0%			
	5-6	3	0		0	0			
	7-8	28	40		0	20			
	9-11	50	40		100	80			
	12 or older	19	20		0	0			
3B.	Age of partner	(N=42)	(N=5)	(N=0)	(N=0)	(N=5)	(N=0)	(N=0)	(N=0)
	Under 5	0%	0%			20%			
	5-6	5	0			0			
	7-8	10	40			20			
	9-11	19	20			60			
	12-15	19	0			0			
	16-39	12	20			0			
	40 or older	0	0			0			
	Child, age not given	33	20			0			
	Adult, age not given	2	0			0			
3C.	Identity of partner	(N=31)	(N=7)	(N=0)	(N=1)	(N=5)	(N=1)	(N=0)	(N=0)
	Sibling	0%	0%		0%	0%	0%		
	Parent	0	0		0	0	0		
	Other relative	16	0		0	0	0		
	Friend or acquaintance	42	86		100	80	100		
	Stranger	10	0		0	0	0		
	Group	29	14		0	20	0		
	Other	3	0		0	0	0		
3D.	If partner was a group, members of the group	(N=8)	(N=1)	(N=0)	(N=0)	(N=1)	(N=0)	(N=0)	(N=0)
	Siblings	0%	0%			100%			
	Parents	0	0			0			
	Other relatives	0	0			0			
	Friends or acquaintances	62	100			0			
	Strangers	0	0			0			
	Some combination of those	29	0			0			

CHILDHOOD AND ADOLESCENT SEXUALITY/Third Prepubertal Homosexual Encounter

	WHM	BHM	WHTM	BHTM	WHF	BHF	WHTF	BHTF
3E. First sexual activity described	(N=41)	(N=7)	(N=0)	(N=1)	(N=5)	(N=1)	(N=0)	(N=0)
Proposition, without subsequent activity	0%	14%		0%	0%	0%		
Looking at bodies, watching masturbation	15	14		0	40	0		
Non-genital physical contact	2	0		0	20	0		
Kissing or necking	0	0		0	0	0		
Manual-genital contact, genital apposition	49	14		100	20	0		
Oral-genital contact	7	0		0	0	0		
Oral-anal or anal-genital contact	5	43		0	0	0		
Rape or attempted rape	0	0		0	0	0		
Other activity not involving contact	10	14		0	0	0		
Other activity involving physical contact	12	0		0	20	100		
3F. Who performed first sexual activity	(N=39)	(N=7)	(N=0)	(N=1)	(N=5)	(N=1)	(N=0)	(N=0)
Respondent	10%	43%		100%	20%	100%		
Partner(s)	15	14		0	0	0		
Both	74	43		0	80	0		
3G. Second sexual activity described	(N=11)	(N=1)	(N=0)	(N=0)	(N=1)	(N=0)	(N=0)	(N=0)
Proposition, without subsequent activity	0%	0%			0%			
Looking at bodies, watching masturbation	0	0			100			
Non-genital physical contact	18	0			0			
Kissing or necking	0	0			0			
Manual-genital contact, genital apposition	9	0			0			
Oral-genital contact	55	100			0			
Oral-anal or anal-genital contact	18	0			0			
Rape or attempted rape	0	0			0			
Other activity not involving contact	0	0			0			
Other activity involving physical contact	0	0			0			
3H. Who performed second sexual activity	(N=9)	(N=1)	(N=0)	(N=0)	(N=1)	(N=0)	(N=0)	(N=0)
Respondent	22%	0%			0%			
Partner(s)	33	0			0			
Both	44	100			100			

131

CHILDHOOD AND ADOLESCENT SEXUALITY/Third Prepubertal Homosexual Encounter

	WHM	BHM	WHTM	BHTM	WHF	BHF	WHTF	BHTF
3I. Respondent's reaction to the experience	(N=32)	(N=7)	(N=0)	(N=0)	(N=5)	(N=0)	(N=0)	(N=0)
Positive feelings	78%	86%			80%			
Enjoyed it but felt guilty	12	0			20			
Mixed feelings	6	0			0			
Negative feelings	3	14			0			
Some other reaction	0	0			0			
No particular reaction	0	0			0			
3J. Were any adults aware of this experience?	(N=44)	(N=7)	(N=0)	(N=1)	(N=3)	(N=1)	(N=0)	(N=0)
No	91%	57%		100%	33%	100%		
Not sure	2	0		0	33	0		
Yes	7	43		0	33	0		
3K. Who was the [first] adult who was aware of the experience?	(N=2)	(N=2)	(N=0)	(N=0)	(N=1)	(N=0)	(N=0)	(N=0)
Respondent's mother	0%	0%			0%			
Respondent's father	0	0			100			
Both parents	50	50			0			
Other adult relative(s)	50	0			0			
Partner's parent(s)	0	0			0			
Some other person	0	50			0			
3L. Emotional reaction of [first] aware adult	(N=2)	(N=2)	(N=0)	(N=0)	(N=1)	(N=0)	(N=0)	(N=0)
Very negative (shocked, horrified)	100%	0%			0%			
Mildly negative	0	50			0			
Indifferent	0	0			100			
Accepting, supportive, amused	0	50			0			
Some other reaction	0	0			0			
3M. First thing the [first] aware adult did	(N=3)	(N=2)	(N=0)	(N=0)	(N=1)	(N=0)	(N=0)	(N=0)
Scolded or punished	67%	0%			0%			
Just stopped the activity	0	0			0			
Supportive or accepting response	0	50			0			
Some other response	0	50			0			
Said or did nothing	33	0			100			

132

CHILDHOOD AND ADOLESCENT SEXUALITY/Third Prepubertal Homosexual Encounter

	WHM	BHM	WHTM	BHTM	WHF	BHF	WHTF	BHTF
3N. Second thing the [first] aware adult did	(N=0)	(N=1)	(N=0)	(N=0)	(N=0)	(N=0)	(N=0)	(N=0)
Scolded or punished		0%						
Just stopped the activity		0						
Supportive or accepting response		0						
Some other response		100						
3O. Were any other adults aware of the experience?	(N=44)	(N=7)	(N=0)	(N=0)	(N=3)	(N=1)	(N=0)	(N=0)
No	100%	100%			100%	100%		
Yes	0	0			0	0		
3P. Did anyone observe the experience?	(N=37)	(N=7)	(N=0)	(N=1)	(N=3)	(N=1)	(N=0)	(N=0)
No; just respondent and partner were present	70%	86%		100%	67%	100%		
Yes; a group experience and/or one or more spectators	30	14		0	33	0		

133

CHILDHOOD AND ADOLESCENT SEXUALITY/Fourth Prepubertal Homosexual Encounter

	WHM	BHM	WHTM	BHTM	WHF	BHF	WHTF	BHTF
Did you have any other experiences with a member of the same sex? What did your fourth such experience consist of?								
4A. Age of respondent	(N=10)	(N=2)	(N=0)	(N=0)	(N=2)	(N=0)	(N=0)	(N=0)
Under 5	0%	0%			0%			
5-6	10	0			0			
7-8	20	50			0			
9-11	60	50			50			
12 or older	10	0			50			
4B. Age of partner	(N=12)	(N=2)	(N=0)	(N=0)	(N=2)	(N=0)	(N=0)	(N=0)
Under 5	0%	0%			0%			
5-6	8	0			0			
7-8	8	50			0			
9-11	25	50			50			
12-15	8	0			50			
16-39	8	0			0			
40 or older	0	0			0			
Child, age not given	33	0			0			
Adult, age not given	8	0			0			

CHILDHOOD AND ADOLESCENT SEXUALITY/Fourth Prepubertal Homosexual Encounter

	WHM	BHM	WHTM	BHTM	WHF	BHF	WHTF	BHTF
4C. Identity of partner	(N=8)	(N=2)	(N=0)	(N=0)	(N=2)	(N=0)	(N=0)	(N=0)
Sibling	0%	0%			0%			
Parent	0	0			0			
Other relative	0	50			0			
Friend or acquaintance	62	50			100			
Stranger	12	0			0			
Group	25	0			0			
4D. If partner was a group, members of the group	(N=2)	(N=0)	(N=0)	(N=0)	(N=0)	(N=0)	(N=0)	(N=0)
Siblings	0%							
Parents	0							
Other relatives	0							
Friends or acquaintances	50							
Strangers	0							
Some combination of these	50							
4E. First sexual activity described	(N=13)	(N=3)	(N=0)	(N=0)	(N=2)	(N=0)	(N=0)	(N=0)
Proposition, without subsequent activity	0%	0%			0%			
Looking at bodies, watching masturbation	23	0			0			
Non-genital physical contact	0	33			0			
Kissing or necking	0	0			50			
Manual-genital contact, genital apposition	46	0			0			
Oral-genital contact	31	0			0			
Oral-anal or anal-genital contact	0	33			0			
Rape or attempted rape	0	0			0			
Other activity not involving contact	0	33			50			
Other activity involving physical contact	0	0			0			
4F. Who performed first sexual activity	(N=12)	(N=3)	(N=0)	(N=0)	(N=2)	(N=0)	(N=0)	(N=0)
Respondent	17%	33%			50%			
Partner(s)	25	0			0			
Both	58	67			50			

135

	WHM	BHM	WHTM	BHTM	WHF	BHF	WHTF	BHTF
4G. Second sexual activity described	(N=6)	(N=0)	(N=0)	(N=0)	(N=1)	(N=0)	(N=0)	(N=0)
Proposition, without subsequent activity	0%				0%			
Looking at bodies, watching masturbation	0				0			
Non-genital physical contact	17				0			
Kissing or necking	0				0			
Manual-genital contact, genital apposition	17				100			
Oral-genital contact	33				0			
Oral-anal or anal-genital contact	33				0			
Rape or attempted rape	0				0			
Other activity not involving contact	0				0			
Other activity involving physical contact	0				0			
4H. Who performed second sexual activity	(N=4)	(N=0)	(N=0)	(N=0)	(N=1)	(N=0)	(N=0)	(N=0)
Respondent	0%				0%			
Partner(s)	25				0			
Both	75				100			
4I. Respondent's reaction to the experience	(N=8)	(N=3)	(N=0)	(N=0)	(N=2)	(N=0)	(N=0)	(N=0)
Positive feelings	80%	100%			100%			
Enjoyed it but felt guilty	20	0			0			
Mixed feelings	0	0			0			
Negative feelings	0	0			0			
Some other reaction	0	0			0			
No particular reaction	0	0			0			
4J. Were any adults aware of this experience?	(N=13)	(N=3)	(N=0)	(N=0)	(N=2)	(N=0)	(N=0)	(N=0)
No	100%	100%			100%			
Not sure	0	0			0			
Yes	0	0			0			
4K. Did anyone observe the experience?	(N=11)	(N=3)	(N=0)	(N=0)	(N=2)	(N=0)	(N=0)	(N=0)
No; just respondent and partner were present	73%	100%			100%			
Yes; a group experience and/or one or more spectators	27	0			0			

CHILDHOOD AND ADOLESCENT SEXUALITY/Onset of Puberty

	WHM	BHM	WHTM	BHTM	WHF	BHF	WHTF	BHTF
	(N=575)	(N=111)	(N=280)	(N=53)	(N=0)	(N=0)	(N=0)	(N=0)
How old were you the first time you "came" (had an ejaculation)?								
Under 10	3%	0%	1%	2%				
10	4	5	3	0				
11	15	10	12	6				
12	33	25	28	21				
13	24	25	23	34				
14	12	16	18	13				
15	5	10	9	13	[not asked of females]			
Over 15	3	9	5	11				
	(N=548)	(N=106)	(N=271)	(N=52)	(N=0)	(N=0)	(N=0)	(N=0)
How did [your first ejaculation] happen?								
Solitary masturbation	66%	48%	52%	48%				
Orgasm during sleep	9	13	36	12				
Homosexual oral-genital contact	3	6	1	0				
Other homosexual genital contact	19	25	1	0	[not asked of females]			
Other homosexual situation	1	0	0	0				
Heterosexual sexual intercourse	1	8	3	27				
Other heterosexual genital contact	0	1	5	13				
Other heterosexual situation	0	0	0	0				
	(N=571)	(N=111)	(N=277)	(N=53)	(N=0)	(N=0)	(N=0)	(N=0)
What was your reaction to this first ejaculation?								
Entirely positive	39%	37%	35%	75%				
Enjoyed it, but was surprised	16	14	14	8				
Enjoyed it, but felt guilty	5	4	5	0				
Mixed feelings	11	6	9	13	[not asked of females]			
Frightened, confused, unprepared for it	13	23	17	2				
Negative feelings	10	12	10	2				
Other reaction, or don't remember	6	5	11	0				

137

CHILDHOOD AND ADOLESCENT SEXUALITY/Onset of Puberty

	WHM	BHM	WHTM	BHTM	WHF	BHF	WHTF	BHTF
	(N=0)	(N=0)	(N=0)	(N=0)	(N=228)	(N=64)	(N=101)	(N=39)
At what age did you begin to menstruate?								
Under 10					2%	8%	2%	3%
10					2	9	3	5
11					18	25	14	21
12	[not asked of males]				25	23	29	23
13					29	14	26	23
14					15	9	19	15
15					4	5	4	10
Over 15					4	6	4	0
	(N=0)	(N=0)	(N=0)	(N=0)	(N=227)	(N=61)	(N=99)	(N=39)
What was your reaction to that first menstruation?*								
Was prepared for it					41%	48%	53%	44%
Knew about it, but emotionally unprepared for it					5	8	3	0
Did not know it would happen	[not asked of males]				18	21	13	10
Generally positive feelings					17	18	32	5
Felt it was a nuisance					12	8	6	3
Negative feelings (resentment, confusion, fear, etc.)					36	43	33	28
It was uncomfortable, painful					5	3	2	3
Some other reaction					9	10	7	13
No particular reaction					18	14	15	31
	(N=0)	(N=0)	(N=0)	(N=0)	(N=229)	(N=64)	(N=100)	(N=39)
During adolescence, would you say that the amount of your menstrual flow was above average, average, or below average?								
Below average					11%	14%	7%	18%
Average	[not asked of males]				72	55	73	74
Above average					17	31	20	8
	(N=0)	(N=0)	(N=0)	(N=0)	(N=229)	(N=64)	(N=100)	(N=39)
How much discomfort did you experience at those times?								
None					26%	25%	23%	33%
Very little	[not asked of males]				26	19	32	18
Some					18	19	27	23
Much					29	38	18	26

138

After you were first able to [ejaculate/menstruate], what was the first sexual encounter you ever had with a member of the opposite sex, whether sexual behavior occurred or was only suggested? Could you tell me something about it?

A. Age of respondent

	(N=470)	(N=91)	(N=272)	(N=52)	(N=217)	(N=62)	(N=98)	(N=36)
Under 10	1%	0%	0%	0%	0%	0%	0%	0%
10-11	1	4	4	4	2	7	3	0
12	4	7	7	13	10	10	5	3
13	9	14	14	27	19	10	11	3
14	14	18	21	21	13	26	16	14
15	13	9	16	19	16	13	21	22
16	12	19	19	8	15	10	16	6
17-18	21	15	10	6	15	18	17	33
Over 18	26	14	10	2	9	8	9	19

B. Age of partner

	(N=440)	(N=90)	(N=239)	(N=50)	(N=218)	(N=59)	(N=95)	(N=37)
Under 10	1%	1%	0%	0%	0%	0%	0%	0%
10-11	2	4	3	6	0	0	0	0
12	4	9	7	14	5	5	3	0
13	11	14	13	8	4	0	5	0
14	11	12	16	18	9	5	9	8
15	12	11	16	28	9	5	11	16
16	12	16	12	12	11	8	19	3
17-18	17	13	10	8	18	25	24	27
Over 18	27	17	18	2	39	42	27	41
Non-adult, age not given	2	1	5	4	4	3	0	5
Adult, age not given	1	0	0	0	2	5	1	0

CHILDHOOD AND ADOLESCENT SEXUALITY/First Actual Postpubertal Heterosexual Encounter

C. Identity of partner

	(N=430)	(N=75)	(N=208)	(N=41)	(N=193)	(N=54)	(N=89)	(N=30)
Sibling	1%	1%	1%	0%	1%	4%	0%	0%
Parent	0	0	0	0	5	0	2	0
Other relative	2	4	0	2	4	0	1	0
Friend, acquaintance, date	69	83	74	88	81	83	87	73
Presumed or actual fiancé(e)	3	0	1	0	3	0	2	10
Spouse	1	3	1	0	1	4	2	17
Stranger	8	7	12	10	5	6	4	0
Prostitute	12	3	8	0	0	0	0	0
Group	2	0	4	0	1	0	1	0
Other	2	0	0	0	1	2	0	0

D. If partner was a group, members of the group

	(N=9)	(N=0)	(N=6)	(N=0)	(N=2)	(N=0)	(N=1)	(N=1)
Siblings	0%		17%		0%		0%	0%
Parents	0		0		0		0	0
Other relatives	0		17		0		0	0
Friends or acquaintances	67		67		100		0	100
Some combination of these	0		0		0		100	0
Strangers	0		0		0		0	0
Prostitutes	0		0		0		0	0
Other, or other combination of these	33		0		0		0	0

E. First sexual activity described

	(N=476)	(N=92)	(N=273)	(N=52)	(N=220)	(N=62)	(N=98)	(N=37)
Proposition, without subsequent activity	3%	1%	1%	0%	4%	2%	7%	3%
Watching others' sexual activity	1	3	3	0	2	2	0	0
Kissing or necking	30	15	39	8	50	37	65	24
Non-genital body contact, light petting	17	12	19	21	15	13	16	16
Manual-genital contact, genital apposition	12	7	12	25	10	2	5	3
Oral-genital contact	3	4	1	0	0	2	0	0
Oral-anal or anal-genital contact	0	1	0	0	0	0	0	0
Sexual intercourse	22	50	16	37	10	34	3	54
Rape or attempted rape	3	0	0	0	3	3	1	0
Other activity not involving contact	3	2	4	0	2	2	0	0
Other activity involving physical contact	7	4	5	10	4	5	2	0

	WHM	BHM	WHTM	BHTM	WHF	BHF	WHTF	BHTF
F. Who performed first sexual activity	(N=434)	(N=89)	(N=230)	(N=51)	(N=212)	(N=61)	(N=95)	(N=37)
Respondent	11%	11%	18%	8%	4%	2%	1%	0%
Partner(s)	10	4	7	4	23	13	31	8
Both	79	84	75	88	73	85	68	92
G. Second sexual activity described	(N=182)	(N=31)	(N=108)	(N=24)	(N=87)	(N=23)	(N=28)	(N=6)
Proposition, without subsequent activity	0%	6%	0%	0%	0%	0%	0%	0%
Watching others' sexual activity	1	0	2	0	0	0	0	0
Kissing or necking	1	0	1	0	1	0	0	0
Non-genital body contact, light petting	48	26	53	8	56	43	75	50
Manual-genital contact, genital apposition	19	13	27	12	24	39	18	17
Oral-genital contact	3	0	1	0	2	4	0	0
Oral-anal or anal-genital contact	0	6	0	0	0	0	0	0
Sexual intercourse	23	42	8	75	11	9	0	17
Rape or attempted rape	0	0	0	0	0	0	0	0
Other activity not involving contact	2	0	2	0	0	0	0	0
Other activity involving physical contact	4	6	6	4	5	4	7	17
H. Who performed second sexual activity	(N=174)	(N=30)	(N=90)	(N=24)	(N=85)	(N=24)	(N=28)	(N=6)
Respondent	17%	17%	21%	8%	8%	9%	0%	0%
Partner(s)	12	13	6	0	28	17	25	17
Both	71	70	73	92	64	74	75	83
I. Respondent's reaction to the experience	(N=457)	(N=90)	(N=259)	(N=51)	(N=215)	(N=60)	(N=94)	(N=37)
Positive feelings	43%	48%	69%	84%	39%	25%	51%	54%
Enjoyed it but felt guilty	4	8	3	0	6	3	7	0
Mixed feelings	11	11	13	8	11	13	7	8
Negative feelings	26	23	12	6	31	42	27	32
Some other reaction	1	1	1	0	2	3	2	0
No particular reaction	16	9	2	2	12	13	5	5
J. Did anyone observe the experience?	(N=338)	(N=85)	(N=220)	(N=43)	(N=205)	(N=60)	(N=89)	(N=37)
No; just respondent and partner were present	89%	96%	95%	98%	95%	97%	91%	100%
Yes; a group experience and/or one or more spectators	11	4	5	2	5	3	9	0

CHILDHOOD AND ADOLESCENT SEXUALITY/First Postpubertal Heterosexual Encounter with Physical Contact

[If the first encounter did not involve contact], can you recall the first encounter which involved physical contact with a member of the opposite sex? Could you tell me something about it?

A. Age of respondent

	WHM	BHM	WHTM	BHTM	WHF	BHF	WHTF	BHTF
	(N=19)	(N=6)	(N=14)	(N=0)	(N=16)	(N=3)	(N=8)	(N=0)
Under 10	0%	0%	0%		0%	33%	0%	
10-11	0	0	0		0	0	0	
12	0	16	0		6	0	0	
13	5	0	0		6	0	0	
14	16	17	21		25	0	12	
15	11	50	29		12	33	12	
16	16	17	7		25	0	25	
17-18	16	0	14		0	33	25	
Over 18	37	0	29		25	0	25	

B. Age of partner

	WHM	BHM	WHTM	BHTM	WHF	BHF	WHTF	BHTF
	(N=15)	(N=6)	(N=11)	(N=0)	(N=17)	(N=3)	(N=8)	(N=0)
Under 10	0%	0%	0%		0%	0%	0%	
10-11	0	0	0		0	0	0	
12	0	17	0		0	0	0	
13	13	0	0		6	0	0	
14	7	0	18		19	0	0	
15	20	17	0		6	0	0	
16	27	50	9		12	33	12	
17-18	0	17	45		12	0	38	
Over 18	33	0	27		41	67	50	
Non-adult, age not given	0	0	0		6	0	0	
Adult, age not given	0	0	0		0	0	0	

CHILDHOOD AND ADOLESCENT SEXUALITY/First Postpubertal Heterosexual Encounter with Physical Contact

	WHM	BHM	WHTM	BHTM	WHF	BHF	WHTF	BHTF
C. Identity of partner	(N=19)	(N=6)	(N=14)	(N=0)	(N=15)	(N=3)	(N=8)	(N=0)
Sibling	0%	0%	0%		0%	0%	0%	
Parent	0	0	0		0	0	0	
Other relative	0	0	0		7	100	0	
Friend, acquaintance, date	74	100	71		67	0	62	
Presumed or actual fiancé(e)	0	0	0		7	0	12	
Spouse	5	0	0		0	0	25	
Stranger	11	0	14		20	0	0	
Prostitute	11	0	0		0	0	0	
Group	0	0	14		0	0	0	
Other	0	0	0		0	0	0	
D. If partner was a group, members of the group	(N=0)	(N=0)	(N=2)	(N=0)	(N=0)	(N=0)	(N=0)	(N=0)
Siblings			0%					
Parents			0					
Other relatives			0					
Friends or acquaintances			0					
Some combination of these			100					
Strangers			0					
Prostitutes			0					
Other, or other combination of these			0					
E. First sexual activity described	(N=19)	(N=6)	(N=14)	(N=0)	(N=13)	(N=3)	(N=8)	(N=0)
Kissing or necking	26%	17%	64%		62%	0%	50%	
Non-genital body contact, light petting	21	17	14		8	67	12	
Manual-genital contact, genital apposition	21	17	7		15	0	0	
Oral-genital contact	11	0	0		0	0	0	
Oral-anal or anal-genital contact	0	0	0		0	0	0	
Sexual intercourse	16	17	14		8	0	38	
Rape or attempted rape	0	0	0		0	0	0	
Other activity	5	33	0		8	33	0	

CHILDHOOD AND ADOLESCENT SEXUALITY/First Postpubertal Heterosexual Encounter with Physical Contact

		WHM	BHM	WHTM	BHTM	WHF	BHF	WHTF	BHTF
F.	**Who performed first sexual activity**	(N=18)	(N=6)	(N=13)	(N=0)	(N=16)	(N=3)	(N=8)	(N=0)
	Respondent	28%	33%	15%		12%	33%	0%	
	Partner(s)	6	17	0		38	33	0	
	Both	67	50	85		50	33	100	
G.	**Second sexual activity described**	(N=6)	(N=4)	(N=8)	(N=0)	(N=6)	(N=2)	(N=3)	(N=0)
	Kissing or necking	0%	0%	0%		0%	0%	0%	
	Non-genital body contact, light petting	50	25	50		67	0	67	
	Manual-genital contact, genital apposition	17	50	38		33	100	33	
	Oral-genital contact	0	0	0		0	0	0	
	Oral-anal or anal-genital contact	0	0	0		0	0	0	
	Sexual intercourse	33	25	0		0	0	0	
	Rape or attempted rape	0	0	0		0	0	0	
	Other activity	0	0	12		0	0	0	
H.	**Who performed second sexual activity**	(N=6)	(N=4)	(N=7)	(N=0)	(N=6)	(N=2)	(N=3)	(N=0)
	Respondent	17%	50%	14%		33%	0%	0%	
	Partner(s)	0	25	14		33	50	0	
	Both	83	25	71		33	50	100	
I.	**Respondent's reaction to the experience**	(N=19)	(N=6)	(N=13)	(N=0)	(N=16)	(N=3)	(N=8)	(N=0)
	Positive feelings	68%	0%	54%		31%	0%	25%	
	Enjoyed it but felt guilty	0	0	8		0	0	12	
	Mixed feelings	5	17	23		19	0	12	
	Negative feelings	21	67	8		19	33	25	
	Some other reaction	0	0	8		6	33	0	
	No particular reaction	5	17	0		25	33	25	
J.	**Did anyone observe the experience?**	(N=18)	(N=5)	(N=13)	(N=0)	(N=15)	(N=3)	(N=7)	(N=0)
	No; just respondent and partner were present	94%	100%	77%		100%	67%	100%	
	Yes; a group experience and/or one or more spectators	6	0	23		0	33	0	

CHILDHOOD AND ADOLESCENT SEXUALITY/First Actual Postpubertal Homosexual Encounter

After you were first able to [ejaculate/menstruate], what was the first sexual encounter you ever had with a member of the same sex, whether sexual behavior occurred or was only suggested? Can you tell me something about it?

A. Age of respondent

	WHM	BHM	WHTM	BHTM	WHF	BHF	WHTF	BHTF
	(N=560)	(N=107)	(N=137)	(N=15)	(N=227)	(N=63)	(N=13)	(N=2)
Under 10	2%	0%	0%	0%	1%	0%	0%	0%
10-11	10	10	1	0	1	5	8	0
12	22	14	13	7	5	8	8	0
13	18	18	13	13	9	10	0	0
14	13	14	15	0	10	6	23	0
15	10	6	12	13	9	10	23	0
16	4	14	6	7	10	17	8	50
17-18	10	14	17	27	19	11	8	0
Over 18	11	10	23	33	37	33	23	50

B. Age of partner

	WHM	BHM	WHTM	BHTM	WHF	BHF	WHTF	BHTF
	(N=540)	(N=104)	(N=117)	(N=14)	(N=222)	(N=62)	(N=14)	(N=2)
Under 10	1%	1%	0%	0%	0%	0%	0%	0%
10-11	8	6	0	0	1	3	7	0
12	13	6	10	7	4	8	7	0
13	12	8	9	7	5	7	0	0
14	9	12	7	7	9	7	14	0
15	8	7	4	0	5	5	7	0
16	5	11	4	0	7	16	14	0
17-18	8	8	11	7	17	8	14	0
Over 18	26	37	45	64	51	44	29	100
Non-adult, age not given	6	4	5	7	1	2	0	0
Adult, age not given	3	0	3	0	2	2	7	0

CHILDHOOD AND ADOLESCENT SEXUALITY/First Actual Postpubertal Homosexual Encounter

	WHM	BHM	WHTM	BHTM	WHF	BHF	WHTF	BHTF
C. Identity of partner	(N=521)	(N=103)	(N=130)	(N=12)	(N=219)	(N=58)	(N=14)	(N=1)
Sibling	5%	1%	5%	0%	0%	0%	0%	0%
Parent	0	0	0	0	0	0	0	0
Other relative	5	7	1	0	2	10	0	0
Friend or acquaintance	61	61	44	33	91	81	86	100
Stranger	21	18	42	50	5	9	0	0
Prostitute	0	0	1	0	0	0	0	0
Group	6	8	7	17	3	0	14	0
Other	1	5	1	0	0	0	0	0
D. If partner was a group, members of the group	(N=30)	(N=7)	(N=7)	(N=1)	(N=6)	(N=0)	(N=2)	(N=0)
Siblings	0%	0%	0%	0%	0%		0%	
Parents	0	0	0	0	0		0	
Other relatives	3	14	0	0	0		0	
Friends or acquaintances	93	86	86	100	83		100	
Some combination of these	3	0	14	0	17		0	
Strangers	0	0	0	0	0		0	
Prostitutes	0	0	0	0	0		0	
Other, or other combination of these	0	0	0	0	0		0	
E. First sexual activity described	(N=565)	(N=107)	(N=144)	(N=15)	(N=228)	(N=63)	(N=14)	(N=3)
Proposition, without subsequent activity	1%	0%	28%	33%	4%	5%	14%	33%
Watching others' sexual activity	11	7	13	27	0	0	7	0
Non-genital physical contact	10	15	2	7	20	19	29	0
Manual-genital contact, genital apposition	47	27	24	13	16	32	14	0
Oral-genital contact	19	25	12	13	3	5	0	33
Kissing or necking	3	6	0	0	41	27	7	33
Oral-anal or anal-genital contact	3	18	1	0	0	0	0	0
Rape or attempted rape	0	1	0	0	0	0	0	0
Other activity not involving contact	2	0	6	0	9	6	21	0
Other activity involving physical contact	4	2	15	7	7	6	7	0

		WHM	BHM	WHTM	BHTM	WHF	BHF	WHTF	BHTF
F.	Who performed first sexual activity	(N=553)	(N=103)	(N=142)	(N=15)	(N=219)	(N=62)	(N=14)	(N=3)
	Respondent	10%	13%	6%	0%	14%	11%	14%	0%
	Partner(s)	28	35	65	53	21	26	43	67
	Both	61	52	30	47	66	63	43	33
G.	Second sexual activity described	(N=146)	(N=32)	(N=13)	(N=3)	(N=92)	(N=25)	(N=1)	(N=0)
	Proposition, without subsequent activity	0%	0%	0%	0%	0%	0%	0%	
	Watching others' sexual activity	3	3	8	0	0	0	0	
	Non-genital physical contact	4	3	8	0	33	32	0	
	Manual-genital contact, genital apposition	33	31	38	33	34	36	100	
	Oral-genital contact	27	25	15	67	21	28	0	
	Kissing or necking	2	3	0	0	4	4	0	
	Oral-anal or anal-genital contact	17	25	8	0	0	0	0	
	Rape or attempted rape	0	3	0	0	0	0	0	
	Other activity not involving contact	6	3	8	0	4	0	0	
	Other activity involving physical contact	7	3	15	0	4	0	0	
H.	Who performed second sexual activity	(N=136)	(N=31)	(N=11)	(N=3)	(N=88)	(N=25)	(N=1)	(N=0)
	Respondent	18%	10%	27%	0%	10%	12%	0%	
	Partner(s)	26	35	45	33	24	32	0	
	Both	56	55	27	67	66	56	100	
I.	Respondent's reaction to the experience	(N=535)	(N=102)	(N=138)	(N=15)	(N=224)	(N=59)	(N=13)	(N=3)
	Positive feelings	59%	47%	17%	27%	72%	63%	31%	0%
	Enjoyed it but felt guilty	10	15	9	0	4	5	0	0
	Mixed feelings	13	17	7	20	12	14	8	0
	Negative feelings	14	14	58	20	7	12	46	67
	Some other reaction	1	0	2	13	4	3	8	0
	No particular reaction	4	8	7	20	2	3	8	33
J.	Did anyone observe the experience?	(N=534)	(N=97)	(N=111)	(N=15)	(N=220)	(N=62)	(N=14)	(N=2)
	No; just respondent and partner were present	93%	92%	90%	87%	93%	98%	79%	50%
	Yes; a group experience and/or one or more spectators	7	8	10	13	7	2	21	50

CHILDHOOD AND ADOLESCENT SEXUALITY/First Postpubertal Homosexual Encounter with Physical Contact

[If the first encounter did not involve contact], can you recall the first encounter which involved physical contact with a member of the same sex? Could you tell me something about it?

A. Age of respondent

	WHM (N=52)	BHM (N=5)	WHTM (N=11)	BHTM (N=2)	WHF (N=30)	BHF (N=7)	WHTF (N=1)	BHTF (N=0)
Under 10	6%	0%	0%	0%	0%	0%	0%	
10-11	10	0	0	0	0	0	0	
12	6	20	9	0	0	14	0	
13	15	0	9	50	0	0	0	
14	10	20	9	0	0	0	0	
15	13	20	9	0	0	0	0	
16	0	0	9	50	7	0	0	
17-18	17	20	18	0	17	29	0	
Over 18	23	20	36	0	77	57	100	

B. Age of partner

	WHM (N=51)	BHM (N=5)	WHTM (N=11)	BHTM (N=2)	WHF (N=28)	BHF (N=6)	WHTF (N=1)	BHTF (N=0)
Under 10	0%	0%	0%	0%	0%	0%	0%	
10-11	10	0	0	0	0	0	0	
12	6	20	0	0	0	0	0	
13	12	0	9	50	0	0	0	
14	10	20	9	0	0	0	0	
15	8	0	0	0	0	0	0	
16	4	20	9	0	0	0	0	
17-18	6	20	0	0	4	17	0	
Over 18	37	0	64	50	93	83	0	
Non-adult, age not given	2	0	0	0	0	0	0	
Adult, age not given	6	20	0	0	4	0	100	

CHILDHOOD AND ADOLESCENT SEXUALITY/First Postpubertal Homosexual Encounter with Physical Contact

	WHM	BHM	WHTM	BHTM	WHF	BHF	WHTF	BHTF
	(N=53)	(N=5)	(N=13)	(N=2)	(N=28)	(N=7)	(N=1)	(N=0)
C. Identity of partner								
Sibling	2%	0%	0%	0%	0%	0%	0%	
Parent	0	0	0	0	0	0	0	
Other relative	0	0	0	50	0	0	0	
Friend or acquaintance	57	60	54	0	89	86	100	
Stranger	34	40	38	50	7	14	0	
Prostitute	0	0	8	0	0	0	0	
Group	4	0	0	0	4	0	0	
Other	4	0	0	0	0	0	0	
	(N=2)	(N=0)	(N=0)	(N=0)	(N=1)	(N=0)	(N=0)	(N=0)
D. If partner was a group, members of the group								
Siblings	0%				0%			
Parents	0				0			
Other relatives	50				0			
Friends or acquaintances	50				0			
Some combination of these	0				0			
Strangers	0				100			
Prostitutes	0				0			
Other, or other combination of these	0				0			
	(N=55)	(N=5)	(N=13)	(N=2)	(N=30)	(N=7)	(N=1)	(N=0)
E. First sexual activity described								
Non-genital physical contact	4%	0%	15%	0%	20%	0%	100%	
Manual-genital contact, genital apposition	38	40	31	50	37	0	0	
Oral-genital contact	33	40	31	0	0	14	0	
Kissing or necking	0	0	0	0	40	57	0	
Oral-anal or anal-genital contact	5	20	0	50	0	0	0	
Rape or attempted rape	0	0	0	0	0	0	0	
Other activity	20	0	23	0	3	29	0	

149

CHILDHOOD AND ADOLESCENT SEXUALITY/First Postpubertal Homosexual Encounter with Physical Contact

	WHM (N=52)	BHM (N=4)	WHTM (N=13)	BHTM (N=2)	WHF (N=30)	BHF (N=5)	WHTF (N=1)	BHTF (N=0)
F. Who performed first sexual activity								
Respondent	13%	50%	15%	0%	7%	0%	0%	
Partner(s)	27	0	62	50	17	40	100	
Both	60	50	23	50	77	60	0	
G. Second sexual activity described	(N=16)	(N=2)	(N=3)	(N=0)	(N=14)	(N=3)	(N=0)	(N=0)
Non-genital physical contact	0%	0%	33%		36%	33%		
Manual-genital contact, genital apposition	25	0	0		21	33		
Oral-genital contact	38	0	33		29	33		
Kissing or necking	12	0	0		14	0		
Oral-anal or anal-genital contact	12	50	0		0	0		
Rape or attempted rape	0	0	0		0	0		
Other activity	12	50	33		0	0		
H. Who performed second sexual activity	(N=16)	(N=1)	(N=3)	(N=0)	(N=12)	(N=3)	(N=0)	(N=0)
Respondent	19%	100%	0%		8%	0%		
Partner(s)	25	0	100		17	67		
Both	56	0	0		75	33		
I. Respondent's reaction to the experience	(N=53)	(N=5)	(N=12)	(N=2)	(N=30)	(N=6)	(N=1)	(N=0)
Positive feelings	49%	60%	8%	0%	77%	67%	0%	
Enjoyed it but felt guilty	9	0	0	50	7	0	0	
Mixed feelings	21	20	17	0	10	33	0	
Negative feelings	19	20	67	50	7	0	100	
Some other reaction	0	0	8	0	0	0	0	
No particular reaction	2	0	0	0	0	0	0	
J. Did anyone observe the experience?	(N=46)	(N=5)	(N=10)	(N=1)	(N=26)	(N=6)	(N=1)	(N=0)
No; just respondent and partner were present	93%	100%	100%	100%	88%	67%	100%	
Yes; a group experience and/or one or more spectators	7	0	0	0	12	33	0	

CHILDHOOD AND ADOLESCENT SEXUALITY/Onset of Sexual Activities

	WHM	BHM	WHTM	BHTM	WHF	BHF	WHTF	BHTF
	(N=575)	(N=111)	(N=283)	(N=52)	(N=227)	(N=64)	(N=97)	(N=38)
How old were you the first time you ever masturbated [self-stimulation]?								
Under 5	1%	0%	1%	2%	6%	5%	1%	3%
5-6	3	1	3	0	10	8	9	0
7-8	5	5	2	6	8	11	5	11
9-11	24	11	16	13	13	22	8	8
12	26	22	22	23	6	6	6	3
13	18	23	19	15	4	9	3	3
14	11	14	14	11	6	8	4	5
15	5	7	9	13	7	6	4	0
16	2	7	4	4	3	6	2	5
17-18	2	4	5	2	5	2	10	3
Over 18	2	5	3	4	22	0	7	0
Never occurred	0	2	2	8	11	17	39	59
	(N=572)	(N=109)	(N=277)	(N=42)	(N=204)	(N=52)	(N=61)	(N=15)
What was your overall reaction to [first self-masturbation]?								
Negative	13%	10%	14%	2%	11%	12%	15%	27%
Neutral	10	24	16	12	22	27	31	60
Positive	77	66	69	86	67	62	54	13
	(N=573)	(N=111)	(N=280)	(N=52)	(N=226)	(N=62)	(N=99)	(N=38)
How old were you the first time you had an orgasm in your sleep?								
Under 10	2%	1%	0%	0%	0%	2%	0%	0%
10-11	4	5	7	2	1	0	0	3
12	11	10	16	8	1	5	0	3
13	13	14	18	15	2	3	0	5
14	15	11	18	9	2	8	2	5
15	9	12	13	30	4	6	2	3
16	7	6	4	13	3	0	2	8
17-18	10	13	7	8	6	6	1	8
Over 18	7	7	4	0	20	19	13	3
Never occurred	22	21	15	13	60	50	79	63

CHILDHOOD AND ADOLESCENT SEXUALITY/Onset of Sexual Activities

	WHM	BHM	WHTM	BHTM	WHF	BHF	WHTF	BHTF
	(N=574)	(N=111)	(N=282)	(N=53)	(N=228)	(N=64)	(N=101)	(N=38)
How old were you when you first reached orgasm by rubbing your body against the body of a female?								
Under 10	0%	0%	1%	0%	1%	6%	0%	0%
10-11	0	2	1	0	0	3	0	0
12	1	4	1	6	1	2	0	0
13	1	4	2	13	2	5	0	0
14	2	5	9	15	1	6	0	0
15	3	3	12	15	3	5	0	0
16	4	7	9	17	4	9	0	0
17-18	7	10	19	13	7	12	0	0
Over 18	10	5	21	2	40	34	0	0
Never occurred	72	62	26	19	39	17	100	100
	(N=160)	(N=42)	(N=209)	(N=42)	(N=138)	(N=53)	(N=0)	(N=0)
What was your overall reaction to [first body-rubbing with female]?								
Negative	14%	7%	6%	0%	2%	4%		
Neutral	19	24	5	2	8	8		
Positive	68	69	89	98	90	89		
	(N=574)	(N=111)	(N=282)	(N=52)	(N=228)	(N=63)	(N=101)	(N=38)
How old were you the first time you masturbated a female?								
Under 10	1%	2%	2%	0%	4%	13%	1%	0%
10-11	0	1	1	4	4	3	2	3
12	1	3	2	8	2	2	0	0
13	1	2	2	11	3	5	0	0
14	2	5	7	8	2	3	0	0
15	3	5	9	4	4	5	0	0
16	5	5	10	9	5	6	0	0
17-18	7	5	22	19	13	16	1	0
Over 18	15	11	33	21	57	40	0	0
Never occurred	65	62	12	15	5	8	96	97

CHILDHOOD AND ADOLESCENT SEXUALITY/Onset of Sexual Activities

	WHM	BHM	WHTM	BHTM	WHF	BHF	WHTF	BHTF
What was your overall reaction to [first orgasm in sleep]?	(N=447)	(N=88)	(N=238)	(N=41)	(N=87)	(N=31)	(N=21)	(N=14)
Negative	21%	24%	17%	7%	8%	16%	0%	21%
Neutral	31	27	34	27	14	16	19	57
Positive	48	49	49	66	78	68	81	21
How old were you the first time you reached orgasm by rubbing your body against the body of a male?	(N=575)	(N=111)	(N=282)	(N=53)	(N=229)	(N=64)	(N=100)	(N=38)
Under 10	1%	2%	1%	0%	0%	2%	0%	0%
10-11	2	5	0	0	1	0	0	0
12	5	6	1	0	0	5	0	0
13	6	3	0	2	1	2	0	0
14	5	7	0	0	2	8	0	5
15	5	5	1	0	1	8	3	5
16	5	9	0	2	3	0	9	3
17-18	11	15	2	0	5	8	12	8
Over 18	32	23	0	4	9	9	24	5
Never occurred	29	26	94	92	78	59	52	72
What was your overall reaction to [first body-rubbing with a male]?	(N=408)	(N=82)	(N=15)	(N=4)	(N=51)	(N=26)	(N=49)	(N=10)
Negative	8%	5%	27%	0%	12%	4%	0%	0%
Neutral	10	7	13	50	20	15	8	40
Positive	82	88	60	50	69	81	92	60

CHILDHOOD AND ADOLESCENT SEXUALITY/Onset of Sexual Activities

	WHM	BHM	WHTM	BHTM	WHF	BHF	WHTF	BHTF
	(N=199)	(N=42)	(N=247)	(N=44)	(N=217)	(N=59)	(N=4)	(N=1)
What was your overall reaction to [first time masturbating a female]?								
Negative	10%	10%	2%	0%	3%	5%	0%	0%
Neutral	31	29	9	11	10	15	25	0
Positive	59	62	90	89	87	80	25	100
	(N=575)	(N=111)	(N=282)	(N=53)	(N=229)	(N=64)	(N=101)	(N=39)
How old were you when you first masturbated a male?								
Under 10	12%	10%	2%	0%	4%	5%	0%	0%
10-11	11	7	1	2	2	3	1	0
12	15	10	4	0	4	3	0	0
13	11	10	2	0	1	3	1	0
14	9	6	4	0	3	3	0	5
15	6	9	2	2	4	5	6	0
16	5	6	1	2	7	5	3	8
17-18	9	17	1	2	13	9	22	21
Over 18	19	22	1	2	31	28	49	28
Never occurred	2	3	82	92	30	36	19	36
	(N=558)	(N=108)	(N=51)	(N=2)	(N=160)	(N=41)	(N=82)	(N=24)
What was your overall reaction to [first time masturbating a male]?								
Negative	8%	14%	24%	0%	36%	39%	24%	25%
Neutral	15	19	27	50	32	32	34	25
Positive	78	67	49	50	32	29	41	50

154

CHILDHOOD AND ADOLESCENT SEXUALITY/Onset of Sexual Activities

	WHM	BHM	WHTM	BHTM	WHF	BHF	WHTF	BHTF
	(N=575)	(N=111)	(N=282)	(N=53)	(N=228)	(N=64)	(N=101)	(N=38)
How old were you the first time a female masturbated you?								
Under 10	1%	0%	2%	2%	4%	6%	1%	0%
10-11	0	2	0	2	3	2	2	3
12	1	1	2	4	2	3	0	0
13	2	3	2	8	3	3	0	0
14	3	4	4	9	2	5	0	0
15	3	6	9	9	4	5	0	0
16	5	8	11	11	7	9	0	0
17-18	8	5	21	26	14	19	1	0
Over 18	19	12	37	21	57	42	0	0
Never occurred	59	59	13	5	4	5	96	97
	(N=231)	(N=45)	(N=245)	(N=47)	(N=219)	(N=61)	(N=4)	(N=1)
What was your overall reaction to [first time masturbated by a female]?								
Negative	10%	11%	4%	4%	6%	11%	50%	0%
Neutral	19	22	3	4	11	10	25	0
Positive	71	67	93	91	83	79	25	100
	(N=575)	(N=111)	(N=282)	(N=53)	(N=229)	(N=63)	(N=101)	(N=37)
How old were you the first time a male masturbated you?								
Under 10	11%	7%	2%	0%	7%	8%	0%	0%
10-11	11	6	1	2	2	2	1	0
12	16	8	4	0	2	5	1	0
13	12	14	3	0	1	6	1	3
14	9	8	4	0	4	9	5	8
15	7	7	2	0	3	3	11	3
16	5	9	1	2	7	3	22	10
17-18	11	18	2	2	19	22	44	15
Over 18	17	20	4	2	26	19	15	30
Never occurred	1	2	77	92	29	20		30
	(N=562)	(N=109)	(N=64)	(N=4)	(N=160)	(N=50)	(N=86)	(N=27)
What was your overall reaction to [first time masturbated by a male]?								
Negative	8%	6%	27%	0%	21%	26%	8%	11%
Neutral	9	12	22	0	20	26	16	15
Positive	83	83	52	100	59	48	76	74

CHILDHOOD AND ADOLESCENT SEXUALITY/Onset of Sexual Activities

	WHM	BHM	WHTM	BHTM	WHF	BHF	WHTF	BHTF
How old were you the first time you had your mouth on a male's genitals?	(N=575)	(N=111)	(N=282)	(N=53)	(N=229)	(N=64)	(N=101)	(N=3)
Under 10	11%	14%	3%	2%	1%	0%	0%	0%
10-11	4	5	0	0	0	0	1	0
12	7	3	1	0	1	0	0	0
13	7	4	0	0	1	3	0	0
14	6	6	1	0	1	0	0	0
15	8	2	1	0	2	3	1	0
16	6	5	1	0	3	3	3	3
17-18	14	18	1	0	10	5	11	3
Over 18	37	38	2	2	41	28	55	6
Never occurred	1	7	88	96	39	58	29	88
What was your overall reaction to [first time performing oral-genital on a male]?	(N=568)	(N=103)	(N=32)	(N=2)	(N=139)	(N=27)	(N=72)	(N=10)
Negative	26%	40%	41%	0%	52%	41%	33%	50%
Neutral	19	20	28	50	21	44	26	20
Positive	54	40	31	50	27	15	40	30
How old were you the first time you had your mouth on a female's genitals?	(N=573)	(N=111)	(N=282)	(N=53)	(N=228)	(N=64)	(N=101)	(N=38)
Under 10	1%	1%	1%	0%	2%	2%	0%	0%
10-11	0	1	0	0	1	0	0	0
12	0	0	0	2	0	0	0	0
13	1	2	1	0	0	2	0	0
14	0	0	1	4	0	3	0	0
15	1	1	5	0	2	0	0	0
16	1	2	4	2	4	3	0	0
17-18	5	4	15	9	10	17	0	0
Over 18	24	13	52	45	73	62	0	0
Never occurred	67	77	22	38	7	11	100	100
What was your overall reaction to [first time performing oral-genital on a female]?	(N=188)	(N=25)	(N=221)	(N=33)	(N=211)	(N=57)	(N=0)	(N=0)
Negative	25%	32%	9%	21%	16%	18%		
Neutral	24	12	14	30	15	28		
Positive	51	56	77	48	69	54		

CHILDHOOD AND ADOLESCENT SEXUALITY/Onset of Sexual Activities

How old were you when you first experienced a female's mouth on your genitals?	WHM	BHM	WHTM	BHTM	WHF	BHF	WHTF	BHTF
	(N=575)	(N=111)	(N=282)	(N=53)	(N=228)	(N=64)	(N=101)	(N=38)
Under 10	1%	3%	1%	0%	2%	2%	0%	0%
10-11	0	0	1	0	0	0	0	0
12	1	1	1	2	0	2	0	0
13	1	5	1	0	0	3	0	0
14	1	0	4	8	3	0	0	0
15	1	2	6	4	4	6	0	0
16		3		8				
17-18	8	5	20	21	10	14	0	0
Over 18	32	23	48	49	75	67	0	3
Never occurred	54	59	18	9	5	6	100	97

What was your overall reaction to [first time receiving oral-genital from a female]?	WHM	BHM	WHTM	BHTM	WHF	BHF	WHTF	BHTF
	(N=264)	(N=44)	(N=231)	(N=46)	(N=216)	(N=60)	(N=0)	(N=1)
Negative	16%	20%	4%	0%	11%	7%		0%
Neutral	20	18	2	11	11	20		0
Positive	64	61	94	89	78	73		100

How old were you when you first experienced a male's mouth on your genitals?	WHM	BHM	WHTM	BHTM	WHF	BHF	WHTF	BHTF
	(N=575)	(N=111)	(N=282)	(N=53)	(N=229)	(N=64)	(N=101)	(N=38)
Under 10	10%	15%	2%	2%	3%	0%	0%	0%
10-11	4	5	0	0	0	2	2	0
12	8	5	2	0	0	0	0	0
13	9	7	1	0	0	2	0	0
14	7	5	2	0	3	2	1	0
15	9	3	2	0	3	3	3	3
16	7	13	1			2		
17-18	16	23	2	2	14	16	12	3
Over 18	31	25	6	6	41	45	59	39
Never occurred	1	0	81	91	36	30	23	55

What was your overall reaction to [first time receiving oral-genital from a male]?	WHM	BHM	WHTM	BHTM	WHF	BHF	WHTF	BHTF
	(N=569)	(N=111)	(N=53)	(N=5)	(N=146)	(N=45)	(N=78)	(N=17)
Negative	11%	14%	25%	0%	16%	20%	17%	18%
Neutral	11	11	17	20	21	31	12	12
Positive	78	75	58	80	64	49	72	71

CHILDHOOD AND ADOLESCENT SEXUALITY/Onset of Sexual Activities

	WHM	BHM	WHTM	BHTM	WHF	BHF	WHTF	BHTF
	(N=575)	(N=111)	(N=46)	(N=4)	(N=229)	(N=64)	(N=101)	(N=38)
How old were you the first time you received anal intercourse?								
Under 10	5%	11%	7%	25%	0%	0%	0%	0%
10-11	3	5	0	0	1	0	0	0
12	3	5	2	0	0	0	0	0
13	3	5	0	25	0	2	0	0
14	5	5	2	0	0	3	0	3
15	4	7	2	0	1	0	1	0
16	5	7	0	0	0	0	1	0
17-18	14	16	7	0	1	0	1	13
Over 18	53	32	9	25	18	22	20	13
Never occurred	6	8	72	25	78	73	78	71
What was your overall reaction to [first time receiving anal intercourse]?	(N=543)	(N=102)	(N=13)	(N=3)	(N=51)	(N=17)	(N=23)	(N=11)
Negative	51%	58%	54%	67%	65%	94%	39%	64%
Neutral	17	15	15	0	14	6	17	0
Positive	32	27	31	33	22	0	43	36
How old were you the first time you performed anal intercourse with a female?	(N=575)	(N=111)	(N=281)	(N=53)	(N=0)	(N=0)	(N=0)	(N=0)
					[not asked of females]			
Under 10	0%	2%	0%	0%				
10-11	0	1	0	0				
12	0	0	0	0				
13	0	3	0	4				
14	0	2	0	2				
15	1	1	1	2				
16	2	2	1	2				
17-18	2	3	2	2				
Over 18	6	8	26	23				
Never occurred	90	79	70	66				
What was your overall reaction to [first time performing anal intercourse with a female]?	(N=55)	(N=23)	(N=83)	(N=18)	(N=0)	(N=0)	(N=0)	(N=0)
					[not asked of females]			
Negative	22%	9%	19%	6%				
Neutral	22	17	34	11				
Positive	56	74	47	83				

CHILDHOOD AND ADOLESCENT SEXUALITY/Onset of Sexual Activities

How old were you the first time you performed anal intercourse with a male?

	WHM	BHM	WHTM	BHTM	WHF	BHF	WHTF	BHTF
	(N=575)	(N=111)	(N=48)	(N=2)	(N=0)	(N=0)	(N=0)	(N=0)
Under 10	2%	7%	6%	0%				
10-11	2	6	0	0		[not asked of females]		
12	2	2	0	0				
13	4	6	2	50				
14	6	5	2	0				
15	5	7	0	0				
16		14	10	0				
17-18	13	17	8	0				
Over 18	59	32		0				
Never occurred	4	2	71	50				

What was your overall reaction to [first time performing anal intercourse with a male]?

	WHM	BHM	WHTM	BHTM	WHF	BHF	WHTF	BHTF
	(N=550)	(N=109)	(N=13)	(N=1)	(N=0)	(N=0)	(N=0)	(N=0)
Negative	10%	10%	38%	0%				
Neutral	17	19	23	0		[not asked of females]		
Positive	73	71	38	100				

How old were you when you first had sexual intercourse?

	WHM	BHM	WHTM	BHTM	WHF	BHF	WHTF	BHTF
	(N=573)	(N=110)	(N=282)	(N=53)	(N=229)	(N=64)	(N=101)	(N=37)
Under 10	2%	5%	1%	4%	5%	10%	0%	3%
10-11	2	4	2	6	3	2	1	0
12	1	5	0	11	2	5	0	3
13	2	7	4	19	4	0	1	3
14	3	9	6	23	0	5	3	8
15	5	7	10	13	4	11	3	5
16	15	12	14	6	6	11	4	5
17-18	31	12	26	13	17	16	20	41
Over 18	37	13	36	6	42	30	62	27
Never occurred		27	2	0	17	12	6	5

What was your overall reaction to [first heterosexual coitus]?

	WHM	BHM	WHTM	BHTM	WHF	BHF	WHTF	BHTF
	(N=361)	(N=79)	(N=269)	(N=51)	(N=191)	(N=56)	(N=95)	(N=35)
Negative	16%	10%	3%	2%	37%	57%	20%	34%
Neutral	25	22	3	2	28	25	26	17
Positive	60	68	94	96	35	18	54	48

CHILDHOOD AND ADOLESCENT SEXUALITY/Onset of Sexual Activities

How old were you the first time you performed oral-anal contact?

	WHM	BHM	WHTM	BHTM	WHF	BHF	WHTF	BHTF
	(N=575)	(N=111)	(N=282)	(N=53)	(N=228)	(N=64)	(N=101)	(N=37)
Under 10	1%	1%	0%	0%	0%	0%	0%	0%
10-11	0	1	0	0	0	0	0	0
12	0	0	0	0	0	2	0	0
13	1	3	0	0	0	0	0	0
14	0	2	0	0	0	0	0	0
15	2	0	1	0	0	0	1	0
16	2	0	0	0	1	2	1	0
17-18	8	9	2	2	0	6	1	5
Over 18	57	44	12	2	16	6	11	3
Never occurred	29	41	84	96	82	84	87	92

What was your overall reaction to [first time performing oral-anal]?

	WHM	BHM	WHTM	BHTM	WHF	BHF	WHTF	BHTF
	(N=409)	(N=65)	(N=44)	(N=2)	(N=41)	(N=10)	(N=13)	(N=3)
Negative	21%	29%	9%	0%	20%	20%	23%	0%
Neutral	27	32	27	50	24	30	23	0
Positive	52	38	64	50	56	50	54	100

How old were you the first time you received oral-anal contact?

	WHM	BHM	WHTM	BHTM	WHF	BHF	WHTF	BHTF
	(N=575)	(N=111)	(N=282)	(N=53)	(N=228)	(N=64)	(N=101)	(N=37)
Under 10	1%	2%	0%	0%	0%	0%	0%	0%
10-11	0	1	0	0	0	0	0	0
12	0	1	0	0	0	0	0	0
13	1	3	0	0	0	0	0	0
14	1	1	0	2	0	0	0	0
15	2	3	1	2	0	0	0	0
16	4	0	0	0	2	0	1	0
17-18	13	20	3	0	1	11	12	5
Over 18	67	56	12	0	17	27	87	3
Never occurred	11	14	83	96	79	62	—	92

What was your overall reaction to [first time receiving oral-anal]?

	WHM	BHM	WHTM	BHTM	WHF	BHF	WHTF	BHTF
	(N=512)	(N=96)	(N=48)	(N=2)	(N=47)	(N=24)	(N=13)	(N=3)
Negative	14%	24%	6%	100%	13%	38%	15%	0%
Neutral	18	23	17	0	32	21	23	0
Positive	68	53	77	0	55	42	62	100

CHILDHOOD AND ADOLESCENT SEXUALITY/Onset of Sexual Activities

	WHM	BHM	WHTM	BHTM	WHF	BHF	WHTF	BHTF
	(N=575)	(N=111)	(N=282)	(N=53)	(N=228)	(N=64)	(N=101)	(N=37)
How old were you the first time you had sex with an animal?								
Under 10	2%	2%	1%	0%	0%	3%	0%	0%
10-11	3	0	0	2	1	2	0	0
12	3	1	1	0	0	2	0	0
13	3	0	1	0	0	0	0	0
14	2	2	1	0	0	0	0	0
15	2	0	0	0	0	0	0	0
16	2	2	0	0	0	0	0	0
17-18	1	0	1	0	0	2	0	0
Over 18	3	0	0	0	3	2	0	0
Never occurred	78	94	94	98	94	92	100	100
	(N=125)	(N=7)	(N=13)	(N=1)	(N=12)	(N=5)	(N=0)	(N=0)
What was your overall reaction to [first animal contact]?								
Negative	20%	57%	8%	0%	25%	20%		
Neutral	39	14	54	0	25	20		
Positive	41	29	38	100	50	60		
	(N=575)	(N=111)	(N=282)	(N=53)	(N=228)	(N=64)	(N=101)	(N=37)
How old were you when you first engaged in sadistic [sexual] activity?								
Under 10	0%	0%	0%	0%	0%	2%	0%	0%
10-11	0	0	0	0	0	0	0	0
12	0	0	0	0	0	0	0	0
13	0	0	0	0	0	0	0	0
14	0	0	0	0	0	0	0	0
15	0	1	0	0	0	0	0	0
16	1	1	0	0	1	0	1	0
17-18	1	1	1	0	1	5	1	0
Over 18	25	14	3	2	7	6	3	0
Never occurred	72	84	95	98	91	88	96	100
	(N=162)	(N=18)	(N=13)	(N=1)	(N=20)	(N=8)	(N=4)	(N=0)
What was your overall reaction to [first sadistic activity]?								
Negative	32%	67%	31%	0%	40%	12%	75%	
Neutral	30	28	23	0	20	25	0	
Positive	38	6	46	100	40	62	25	

161

CHILDHOOD AND ADOLESCENT SEXUALITY/Onset of Sexual Activities

	WHM	BHM	WHTM	BHTM	WHF	BHF	WHTF	BHTF
How old were you when you first engaged in masochistic [sexual] activity?	(N=575)	(N=111)	(N=282)	(N=53)	(N=228)	(N=64)	(N=101)	(N=37)
Under 10	0%	0%	0%	0%	0%	0%	0%	0%
10-11	1	0	0	0	0	0	0	0
12	0	0	0	0	0	0	0	0
13	0	0	0	0	0	0	0	0
14	0	0	0	0	0	0	0	0
15	0	1	0	0	0	0	0	0
16	0	0	0	0	1	2	0	0
17-18	0	1	0	0	0	2	0	0
Over 18	23	10	2	0	7	6	0	3
Never occurred	75	88	97	100	91	91	100	97
What was your overall reaction to [first masochistic activity]?	(N=141)	(N=13)	(N=6)	(N=0)	(N=20)	(N=6)	(N=0)	(N=1)
Negative	33%	54%	50%		25%	33%		100%
Neutral	25	31	0		30	33		0
Positive	42	15	50		45	33		0
Is there any other technique that is important to you that we haven't mentioned?	(N=575)	(N=110)	(N=282)	(N=53)	(N=227)	(N=63)	(N=101)	(N=38)
No	79%	96%	95%	96%	84%	59%	96%	97%
Yes	21	4	5	4	16	41	4	3
How old were you the first time you engaged in [other activity]?	(N=118)	(N=4)	(N=13)	(N=2)	(N=37)	(N=26)	(N=4)	(N=1)
Under 10	5%	0%	0%	0%	3%	0%	0%	0%
10-11	3	0	0	0	0	0	0	0
12	1	0	0	0	0	0	25	0
13	3	0	0	0	3	4	25	0
14	2	0	0	0	0	0	0	0
15	3	0	0	0	0	0	0	0
16	3	0	8	0	8	4	0	0
17-18	10	0	23	50	5	19	0	0
Over 18	70	100	69	50	81	73	50	100

CHILDHOOD AND ADOLESCENT SEXUALITY/Onset of Sexual Activities; Incidence of Rape

	WHM	BHM	WHTM	BHTM	WHF	BHF	WHTF	BHTF
What was your overall reaction to [first experience with other activity]?	(N=114)	(N=4)	(N=13)	(N=2)	(N=35)	(N=26)	(N=4)	(N=1)
Negative	6%	25%	0%	0%	9%	4%	0%	0%
Neutral	12	0	15	0	6	35	0	0
Positive	82	75	85	100	86	62	100	100
Did respondent mention actively performing rape in any prepubertal heterosexual encounter?	(N=281)	(N=52)	(N=165)	(N=38)	(N=145)	(N=38)	(N=44)	(N=9)
No	100%	100%	100%	100%	100%	100%	100%	100%
Yes	0	0	0	0	0	0	0	0
Did respondent mention actively performing rape in any prepubertal homosexual encounter?	(N=372)	(N=62)	(N=75)	(N=11)	(N=96)	(N=29)	(N=34)	(N=3)
No	100%	98%	100%	100%	100%	100%	100%	100%
Yes	0	2	0	0	0	0	0	0
Did respondent mention actively performing rape in the first postpubertal heterosexual encounter involving physical contact?	(N=397)	(N=83)	(N=239)	(N=48)	(N=196)	(N=60)	(N=88)	(N=29)
No	100%	100%	100%	100%	100%	100%	100%	100%
Yes	0	0	0	0	0	0	0	0
Did respondent mention actively performing rape in the first postpubertal homosexual encounter involving physical contact?	(N=502)	(N=97)	(N=137)	(N=16)	(N=163)	(N=44)	(N=42)	(N=4)
No	100%	100%	100%	100%	100%	100%	100%	100%
Yes	0	0	0	0	0	0	0	0

CHILDHOOD AND ADOLESCENT SEXUALITY/Incidence of Rape

	WHM	BHM	WHTM	BHTM	WHF	BHF	WHTF	BHTF
Did respondent mention being raped in the first prepubertal heterosexual encounter?	(N=302)	(N=55)	(N=173)	(N=38)	(N=154)	(N=38)	(N=45)	(N=9)
No	100%	100%	100%	100%	97%	97%	96%	100%
Yes	0	0	0	0	3	3	4	0
Did respondent mention being raped in the first prepubertal homosexual encounter?	(N=381)	(N=62)	(N=75)	(N=11)	(N=95)	(N=32)	(N=34)	(N=3)
No	99%	100%	100%	100%	100%	100%	100%	100%
Yes	1	0	0	0	0	0	0	0
Did respondent mention being raped in any prepubertal heterosexual encounter?	(N=294)	(N=53)	(N=172)	(N=40)	(N=137)	(N=37)	(N=38)	(N=9)
No	100%	100%	100%	100%	96%	97%	95%	100%
Yes	0	0	0	0	4	3	5	0
Did respondent mention being raped in any prepubertal homosexual encounter?	(N=360)	(N=60)	(N=73)	(N=10)	(N=93)	(N=30)	(N=34)	(N=3)
No	99%	100%	99%	100%	100%	100%	100%	100%
Yes	1	0	1	0	0	0	0	0
Did respondent mention being raped in the first postpubertal heterosexual encounter involving physical contact?	(N=309)	(N=68)	(N=218)	(N=44)	(N=185)	(N=52)	(N=85)	(N=27)
No	100%	100%	100%	100%	97%	96%	99%	100%
Yes	0	0	0	0	3	4	1	0
Did respondent mention being raped in the first postpubertal homosexual encounter involving physical contact?	(N=447)	(N=93)	(N=53)	(N=5)	(N=123)	(N=37)	(N=9)	(N=0)
No	100%	98%	100%	100%	100%	100%	100%	
Yes	0	2	0	0	0	0	0	

CHILDHOOD AND ADOLESCENT SEXUALITY/Incidence of Rape

	WHM	BHM	WHTM	BHTM	WHF	BHF	WHTF	BHTF
Has a person of the same sex ever attempted to use or threatened to use physical force to get you into sexual activity against your will?	(N=575)	(N=111)	(N=284)	(N=53)	(N=229)	(N=64)	(N=101)	(N=39)
Yes	24%	35%	9%	8%	11%	14%	2%	5%
No	76	65	91	92	89	86	98	95
How old were you at the time?	(N=139)	(N=39)	(N=25)	(N=4)	(N=25)	(N=9)	(N=2)	(N=2)
Under 10	6%	5%	12%	25%	0%	11%	0%	50%
10-11	4	3	0	0	0	0	0	0
12	3	3	12	0	4	0	0	0
13	2	8	8	0	0	0	0	0
14	4	8	20	0	0	0	0	0
15	6	8	12	50	0	0	0	0
16	3	10	0	0	4	0	0	0
17-18	9	21	12	0	8	11	0	50
Over 18	63	36	24	25	84	78	100	0

CHILDHOOD AND ADOLESCENT SEXUALITY/Adolescent Heterosexual Frequency

	WHM	BHM	WHTM	BHTM	WHF	BHF	WHTF	BHTF
Between the ages of 14 and 17, how often did you engage in necking, that is, prolonged hugging and kissing with a member of the opposite sex?	(N=575)	(N=111)	(N=284)	(N=53)	(N=229)	(N=64)	(N=100)	(N=39)
Never	30%	23%	11%	2%	19%	9%	14%	10%
Once	3	1	2	0	1	3	1	0
2-12 times	27	27	17	8	26	44	25	31
13-15 times	19	24	27	17	20	27	20	25
Over 50 times	21	24	42	74	34	17	40	33
During this time, how often did you caress the clothed breasts of a female?	(N=565)	(N=111)	(N=283)	(N=53)	(N=0)	(N=0)	(N=0)	(N=0)
					[not asked of females]			
Never	46%	32%	19%	2%				
Once	6	3	4	0				
2-12 times	26	29	26	19				
13-50 times	14	25	27	21				
Over 50 times	8	12	23	58				
During this time, how often did a male caress your clothed breasts?	(N=0)	[not asked of males]	(N=0)	(N=0)	(N=229)	(N=64)	(N=100)	(N=39)
Never					32%	20%	36%	28%
Once					6	9	7	3
2-12 times					32	47	24	36
13-50 times					15	10	14	23
Over 50 times					14	14	19	10
How often did you caress the bare breasts of a female?	(N=573)	(N=111)	(N=284)	(N=53)	(N=0)	(N=0)	(N=0)	(N=0)
					[not asked of females]			
Never	66%	44%	31%	8%				
Once	4	5	7	4				
2-12 times	16	30	19	18				
13-50 times	10	17	20	39				
Over 50 times	4	5	14	30				

166

CHILDHOOD AND ADOLESCENT SEXUALITY/Adolescent Heterosexual Frequency

	WHM	BHM	WHTM	BHTM	WHF	BHF	WHTF	BHTF
How often did a male caress your bare breasts?	(N=0)	(N=0)	(N=0)	(N=0)	(N=229)	(N=64)	(N=100)	(N=39)
					55%	48%	59%	54%
Never		[not asked of males]			6	8	8	5
Once					20	29	14	23
2-12 times					11	8	5	8
13-50 times					9	6	14	10
Over 50 times								
During this age period, how often did you touch a [opposite-sex genitalia]?	(N=575)	(N=111)	(N=284)	(N=53)	(N=229)	(N=63)	(N=100)	(N=39)
Never	67%	39%	38%	8%	61%	48%	68%	79%
Once	7	7	8	2	7	13	8	3
2-12 times	19	34	24	21	19	27	11	10
13-50 times	7	16	21	36	7	5	7	6
Over 50 times	2	4	9	34	6	8	6	3
How often did a member of the opposite sex touch your [vagina/penis]?	(N=575)	(N=111)	(N=283)	(N=53)	(N=229)	(N=64)	(N=100)	(N=39)
Never	65%	31%	46%	11%	55%	41%	67%	62%
Once	6	6	5	4	8	14	7	5
2-12 times	20	46	27	20	24	30	7	18
13-50 times	6	13	15	34	7	9	9	11
Over 50 times	2	5	7	30	6	6	10	5
How often did you engage in sexual intercourse with a member of the opposite sex?	(N=575)	(N=111)	(N=284)	(N=53)	(N=229)	(N=64)	(N=100)	(N=39)
Never	76%	39%	53%	9%	76%	53%	83%	64%
Once	4	5	4	0	3	11	1	5
2-12 times	14	38	21	19	12	22	4	11
13-50 times	3	15	13	32	4	8	4	10
Over 50 times	2	4	8	40	5	6	8	10

167

CHILDHOOD AND ADOLESCENT SEXUALITY/Adolescent Homosexual Frequency

	WHM	BHM	WHTM	BHTM	WHF	BHF	WHTF	BHTF
When you were of high school age, how often did you have homosexual relations?	(N=575)	(N=111)	(N=0)	(N=0)	(N=229)	(N=64)	(N=0)	(N=0)
Never	23%	19%			70%	50%		
Once	5	5	[not asked of		5	9	[not asked of	
2-12 times	27	29	heterosexuals]		10	20	heterosexuals]	
13-50 times	21	26			6	6		
More than 50 times	25	22			9	14		

168

CHILDHOOD AND ADOLESCENT SEXUALITY/Mothers' Sexual Attitudes

During the time you lived with your parents, to what extent would your mother have agreed with the following list of statements?

	WHM	BHM	WHTM	BHTM	WHF	BHF	WHTF	BHTF
	(N=543)	(N=101)	(N=276)	(N=53)	(N=219)	(N=63)	(N=98)	(N=39)
A. Television shows like "Laugh-In" are obscene; jokes about sex do not belong on television.								
Strongly disagree	11%	12%	8%	9%	14%	8%	11%	5%
Disagree	44	60	52	45	38	40	36	46
Agree	28	20	28	42	24	35	30	33
Strongly agree	17	8	12	4	24	17	23	15
	(N=545)	(N=102)	(N=278)	(N=53)	(N=220)	(N=63)	(N=97)	(N=39)
B. Talk about sex does not belong in the home.								
Strongly disagree	13%	14%	14%	17%	19%	13%	15%	21%
Disagree	41	56	54	49	32	48	46	44
Agree	31	24	21	26	27	30	25	21
Strongly agree	14	7	11	8	22	10	13	15
	(N=543)	(N=102)	(N=278)	(N=53)	(N=218)	(N=63)	(N=98)	(N=39)
C. Sex before marriage is immoral.								
Strongly disagree	4%	7%	5%	13%	6%	6%	4%	5%
Disagree	20	41	25	26	15	21	10	28
Agree	40	41	38	45	31	27	33	23
Strongly agree	36	11	32	15	48	46	53	44
	(N=541)	(N=101)	(N=277)	(N=53)	(N=216)	(N=62)	(N=95)	(N=39)
D. An adolescent who masturbates should be punished or at least spoken to severely.								
Strongly disagree	8%	9%	8%	15%	8%	10%	13%	18%
Disagree	37	31	40	34	30	31	23	46
Agree	35	49	37	40	33	44	40	15
Strongly agree	20	12	16	11	29	16	24	21

CHILDHOOD AND ADOLESCENT SEXUALITY/Mother Surrogates' Sexual Attitudes

During the time you lived with your [mother surrogate], to what extent would she have agreed with the following list of statements?

	WHM	BHM	WHTM	BHTM	WHF	BHF	WHTF	BHTF
A. Television shows like "Laugh-In" are obscene; jokes about sex do not belong on television.	(N=61)	(N=25)	(N=16)	(N=3)	(N=25)	(N=14)	(N=8)	(N=2)
Strongly disagree	10%	8%	31%	33%	20%	0%	12%	0%
Disagree	36	40	50	33	8	36	38	50
Agree	26	32	19	0	32	29	12	50
Strongly agree	28	20	0	33	40	36	38	0
B. Talk about sex does not belong in the home.	(N=61)	(N=25)	(N=16)	(N=3)	(N=26)	(N=14)	(N=8)	(N=2)
Strongly disagree	8%	4%	25%	0%	20%	21%	25%	0%
Disagree	39	44	44	33	28	29	38	100
Agree	25	44	25	67	20	21	12	0
Strongly agree	28	8	6	0	32	29	25	0
C. Sex before marriage is immoral.	(N=60)	(N=25)	(N=16)	(N=3)	(N=26)	(N=14)	(N=8)	(N=2)
Strongly disagree	3%	4%	19%	0%	4%	7%	12%	0%
Disagree	18	40	31	0	8	21	25	0
Agree	33	44	31	33	32	21	25	50
Strongly agree	45	12	19	67	56	50	38	50
D. An adolescent who masturbates should be punished or at least spoken to severely.	(N=61)	(N=25)	(N=16)	(N=3)	(N=26)	(N=14)	(N=8)	(N=2)
Strongly disagree	3%	4%	0%	0%	16%	7%	12%	0%
Disagree	36	32	44	33	16	21	25	50
Agree	30	60	56	33	20	36	25	50
Strongly agree	31	4	0	33	48	36	38	0

To what extent would your father have agreed with the same list of statements?

	WHM	BHM	WHTM	BHTM	WHF	BHF	WHTF	BHTF
A. Television shows like "Laugh-In" are obscene; jokes about sex do not belong on television.	(N=511)	(N=90)	(N=262)	(N=49)	(N=194)	(N=56)	(N=96)	(N=33)
Strongly disagree	12%	9%	11%	12%	12%	16%	11%	27%
Disagree	48	60	54	45	46	41	38	42
Agree	27	21	28	37	23	30	31	18
Strongly agree	13	10	6	6	19	12	20	12
B. Talk about sex does not belong in the home.	(N=511)	(N=90)	(N=263)	(N=49)	(N=195)	(N=56)	(N=97)	(N=33)
Strongly disagree	13%	8%	13%	12%	12%	16%	18%	24%
Disagree	42	63	56	53	41	41	52	52
Agree	32	26	24	27	28	27	16	21
Strongly agree	13	3	6	8	19	16	14	3
C. Sex before marriage is immoral.	(N=510)	(N=90)	(N=261)	(N=49)	(N=194)	(N=56)	(N=97)	(N=33)
Strongly disagree	9%	18%	9%	18%	6%	12%	4%	21%
Disagree	31	46	35	43	26	30	19	18
Agree	41	32	44	31	31	29	37	24
Strongly agree	19	4	12	8	37	29	40	36
D. An adolescent who masturbates should be punished or at least spoken to severely.	(N=510)	(N=89)	(N=259)	(N=49)	(N=189)	(N=55)	(N=93)	(N=33)
Strongly disagree	10%	8%	8%	12%	10%	11%	11%	18%
Disagree	41	47	44	43	37	35	31	42
Agree	34	37	41	33	30	35	35	21
Strongly agree	15	8	8	12	23	20	23	18

CHILDHOOD AND ADOLESCENT SEXUALITY/Father Surrogates' Sexual Attitudes

	WHM	BHM	WHTM	BHTM	WHF	BHF	WHTF	BHTF
During the time you lived with your [father surrogate], to what extent would he have agreed with the following list of statements?								
A. Television shows like "Laugh-In" are obscene; jokes about sex do not belong on television.	(N=83)	(N=30)	(N=30)	(N=6)	(N=41)	(N=16)	(N=10)	(N=8)
Strongly disagree	18%	13%	17%	33%	27%	12%	10%	0%
Disagree	36	63	53	50	20	38	40	38
Agree	31	20	23	17	17	12	40	38
Strongly agree	14	3	7	0	37	38	10	25
B. Talk about sex does not belong in the home.	(N=83)	(N=31)	(N=29)	(N=6)	(N=42)	(N=5)	(N=10)	(N=8)
Strongly disagree	14%	13%	10%	17%	17%	6%	20%	0%
Disagree	45	45	48	50	33	50	30	62
Agree	29	42	28	33	21	19	40	38
Strongly agree	12	0	14	0	29	25	10	0
C. Sex before marriage is immoral.	(N=83)	(N=31)	(N=30)	(N=6)	(N=42)	(N=16)	(N=10)	(N=8)
Strongly disagree	11%	3%	7%	50%	10%	6%	10%	0%
Disagree	42	68	47	50	19	31	20	50
Agree	33	26	33	0	29	38	40	38
Strongly agree	14	3	13	0	43	25	30	12
D. An adolescent who masturbates should be punished or at least spoken to severely.	(N=83)	(N=30)	(N=29)	(N=6)	(N=38)	(N=16)	(N=10)	(N=8)
Strongly disagree	8%	10%	3%	33%	8%	0%	10%	12%
Disagree	47	47	48	50	26	44	60	25
Agree	33	40	45	17	21	31	20	38
Strongly agree	12	3	3	0	45	25	10	25

172

[Completed by the interviewer:]
Appearance of respondent

	(N=575)	(N=111)	(N=284)	(N=50)	(N=229)	(N=64)	(N=101)	(N=39)
Somewhat ugly, homely	10%	12%	7%	0%	19%	8%	13%	0%
Average	59	60	60	72	50	47	55	85
Good-looking	31	28	33	28	31	45	32	15

[Completed by the interviewer:]
Appearance of respondent

	(N=574)	(N=111)	(N=284)	(N=50)	(N=228)	(N=64)	(N=101)	(N=39)
Very feminine (effeminate)	4%	4%	0%	0%	4%	12%	7%	13%
Somewhat feminine (effeminate)	25	26	1	0	14	14	17	77
Neither especially feminine nor especially masculine	48	41	34	24	42	34	72	10
Somewhat masculine	18	23	54	26	32	33	4	0
Very masculine	5	6	11	50	7	6	0	0

PART II

Causal and Comparative Analyses

White Males

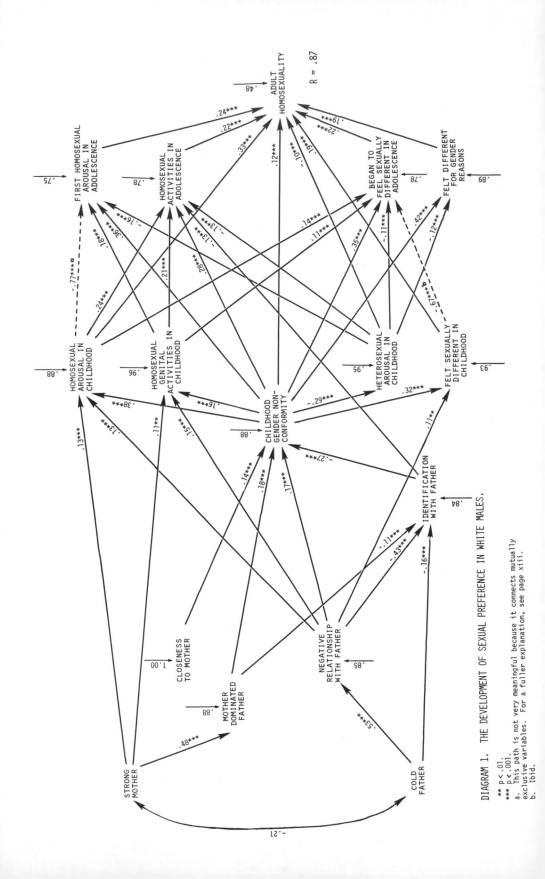

DIAGRAM 1. THE DEVELOPMENT OF SEXUAL PREFERENCE IN WHITE MALES.

** p < .01.
*** p < .001.
a. This path is not very meaningful because it connects mutually
exclusive variables. For a fuller explanation, see page xiii.
b. Ibid.

Correlations, Means, and Standard Deviations for Variables in the Model: WHITE MALES

	(1)	(2)	(3)	(4)	(5)	(6)	(7)	(8)	(9)	(10)	(11)	(12)	(13)	(14)	(15)	(16)
1 Strong mother		-.21	.48	.07	-.07	-.00	.09	.12	-.07	.15	.11	.17	.02	-.03	.12	.17
2 Cold father			-.05	.05	.53	-.38	.21	.09	-.00	.13	.11	.15	.05	.02	.03	.16
3 Mother dominated father				-.02	.05	-.12	.22	.09	-.07	.18	.17	.24	.01	.02	.15	.21
4 Closeness to mother					.10	-.07	.17	.08	-.14	.10	.10	.21	.06	.06	.08	.25
5 Negative relationship with father						-.52	.33	.20	-.08	.25	.22	.31	.07	.01	.12	.28
6 Identification with father							-.39	-.17	.19	-.21	-.20	-.35	-.12	-.08	-.19	-.35
7 Childhood gender nonconformity								.22	-.29	.44	.36	.52	.23	.10	.45	.64
8 Homosexual genital activities in childhood									-.02	.54	.33	.43	.04	-.15	.15	.40
9 Heterosexual arousal in childhood										-.04	-.16	-.25	-.11	-.23	-.24	-.36
10 Homosexual arousal in childhood											.47	.51	-.04	-.51	.25	.52
11 Felt sexually different in childhood												.33	-.43	-.17	.25	.39
12 Homosexual activities in adolescence													.29	.25	.42	.75
13 Began to feel sexually different in adolescence														.32	.16	.36
14 First homosexual arousal in adolescence															.12	.23
15 Felt different for gender reasons during high school																.56
16 Adult homosexuality																

Variable Number:	(1)	(2)	(3)	(4)	(5)	(6)	(7)	(8)	(9)	(10)	(11)	(12)	(13)	(14)	(15)	(16)
Mean	15.95	2.86	.98	.38	2.25	-.18	-.00	1.31	.42	.49	.30	1.56	.30	.22	.67	.33
Standard Deviation	4.86	1.72	.83	.49	1.31	1.72	.75	1.75	.49	.50	.46	.79	.46	.41	.47	.47

Effects of Childhood and Adolescent Experiences on the Development of Adult Homosexuality: WHITE MALES. R = .87.

Variable	Total Effects	Standardized Path Coefficient (β)	Unstandardized Path Coefficient (b)
First homosexual arousal in adolescence	.244	.244***	.278***
Homosexual activities in adolescence	.225	.225***	.134***
Homosexual arousal in childhood	.225	.329***	.309***
Heterosexual arousal in childhood	-.217	-.102***	-.097***
Began to feel sexually different in adolescence	.216	.216***	.221***
Homosexual genital activities in childhood	.115	--	--
Felt sexually different in childhood	.042	.187***	.192***
Childhood gender nonconformity	.605	.118***	.075***
Felt different for gender reasons, high school	.193	.193***	.194***
Negative relationship with father	.236	--	--
Identification with father	-.193	--	--
Cold father	.157	--	--
Mother dominated father	.128	--	--
Strong mother	.103	--	--
Closeness to mother	.082	--	--

NOTE: "Total Effects" refers to the sum of all the pathways from a given variable to adult sexual preference which are shown in Diagram 1. This value represents the portion of the zero-order correlation (r) which is accounted for by the paths in Diagram 1; the unaccounted-for portion is regarded as "extraneous" effects--i.e., those which are spurious or due to variables not included in the model.

***p < .001.

Effects of Earlier Childhood Experiences on Later Childhood and Adolescent
Experiences As Demonstrated in Diagram 1: WHITE MALES.

DEPENDENT VARIABLE: First homosexual arousal in adolescence (R = .67).			
Independent variable	Total Effects	Standardized Path Coefficient (β)	Unstandardized Path Coefficient (b)
Homosexual arousal in childhood	-.774	-.774***	-.641***
Homosexual genital activities in childhood	.180	.180***	.042***
Heterosexual arousal in childhood	-.160	-.160***	-.134***
Felt sexually different in childhood	--	--	--
Childhood gender nonconformity	.134	.357***	.198***
Strong mother	-.064	--	--
Negative relationship with father	-.037	--	--
Identification with father	-.036	--	--
Mother dominated father	.028	--	--
Closeness to mother	.018	--	--
Cold father	-.014	--	--

DEPENDENT VARIABLE: Homosexual activities in adolescence (R = .66).			
Independent variable	Total Effects	Standardized Path Coefficient (β)	Unstandardized Path Coefficient (b)
Homosexual arousal in childhood	.243	.243***	.383***
Homosexual genital activities in childhood	.208	.208***	.094***
Heterosexual arousal in childhood	-.126	-.126***	-.201***
Felt sexually different in childhood	--	--	--
Childhood gender nonconformity	.446	.282***	.299***
Identification with father	-.248	-.127***	-.058***
Negative relationship with father	.244	--	--
Cold father	.170	--	--
Mother dominated father	.106	--	--
Strong mother	.105	--	--
Closeness to mother	.060	--	--

DEPENDENT VARIABLE: Homosexual arousal in childhood (R = .47).			
Independent variable	Total Effects	Standardized Path Coefficient (β)	Unstandardized Path Coefficient (b)
Childhood gender nonconformity	.385	.385***	.258***
Negative relationship with father	.241	.132***	.050***
Strong mother	.164	.126***	.013***
Cold father	.145	--	--
Identification with father	-.104	--	--
Mother dominated father	.079	--	--
Closeness to mother	.052	--	--

DEPENDENT VARIABLE: Heterosexual arousal in childhood (R = .29).

Independent variable	Total Effects	Standardized Path Coefficient (β)	Unstandardized Path Coefficient (b)
Childhood gender nonconformity	-.287	-.287***	-.190***
Negative relationship with father	-.082	--	--
Identification with father	.078	--	--
Mother dominated father	-.059	--	--
Cold father	-.056	--	--
Closeness to mother	-.029	--	--

DEPENDENT VARIABLE: Began to feel sexually different in adolescence (R = .62).

Independent variable	Total Effects	Standardized Path Coefficient (β)	Unstandardized Path Coefficient (b)
Felt sexually different in childhood	-.672	-.672***	-.676***
Homosexual arousal in childhood	.138	.138***	.127***
Homosexual genital activities in childhood	.111	.111***	.029***
Heterosexual arousal in childhood	-.110	-.110***	-.103***
Childhood gender nonconformity	.236	.350***	.216***
Identification with father	-.064	--	--
Strong mother	.054	--	--
Mother dominated father	.049	--	--
Closeness to mother	.032	--	--
Cold father	.014	--	--
Negative relationship with father	.007	--	--

DEPENDENT VARIABLE: Homosexual genital activities in childhood (R = .28).

Independent variable	Total Effects	Standardized Path Coefficient (β)	Unstandardized Path Coefficient (b)
Childhood gender nonconformity	.163	.163***	.383***
Negative relationship with father	.196	.150***	.201***
Strong mother	.129	.113**	.041**
Cold father	.111	--	--
Identification with father	-.044	--	--
Mother dominated father	.034	--	--
Closeness to mother	.022	--	--

DEPENDENT VARIABLE: Felt sexually different in childhood (R = .37).

Independent variable	Total Effects	Standardized Path Coefficient (β)	Unstandardized Path Coefficient (b)
Childhood gender nonconformity	.322	.322***	.197***
Negative relationship with father	.205	.114**	.040**
Cold father	.123	--	--
Identification with father	-.087	--	--
Mother dominated father	.066	--	--
Closeness to mother	.043	--	--
Strong mother	.032	--	--

DEPENDENT VARIABLE: Childhood gender nonconformity (R = .47).

Independent variable	Total Effects	Standardized Path Coefficient (β)	Unstandardized Path Coefficient (b)
Negative relationship with father	.284	.169***	.096***
Identification with father	-.271	-.271***	-.118***
Mother dominated father	.206	.177***	.159***
Cold father	.195	--	--
Closeness to mother	.135	.135***	.208***
Strong mother	.100	--	--

DEPENDENT VARIABLE: Felt different for gender reasons during high school (R = .46).

Independent variable	Total Effects	Standardized Path Coefficient (β)	Unstandardized Path Coefficient (b)
Heterosexual arousal in childhood	-.123	-.123***	-.117***
Homosexual arousal in childhood	--	--	--
Homosexual genital activities in childhood	--	--	--
Felt sexually different in childhood	--	--	--
Childhood gender nonconformity	.450	.415***	.261***
Negative relationship with father	.128	--	--
Identification with father	-.122	--	--
Mother dominated father	.093	--	--
Cold father	.088	--	--
Closeness to mother	.061	--	--
Strong mother	.045	--	--

DEPENDENT VARIABLE: Negative relationship with father (R = .53).

Independent variable	Total Effects	Standardized Path Coefficient (β)	Unstandardized Path Coefficient (b)
Cold father	.532	.532***	.407***
Mother dominated father	--	--	--
Strong mother	--	--	--

DEPENDENT VARIABLE: Identification with father (R = .54).			
Independent variable	Total Effects	Standardized Path Coefficient (β)	Unstandardized Path Coefficient (b)
Negative relationship with father	-.425	-.425***	-.556***
Cold father	-.388	-.162***	-.162***
Mother dominated father	-.108	-.108***	-.224***
Strong mother	-.052	--	--
Closeness to mother	--	--	--

DEPENDENT VARIABLE: Mother dominated father (R = .48).			
Independent variable	Total Effects	Standardized Path Coefficient (β)	Unstandardized Path Coefficient (b)
Strong mother	.484	.484***	.083***
Cold father	--	--	--

NOTE: Closeness to Mother does not appear as a dependent variable in this table because the diagram illustrates no antecedents for it.

**p < .01.
***p < .001.

Selected Statistics from Fully Recursive Path Model: WHITE MALES[a]. R = .88.

Variable	Total Effects[b]	Standardized Path Coefficient (β)	Unstandardized Path Coefficient (b)
First homosexual arousal in adolescence	.245	.245***	.279***
Began to feel sexually different in adolescence	.212	.212***	.217***
Homosexual arousal in childhood	.201	.311***	.189***
Heterosexual arousal in childhood	-.200	-.096***	-.191***
Homosexual activities in adolescence	.194	.194***	.116***
Homosexual genital activities in childhood	.159	.051***	.043***
Felt sexually different in childhood	.035	.176	.036
Childhood gender nonconformity	.542	.113***	.342***
Felt different for gender reasons, high school	.198	.198***	.199***
Identification with father	-.252	-.029***	-.069***
Negative relationship with father	.222	-.030***	.080***
Closeness to mother	.222	.082***	.215***
Strong mother	.212	.025***	.021***
Cold father	.207	.028***	.057***
Mother dominated father	.157	-.005***	.089***

[a]The fully recursive path model allows paths from every "upstream" variable to each "downstream" variable, including those paths which fail to meet our criteria of statistical and/or substantive significance.

[b]"Total Effects" refers to the sum of all the influences which the given variable would have on adult sexual preference if it had paths to every "downstream" variable in Diagram 1. This value represents the portion of the zero-order correlation (r) which would be accounted for by such an all-possible-paths diagram; the unaccounted-for portion is "extraneous" effects--i.e., those that are spurious or due to variables not included in the model.

***p < .001.

Preliminary Homosexual-Heterosexual Differences Regarding Mothers: WHITE MALES.[a]

Mother-Son Relationships	WHM (N=575)	WHTM (N=284)	Eta[b]
Mentioned having felt close to mother	47%	21%	.251***
Communicated more easily with mother than with father	81%	58%	.258***
Overprotective mother	43%	21%	.175***
Was mother's favorite child	55%	42%	.123***
Seductive mother	no significant difference		
Hostile-rejecting mother	no significant difference		
Mothers' Personal Traits			
Strong mother (strong, active, dominant, independent)	57%	39%	.170***
Mother stronger than father	53%	30%	.211***
Mother made most of the decisions about the children	70%	54%	.162***
Pleasant mother (pleasant, adequate, warm, relaxed)	no significant difference		
Positive image of mother (one-word description)	no significant difference		
Identification with Mother			
Felt similar to mother	no significant difference		
Wanted to be like mother	no significant difference		

[a]Interview items from which these data were derived, and the distribution of responses to them, are given in full in Part I, pages 2-21.

[b]Eta, rather than eta-squared, is presented because it is more comparable to the zero-order correlation coefficient r.

***p< .001.

Preliminary Homosexual-Heterosexual Differences Regarding Fathers: WHITE MALES[a].

Father-Son Relationships	WHM (N=575)	WHTM (N=284)	Eta[b]
Relationship described in positive terms	23%	52%	.307***
Negative feelings toward father	48%	29%	.192***
Dislike or hatred of father	29%	12%	.195***
Not close to father	59%	38%	.233***
Admiration or respect for father	18%	31%	.327***
Was father's favorite child	17%	32%	.166***
Detached-hostile father	52%	37%	.179***

Fathers' Personal Traits			
Strong father	47%	63%	.159***
Submissive father	44%	31%	.107**
Warm father	35%	56%	.164***
Negative image of father (one-word description)	55%	40%	.244***
Father made most of the decisions about the children	30%	46%	.162***
Masculine father	no significant difference		
Independent father	no significant difference		
Active father	no significant difference		
Relaxed father	no significant difference		

Identification with Father			
Felt little or not at all similar to father	72%	34%	.367***
Wanted very much or somewhat to be like father	35%	61%	.257***
Mother discouraged identification with father	48%	31%	.150***
Felt more similar to mother than to father	72%	37%	.356***
Wanted to be more like mother than like father	59%	24%	.333***

[a] Interview items from which these data were derived, and the distribution of responses to them, are given in full in Part I, pages 22-43.

[b] Eta, rather than eta-squared, is presented because it is more comparable to the zero-order correlation coefficient r.

**p $<$ .01.
***p $<$ .001.

Preliminary Homosexual-Heterosexual Differences Regarding Mother-Father
Relationships: WHITE MALES[a].

Marital Relationship	WHM (N=575)	WHTM (N=284)	Eta[b]
Mother's affection for father		no significant difference	
Father's affection for mother		no significant difference	
Amount of friction or bad feeling between parents		no significant difference	
Amount of disagreement over decisions about the children		no significant difference	
Mother would marry father again		no significant difference	
Father would marry mother again		no significant difference	
Broken home (did not live continuously with both parents until age 17)		no significant difference	

Marital Dominance			
Father tended to dominate mother	29%	49%	.212***
Mother tended to dominate father	39%	22%	.212***

[a]Interview items from which these data were derived, and the distribution of responses to them, are given in full in Part I, pages 44-52.

[b]Eta, rather than eta-squared, is presented because it is more comparable to the zero-order correlation coefficient r.

***p < .001.

Preliminary Homosexual-Heterosexual Differences Regarding Brothers and Sisters:
WHITE MALES[a].

Birth Order and Sibling Constellation	WHM (N=575)	WHTM (N=284)	Eta[b]
Was an only child		no significant difference	
Was the only son		no significant difference	
Was the youngest child		no significant difference	
Was the youngest son		no significant difference	
Was the oldest child		no significant difference	
Was the oldest son		no significant difference	
Number of brothers		no significant difference	
Number of younger brothers		no significant difference	
Number of older brothers		no significant difference	
Number of sisters		no significant difference	
Number of younger sisters		no significant difference	
Number of older sisters		no significant difference	
Ratio of brothers to sisters (including respondent)		no significant difference	
Age difference between respondent and brother(s)		no significant difference	
Age difference between respondent and sister(s)		no significant difference	

Closeness and Similarity to Siblings			
Felt close to brother(s)		no significant difference	
Felt similar to brother(s)		no significant difference	
Felt very close to sister(s)	54%	37%	.152***
Felt similar to sister(s)		no significant difference	

Sibling Sex Play			
Engaged in sex play with sister(s)		no significant difference	
Engaged in sex play with brother(s)	29%	8%	.233***

[a]Interview items from which these data were derived, and the distribution of responses to them, are given in full in Part I, pages 53-73.

[b]Eta, rather than eta-squared, is presented because it is more comparable to the zero-order correlation coefficient r.

***$p < .001$.

Preliminary Homosexual-Heterosexual Differences Regarding Gender Conformity:
WHITE MALES[a].

Play Activities	WHM (N=575)	WHTM (N=284)	Eta[b]
Enjoyed boys' activities (e.g., football, baseball) very much	11%	70%	.608***
Enjoyed girls' activities (e.g., house, hopscotch, jacks) very much	46%	11%	.392***
Enjoyed "neuter" activities (e.g., reading, drawing) very much	68%	34%	.347***
Dressed in female clothing and pretended to be a girl	37%	10%	.284***
Gender Traits			
Relatively masculine while growing up	18%	67%	.520***
Relatively strong while growing up	25%	41%	.226***
Relatively passive while growing up	22%	8%	.208***
Relatively submissive while growing up	20%	3%	.243***
Parents' Desire for a Daughter			
Mother had hoped respondent would be a girl		no significant difference	
Father had hoped respondent would be a girl		no significant difference	

[a] Interview items from which these data were derived, and the distribution of responses to them, are given in full in Part I, pages 74-76.

[b] Eta, rather than eta-squared, is presented because it is more comparable to the zero-order correlation coefficient r.

***$p < .001$.

Preliminary Homosexual-Heterosexual Differences Regarding Experiences Outside the Family Circle: WHITE MALES[a].

Relationships with Peers	WHM (N=575)	WHTM (N=284)	Eta[b]
Low social involvement during grade school	43%	20%	.252***
Low social involvement during high school	45%	17%	.258***
More than half of respondent's friends were girls during grade school	19%	1%	.317***
More than half of respondent's friends were girls during high school	12%	2%	.113*
Had an especially close male friend during grade school	no significant difference		
Had an especially close male friend during high school	no significant difference		

Feeling Different			
Felt different from other boys during grade school	72%	39%	.286***
Felt different from other boys during high school	86%	45%	.412***
Felt different during grade school because of:[c]			.280***
Dislike of sports	48%	21%	
Sexual interest in other boys	18%	1%	
"Feminine" traits or interests	23%	1%	
Felt different during high school because of:[c]			.359***
Dislike of sports	34%	13%	
Sexual interest in other boys	57%	2%	
"Feminine" traits or interests	12%	1%	
Felt sexually different from other boys while growing up	84%	11%	.700***

Labeling			
Someone suggested respondent was sexually different or homosexual while he was growing up	53%	5%	.474***
Age at which this labeling took place	no significant difference		

Dating Experiences			
Recalled positive feelings about dating	42%	71%	.290***
Dated because it was expected	28%	9%	.408***
Frequency of dating	no significant difference		
Opportunity to get involved with girls	no significant difference		
Mother's encouragement to date	no significant difference		
Father's encouragement to date	no significant difference		
Physical appearance while growing up: ugly/good-looking	no significant difference		

Happiness and Self-Esteem			
Relatively unhappy during adolescence	42%	30%	.239***
Negative self-image (one-word description)	64%	42%	.224***
Relatively inadequate while growing up	28%	14%	.292***
Relatively "uptight" while growing up	45%	25%	.224***

[a]Interview items from which these data were derived, and the distribution of responses to them, are given in full in Part I, pages 77-88.

[b]Eta, rather than eta-squared, is presented because it is more comparable to the zero-order correlation coefficient r.

[c]Percentages are based on those respondents who did report having felt different from other boys during that time.

**p < .01.
***p < .001.

Preliminary Homosexual-Heterosexual Differences Regarding Childhood and
Adolescent Sexuality: WHITE MALES[a].

Pre-adult Homosexual Experiences[b]	WHM (N=575)	WHTM (N=284)	Eta[c]
Sexual feelings predominantly homosexual	59%	1%	.753***
Sexually aroused by a male	95%	20%	.776***
Average age at first homosexual arousal	11.6 yrs.	12.9 yrs.	.170***
Enjoyed first homosexual encounter	62%	29%	.355***
Sexual behaviors predominantly homosexual	56%	2%	.700***
Had a homosexual encounter involving physical contact	91%	36%	.531***
Had oral-genital homosexual contact	72%	15%	.541***
Engaged in homosexual body-rubbing	39%	5%	.356***
Engaged in homosexual masturbation	84%	21%	.626***
First homosexual encounter involved no physical contact	27%	51%	.219***
Played an active role in first homosexual encounter	83%	64%	.181***
Average age at first homosexual encounter	9.7 yrs.	11.6 yrs.	.217***
First homosexual partner was:			.124**
A much older man	no significant difference		
A friend or acquaintance	53%	42%	
A stranger	10%	21%	
First homosexual encounter involved only one partner	no significant difference		
An adult became aware of first homosexual encounter	no significant difference		
Response of this "aware adult"	no significant difference		

Pre-adult Heterosexual Experiences[b]			
Sexual feelings exclusively heterosexual	5%	72%	.753***
Sexually aroused by a female	62%	98%	.380***
Average age at first heterosexual arousal	13.1 yrs.	11.6 yrs.	.248***
Enjoyed first heterosexual encounter	49%	71%	.180***
Sexual behaviors exclusively heterosexual	8%	80%	.700***
Pre-adult sexual orientation was exclusive and the same as adult orientation (exclusively homosexual among WHMs or heterosexual among WHTMs)	26%	69%	.734***
Sexual orientation did not vary during childhood and adolescence	55%	81%	.280***
Pre-adult sexual feelings and behaviors were not congruent in the degree of homosexuality/heterosexuality	49%	23%	.242***
Had a sexual encounter with a female	79%	94%	.192***
Had a heterosexual encounter involving physical contact	74%	90%	.168***
Engaged in heterosexual coitus	32%	62%	.282***
Had heterosexual oral-genital contact	17%	37%	.230***
Engaged in heterosexual masturbation	26%	58%	.310***
Engaged in heterosexual body-rubbing	18%	54%	.368***
Relatively frequent light petting	8%	23%	.314***
Relatively frequent heavy petting and coitus	12%	34%	.304***
Identity of first heterosexual partner	no significant difference		
Response of adult(s) who became aware of first heterosexual encounter:			.238**
Said or did nothing	11%	29%	
Rebuked or punished respondent	no significant difference		
Age difference between respondent and first heterosexual partner	no significant difference		

191

Comparisons of Homosexual and Heterosexual Experiences[b]

First sexual encounter was a homosexual one	39%	62%	.228***
First sexual arousal was homosexual	53%	22%	.280***
Enjoyed first homosexual encounter more than first heterosexual encounter	33%	10%	.346***

Age at Puberty/Other Sexual Outlets

Age at first ejaculation	no significant difference		
Masturbated while growing up	no significant difference		
Age at first masturbation	no significant difference		
Orgasm during sleep while growing up	no significant difference		
First ejaculation occurred during sleep	9%	36%	.337***
First ejaculation occurred during a homosexual encounter	24%	3%	.261***

Parents' Sexual Attitudes

Mother believed premarital sex is immoral	no significant difference		
Mother believed adolescents who masturbate should be scolded or punished	no significant difference		
Mother believed talk about sex does not belong in the home	no significant difference		
Mother believed TV jokes about sex are improper	no significant difference		
Father believed premarital sex is immoral	no significant difference		
Father believed adolescents who masturbate should be scolded or punished	no significant difference		
Father believed talk about sex does not belong in the home	45%	30%	.121***
Father believed TV jokes about sex are improper	no significant difference		

[a]Interview items from which these data were derived, and the distribution of responses to them, are given in full in Part I, pages 89-173.

[b]Unless otherwise indicated, these variables refer to sexual feelings and behaviors before age nineteen.

[c]Eta, rather than eta-squared, is presented because it is more comparable to the zero-order correlation coefficient r.

**p < .01.
***p < .001.

192

PART III

Causal and Comparative Analyses

White Females

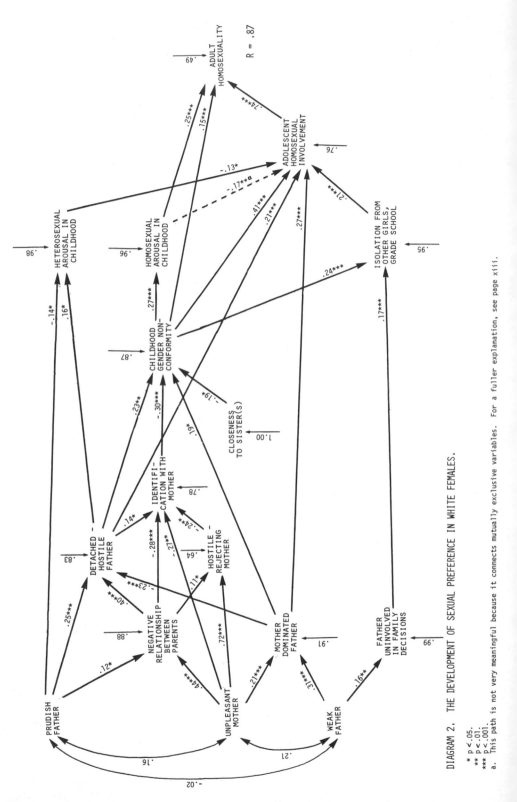

DIAGRAM 2. THE DEVELOPMENT OF SEXUAL PREFERENCE IN WHITE FEMALES.

* p < .05.
** p < .01.
*** p < .001.
a. This path is not very meaningful because it connects mutually exclusive variables. For a fuller explanation, see page xiii.

Correlations, Means, and Standard Deviations for Variables in the Model: WHITE FEMALES.

	(1)	(2)	(3)	(4)	(5)	(6)	(7)	(8)	(9)	(10)	(11)	(12)	(13)	(14)	(15)	(16)
1 Unpleasant mother		.16	.21	.08	.27	.46	.15	.76	-.56	-.07	.23	.05	.14	-.02	.26	.26
2 Prudish father			-.02	.02	-.05	.20	.34	.15	-.13	-.10	.04	-.01	-.00	-.09	.08	.13
3 Weak father				.16	.35	.15	.00	.26	-.12	.07	.16	.09	.10	-.01	.17	.14
4 Father uninvolved in family decisions					.13	.05	.05	.08	-.05	.05	.13	.21	.01	-.06	.24	.22
5 Mother dominated father						.03	-.23	.26	-.11	.00	.17	.09	.10	.03	.29	.22
6 Negative interparental relationship							.44	.44	-.44	-.05	.28	.02	.08	-.00	.20	.23
7 Detached-hostile father								.17	-.06	-.07	.22	-.09	.17	.12	.17	.29
8 Hostile-rejecting mother									-.54	-.14	.28	.07	.18	.00	.27	.30
9 Identification with mother										.16	-.37	-.22	-.11	.07	-.33	-.35
10 Closeness to sister(s)											-.25	-.16	-.04	.08	-.11	-.19
11 Childhood gender nonconformity												.27	.27	-.03	.52	.60
12 Isolation from other girls during grade school													-.07	-.04	.34	.32
13 Homosexual arousal in childhood														.08	-.02	.28
14 Heterosexual arousal in childhood															-.14	-.11
15 Adolescent homosexual involvement																.81
16 Adult homosexuality																

Variable Number:	(1)	(2)	(3)	(4)	(5)	(6)	(7)	(8)	(9)	(10)	(11)	(12)	(13)	(14)	(15)	(16)
Mean	-.01	1.46	.00	2.20	.97	5.11	-.02	.03	.01	.66	-.00	-.00	.20	.22	.07	.69
Standard Deviation	.93	.94	.43	2.38	.84	4.28	1.88	1.82	.87	.47	.90	.71	.40	.42	1.77	.46

Effects of Childhood and Adolescent Experiences on the Development of Adult
Homosexuality: WHITE FEMALES. R = .87.

Variable	Total Effects	Standardized Path Coefficient (β)	Unstandardized Path Coefficient (b)
Adolescent homosexual involvement	.739	.739***	.193***
Homosexual arousal in childhood	.132	.255***	.293***
Heterosexual arousal in childhood	-.099	--	--
Childhood gender nonconformity	.525	.147***	.075***
Isolation from other girls, grade school	.155	--	--
Mother dominated father	.244	--	--
Detached-hostile father	.235	--	--
Unpleasant mother	.184	--	--
Identification with mother	-.159	--	--
Negative interparental relationship	.142	--	--
Closeness to sister(s)	-.098	--	--
Prudish father	.091	--	--
Weak father	.080	--	--
Hostile-rejecting mother	.038	--	--
Father uninvolved in family decisions	.027	--	--

NOTE: "Total Effects" refers to the sum of all the pathways from a given variable to adult
sexual preference which are shown in Diagram 2. This value represents the portion of
the zero-order correlation (r) which is accounted for by the paths in Diagram 2; the
unaccounted-for portion is regarded as "extraneous" effects -- i.e., those which are
spurious or due to variables not included in the model.

***p < .001.

Effects of Earlier Childhood Experiences on Later Childhood and Adolescent
Experiences As. Demonstrated in Diagram 2: WHITE FEMALES.

DEPENDENT VARIABLE: Adolescent homosexual involvement (R = .65).

Independent variable	Total Effects	Standardized Path Coefficient (β)	Unstandardized Path Coefficient (b)
Homosexual arousal in childhood	-.167	-.167**	-.736**
Heterosexual arousal in childhood	-.134	-.134*	-.570*
Childhood gender nonconformity	.417	.412***	.803***
Isolation from other girls, grade school	.210	.210***	.525***
Mother dominated father	.287	.267***	.564***
Detached-hostile father	.264	.209***	.197***
Unpleasant mother	.179	--	--
Negative interparental relationship	.144	--	--
Identification with mother	-.126	--	--
Prudish father	.104	--	--
Weak father	.095	--	--
Closeness to sister(s)	-.078	--	--
Father uninvolved in family decisions	.036	--	--
Hostile-rejecting mother	.030	--	--

DEPENDENT VARIABLE: Homosexual arousal in childhood (R = .27).

Independent variable	Total Effects	Standardized Path Coefficient (β)	Unstandardized Path Coefficient (b)
Childhood gender nonconformity	.273	.273***	.121***
Identification with mother	-.083	--	--
Unpleasant mother	.065	--	--
Closeness to sister(s)	-.051	--	--
Detached-hostile father	.050	--	--
Negative interparental relationship	.045	--	--
Mother dominated father	.041	--	--
Hostile-rejecting mother	.020	--	--
Prudish father	.018	--	--
Weak father	.013	--	--
Father uninvolved in family decisions	--	--	--

DEPENDENT VARIABLE: Heterosexual arousal in childhood (R = .18).			
Independent variable	Total Effects	Standardized Path Coefficient (β)	Unstandardized Path Coefficient (b)
Childhood gender nonconformity	--	--	--
Detached-hostile father	.165	.165*	.037*
Prudish father	-.093	-.143*	-.064*
Negative interparental relationship	.066	--	--
Mother dominated father	-.038	--	--
Unpleasant mother	.021	--	--
Weak father	-.012	--	--
Closeness to sister(s)	--	--	--
Identification with mother	--	--	--
Hostile-rejecting mother	--	--	--
Father uninvolved in family decisions	--	--	--

DEPENDENT VARIABLE: Childhood gender nonconformity (R = .49).			
Independent variable	Total Effects	Standardized Path Coefficient (β)	Unstandardized Path Coefficient (b)
Identification with mother	-.303	-.303***	-.314***
Unpleasant mother	.237	--	--
Closeness to sister(s)	-.187	-.187*	-.358*
Detached-hostile father	.185	.227**	.109**
Negative interparental relationship	.165	--	--
Mother dominated father	.149	.191*	.206*
Hostile-rejecting mother	.072	--	--
Prudish father	.067	--	--
Weak father	.046	--	--
Father uninvolved in family decisions	--	--	--

DEPENDENT VARIABLE: Isolation from other girls, grade school (R = .32).			
Independent variable	Total Effects	Standardized Path Coefficient (β)	Unstandardized Path Coefficient (b)
Childhood gender nonconformity	.242	.242***	.189***
Father uninvolved in family decisions	.173	.173***	.051***
Identification with mother	-.073	--	--
Unpleasant mother	.062	--	--
Closeness to sister(s)	-.045	--	--
Detached-hostile father	.045	--	--
Negative interparental relationship	.041	--	--
Weak father	.038	--	--
Mother dominated father	.036	--	--
Hostile-rejecting mother	.023	--	--
Prudish father	.016	--	--

DEPENDENT VARIABLE: Mother dominated father (R = .41).

Independent variable	Total Effects	Standardized Path Coefficient (β)	Unstandardized Path Coefficient (b)
Weak father	.309	.309***	.601***
Unpleasant mother	.209	.209***	.188***
Prudish father	--	--	--

DEPENDENT VARIABLE: Detached-hostile father (R = .56).

Independent variable	Total Effects	Standardized Path Coefficient (β)	Unstandardized Path Coefficient (b)
Negative interparental relationship	.400	.400***	.176***
Prudish father	.310	.253***	.508***
Mother dominated father	-.227	-.227***	-.509***
Unpleasant mother	.130	--	--
Weak father	-.070	--	--
Father uninvolved in family decisions	--	--	--

DEPENDENT VARIABLE: Identification with mother (R = .62).

Independent variable	Total Effects	Standardized Path Coefficient (β)	Unstandardized Path Coefficient (b)
Unpleasant mother	-.553	-.267**	-.251**
Negative interparental relationship	-.245	-.276***	-.056***
Hostile-rejecting mother	-.239	-.239**	-.115**
Detached-hostile father	.140	.140*	.065*
Mother dominated father	-.032	--	--
Weak father	-.010	--	--
Prudish father	.006	--	--
Father uninvolved in family decisions	--	--	--

DEPENDENT VARIABLE: Negative interparental relationship (R = .48).

Independent variable	Total Effects	Standardized Path Coefficient (β)	Unstandardized Path Coefficient (b)
Unpleasant mother	.443	.443	2.037***
Prudish father	.122	.122*	.559*
Weak father	--	--	--

DEPENDENT VARIABLE: Hostile-rejecting mother (R = .77).

Independent variable	Total Effects	Standardized Path Coefficient (β)	Unstandardized Path Coefficient (b)
Unpleasant mother	.763	.716***	1.403***
Negative interparental relationship	.106	.106*	.045*
Prudish father	.013	--	--
Father uninvolved in family decisions	--	--	--
Mother dominated father	--	--	--
Weak father	--	--	--

DEPENDENT VARIABLE: Father uninvolved in family decisions (R = .16).			
Independent variable	Total Effects	Standardized Path Coefficient (ß)	Unstandardized Path Coefficient (b)
Weak father	.155	.155**	.857**
Unpleasant mother	--	--	--
Prudish father	--	--	--

NOTE: Closeness to Sister(s) does not appear as a dependent variable in this table because the diagram illustrates no antecedents for it.

*p < .05.
**p < .01.
***p < .001.

Selected Statistics from Fully Recursive Path Model: WHITE FEMALES[a]. R = .88.

Variable	Total Effects[b]	Standardized Path Coefficient (ß)	Unstandardized Path Coefficient (b)
Adolescent homosexual involvement	.703	.703***	.184***
Homosexual arousal in childhood	.126	.252	.145
Heterosexual arousal in childhood	-.117	-.028	-.130
Childhood gender nonconformity	.452	.110***	.230***
Isolation from other girls, grade school	.181	.055*	.118*
Identification with mother	-.338	-.047***	-.178***
Detached-hostile father	.293	.104**	.072**
Unpleasant mother	.224	-.046*	.111*
Father uninvolved in family decisions	.177	.020*	.034*
Hostile-rejecting mother	.161	.026	.041
Mother dominated father	.157	-.001	.087
Negative interparental relationship	.147	-.020	.016
Closeness to sister(s)	-.123	-.042	-.120
Prudish father	.101	.029	.050
Weak father	.098	-.023	.105

[a]The fully recursive path model allows paths from every "upstream" variable to each "downstream" variable, including those paths which fail to meet our criteria of statistical and/or substantive significance.

[b]"Total Effects" refers to the sum of all the influences which the given variable would have on adult sexual preference if it had paths to every "downstream" variable in Diagram 2. This value represents the portion of the zero-order correlation (r) which would be accounted for by such an all-possible-paths diagram; the unaccounted-for portion is "extraneous" effects--i.e., those that are spurious or due to variables not included in the model.

*p < .05.
**p < .01.
***p < .001.

Preliminary Homosexual-Heterosexual Differences Regarding Mothers: WHITE FEMALES.[a]

Mother-Daughter Relationships	WHF (N=229)	WHTF (N=101)	Eta[b]
Relationship described in negative terms	49%	21%	.290***
Hostile-rejecting mother	21%	11%	.155*[c]
Communicated more easily with mother than with father	58%	69%	.235***
Was mother's favorite child	no significant difference		
Controlling mother	no significant difference		
Overprotective/unprotective mother	no significant difference		

Mothers' Personal Traits

	WHF	WHTF	Eta
Negative image of mother (one-word description)	48%	20%	.275***
Pleasant mother (pleasant, adequate, warm, relaxed)	19%	40%	.245***
Mother very happy about being a woman	38%	62%	.163**
Mother made most of the decisions about the children	67%	45%	.202***
Feminine mother	no significant difference		
Domineering mother	no significant difference		

Identification with Mother

	WHF	WHTF	Eta
Did not want at all to be like mother	47%	15%	.310***
Did not feel at all similar to mother	45%	15%	.340***
Father encouraged identification with mother	22%	46%	.288***

[a]Interview items from which these data were derived, and the distribution of responses to them, are given in full in Part I, pages 2-21.

[b]Eta, rather than eta-squared, is presented because it is more comparable to the zero-order correlation coefficient r.

[c]Probability and eta are based on comparison of the heterosexual women with the homosexual women who had not been exposed to theories about homosexuality.

*p $<$ .05.
**p $<$ .01.
***p $<$ .001.

Preliminary Homosexual-Heterosexual Differences Regarding Fathers: WHITE FEMALES[a].

Father-Daughter Relationships	WHF (N=229)	WHTF (N=101)	Eta[b]
Relationship described in positive terms	36%	73%	.304***
Negative feelings toward father	45%	23%	.214***
Controlling father	40%	51%	.160*[c]
Communicated as easily with father as with mother	23%	36%	.235***
Detached-hostile father	35%	19%	.207***
Seductive father	no significant difference		
Was father's favorite child	no significant difference		

Fathers' Personal Traits

Negative image of father (one-word description)	58%	30%	.292***
Strong father (strong, active, adequate, dominant, independent)	21%	53%	.298***
Father made most of the decisions about the children	14%	25%	.202***
Cold father	39%	14%	.188***

Identification with Father

Did not want at all to be like father	34%	11%	.201***
Felt little or not at all similar to father	56%	28%	.154*
Wanted to be more like mother than like father	no significant difference		
Felt more similar to mother than to father	no significant difference		

[a]Interview items from which these data were derived, and the distribution of responses to them, are given in full in Part I, pages 22-43.

[b]Eta, rather than eta-squared, is presented because it is more comparable to the zero-order correlation coefficient r.

[c]Probability and eta are based on comparison of the heterosexual women with the homosexual women who had not been exposed to theories about homosexuality.

*$p < .05$.
***$p < .001$.

Preliminary Homosexual-Heterosexual Differences Regarding Mother-Father
Relationships: WHITE FEMALES[a].

Marital Relationships	WHF (N=229)	WHTF (N=101)	Eta[b]
Mother had little or no affection for father	31%	12%	.254***
Father had little or no affection for mother	24%	9%	.238***
A great deal of friction or bad feeling between parents	37%	24%	.214**
Mother would marry father again	no significant difference		
Father would marry mother again	no significant difference		
Amount of disagreement over decisions about the children	no significant difference		
Broken home (did not live continuously with both parents until age 17)	38%	25%	.125*
Reason for family breakup	no significant difference		
Age at family breakup	no significant difference		
Which parent was absent after family breakup	no significant difference		
With whom respondent lived after family breakup	no significant difference		
Marital Dominance			
Mother tended to dominate father	41%	17%	.217***

[a]Interview items from which these data were derived, and the distribution of responses to them, are given in full in Part I, pages 44-52.

[b]Eta, rather than eta-squared, is presented because it is more comparable to the zero-order correlation coefficient r.

  *p$<$.05.
 **p$<$.01.
***p$<$.001.

Preliminary Homosexual-Heterosexual Differences Regarding Brothers and Sisters: WHITE FEMALES[a].

Birth Order and Sibling Constellation	WHF (N=229)	WHTF (N=101)	Eta[b]
Was an only child		no significant difference	
Was the only daughter		no significant difference	
Was the youngest child		no significant difference	
Was the youngest daughter		no significant difference	
Was the oldest child		no significant difference	
Was the oldest daughter		no significant difference	
Number of brothers		no significant difference	
Number of younger brothers		no significant difference	
Number of older brothers		no significant difference	
Number of sisters		no significant difference	
Number of younger sisters		no significant difference	
Number of older sisters		no significant difference	
Ratio of brothers to sisters (including respondent)		no significant difference	
Age difference between respondent and brother(s)		no significant difference	
Age difference between respondent and sister(s)		no significant difference	

Closeness and Similarity to Siblings

	WHF	WHTF	Eta
Felt close to brother(s)		no significant difference	
Felt close to sister(s)	60%	79%	.217**
Identity of sibling to whom respondent felt closest		no significant difference	
Felt similar to brother(s)		no significant difference	
Felt similar to sister(s)	25%	52%	.264***
Identity of sibling to whom respondent felt most similar:			.241*
A sister	39%	60%	
An older brother	30%	11%	

Sibling Sex Play

	WHF	WHTF	Eta
Engaged in sex play with sister(s)		no significant difference	
Engaged in sex play with brother(s)		no significant difference	

[a] Interview items from which these data were derived, and the distribution of responses to them, are given in full in Part I, pages 53-73.

[b] Eta, rather than eta-squared, is presented because it is more comparable to the zero-order correlation coefficient r.

*$p < .05$.
**$p < .01$.
***$p < .001$.

Preliminary Homosexual-Heterosexual Differences Regarding Gender Conformity:
WHITE FEMALES.[a]

Gender Traits	WHF (N=229)	WHTF (N=101)	Eta[b]
Relatively masculine while growing up	62%	10%	.549***
Relatively dominant while growing up	33%	21%	.147*
Weak/strong while growing up	no significant difference		
Passive/active while growing up	no significant difference		
Dependent/independent while growing up	no significant difference		

Play Activities			
Enjoyed girls' activities (e.g., house, hopscotch, jacks) very much	14%	55%	.486***
Enjoyed boys' activities (e.g., football, baseball) very much	71%	28%	.360***
Enjoyed "neuter" activities (e.g., reading, drawing)	no significant difference		
Dressed in male clothing and pretended to be a boy	49%	7%	.405***

Parents' Desire for a Son			
Mother had hoped respondent would be a boy	no significant difference		
Father had hoped respondent would be a boy	no significant difference		

[a]Interview items from which these data were derived, and the distribution of responses to them, are given in full in part I, pages 74-76.

[b]Eta, rather than eta-squared, is presented because it is more comparable to the zero-order correlation coefficient r.

*p < .05.
***p < .001.

Preliminary Homosexual-Heterosexual Differences Regarding Experiences Outside
the Family Circle: WHITE FEMALES.[a]

Relationships with Peers	WHF (N=229)	WHTF (N=101)	Eta[b]
Low social involvement during grade school	38%	14%	.224**
Low social involvement during high school	38%	20%	.165**
More than half of respondent's friends were boys during grade school	22%	4%	.203***
Had an especially close female friend during grade school	70%	84%	.147**
Had an especially close male friend during high school	50%	70%	.285***

Feeling Different			
Felt different from other girls during grade school	72%	54%	.191***
Felt different from other girls during high school	81%	67%	.338***
Felt different during grade school because of:[c]			.436***
"Masculine" traits or interests	34%	9%	
Interest in sports	20%	2%	
Physical appearance	18%	29%	
Felt different during high school because of lack of interest in boys[c]	52%	6%	.326***
Felt sexually different from other girls while growing up	74%	10%	.593***

Labeling			
Someone suggested respondent was sexually different or homosexual while she was growing up	36%	0%	.385***

Dating Experiences			
Recalled positive feelings about dating	49%	73%	.262***
Dated because it was expected	21%	11%	.466***
Frequency of dating	no significant difference		
Opportunity to get involved with boys	no significant difference		
Mother's encouragement to date	no significant difference		
Father's encouragement to date	no significant difference		
Physical appearance while growing up: ugly/good-looking	no significant difference		

Happiness and Self-Esteem

Relatively happy during adolescence	46%	68%	.200***
Relatively "uptight" while growing up	49%	35%	.142*
Relatively inadequate while growing up	30%	18%	.160**
Negative self-image (one-word description)	58%	40%	.208*

[a]Interview items from which these data were derived, and the distribution of responses to them, are given in full in Part I, pages 77-88.

[b]Eta, rather than eta-squared, is presented because it is more comparable to the zero-order correlation coefficient r.

[c]Percentages are based on those respondents who did report having felt different from other girls during that time.

*p < .05.
**p < .01.
***p < .001.

Preliminary Homosexual-Heterosexual Differences Regarding Childhood and
Adolescent Sexuality: WHITE FEMALES.[a]

Pre-adult Homosexual Experiences[b]	WHF (N=229)	WHTF (N=101)	Eta[c]
Sexual feelings predominantly homosexual	44%	0%	.652***
Sexually aroused by a female	70%	6%	.592***
Average age at first homosexual arousal	no significant difference		
Enjoyed first homosexual encounter	73%	29%	.441***
Had a sexual encounter with a female	74%	42%	.303***
Had a homosexual encounter involving physical contact	95%	76%	.310***
Engaged in homosexual masturbation	41%	4%	.373***
Had oral-genital homosexual contact	22%	0%	.282***
Engaged in homosexual body-rubbing	20%	0%	.272***
Sexual behaviors predominantly homosexual	22%	1%	.475***
First homosexual partner was a friend or acquaintance	77%	56%	.190**
First homosexual encounter took place with a group	32%	10%	.246***
Average age at first homosexual encounter	11.4 yrs.	9.7 yrs.	.173*
Age difference between respondent and first homosexual partner	no significant difference		
Played an active role in first homosexual encounter	no significant difference		
An adult became aware of first homosexual encounter	no significant difference		
Response of this "aware adult"	no significant difference		

Pre-adult Heterosexual Experiences[b]			
Sexual feelings exclusively heterosexual	11%	81%	.652***
Sexually aroused by a male	64%	92%	.292***
Average age at first heterosexual arousal	no significant difference		
Enjoyed first heterosexual encounter	no significant difference		
Sexual behaviors exclusively heterosexual	36%	94%	.475***
Pre-adult sexual orientation was exclusive and the same as adult orientation (exclusively homosexual among WHFs or heterosexual among WHTFs)	8%	82%	.585***
Sexual orientation did not vary during childhood and adolescence	49%	88%	.362***
Pre-adult sexual feelings and behaviors were not congruent in the degree of homosexuality/ heterosexuality	64%	15%	.420***
Engaged in heterosexual body-rubbing	14%	24%	.129*
First heterosexual encounter involved genital contact	41%	23%	.178**
Average age at first heterosexual encounter	9.7 yrs.	11.4 yrs.	.216***
Average age at first heterosexual body-rubbing	15.0 yrs.	16.5 yrs.	.328*
Relatively frequent light petting	no significant difference		
Relatively frequent heavy petting and coitus	no significant difference		
Relatively frequent heterosexual masturbation	no significant difference		
Raped before age 19	no significant difference		
Had a sexual encounter with a male	no significant difference		
Identity of first heterosexual partner	no significant difference		
Played an active role in first heterosexual encounter	no significant difference		
An adult became aware of first heterosexual encounter	no significant difference		
Response of this "aware adult"	no significant difference		

Comparisons of Homosexual and Heterosexual Experiences[b]

First sexual arousal was homosexual	no significant difference		
First sexual encounter was a homosexual one	65%	31%	.253***
Enjoyed first homosexual encounter more than first heterosexual encounter	57%	18%	.314***
Type of activities in each encounter	no significant difference		

Age at Puberty/Other Sexual Outlets

Age at first menstruation	no significant difference		
Preparation for first menstruation	no significant difference		
Reaction to first menstruation	no significant difference		
Amount of menstrual flow during adolescence	no significant difference		
Discomfort during menstruation in adolescence	no significant difference		
Masturbated while growing up	67%	54%	.126*
Age at first masturbation	no significant difference		
Orgasm during sleep while growing up	no significant difference		
Age at first orgasm during sleep	no significant difference		
Enjoyment of masturbation	no significant difference		
Enjoyment of orgasm during sleep	no significant difference		

Parents' Sexual Attitudes

Mother believed premarital sex is immoral	no significant difference		
Mother believed adolescents who masturbate should be scolded or punished	no significant difference		
Mother believed talk about sex does not belong in the home	no significant difference		
Mother believed TV jokes about sex are improper	no significant difference		
Father believed premarital sex is immoral	no significant difference		
Father believed adolescents who masturbate should be scolded or punished	no significant difference		
Father believed talk about sex does not belong in the home	47%	31%	.134*
Father believed TV jokes about sex are improper	no significant difference		

[a]Interview items from which these data were derived, and the distribution of responses to them, are given in full in Part I, pages 89-173.

[b]Unless otherwise indicated, these variables refer to sexual feelings and behaviors before age nineteen.

[c]Eta, rather than eta-squared, is presented because it is more comparable to the zero-order correlation coefficient r.

*p < .05.
**p < .01.
***p < .001.

PART IV

Causal Analyses — Various

Types of Homosexual

Men and Women

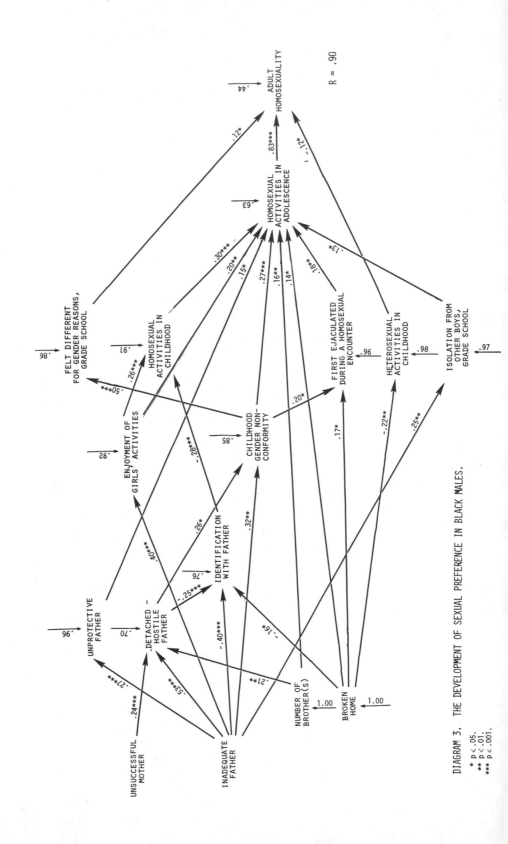

DIAGRAM 3. THE DEVELOPMENT OF SEXUAL PREFERENCE IN BLACK MALES.

* p < .05.
** p < .01.
*** p < .001.

Correlations, Means, and Standard Deviations for Variables in the Model: BLACK MALES.

	(1)	(2)	(3)	(4)	(5)	(6)	(7)	(8)	(9)	(10)	(11)	(12)	(13)	(14)	(15)	(16)
1 Unsuccessful mother		.30	.16	.26	.07	.44	-.25	.05	.28	.13	.08	.11	.13	-.10	.22	.21
2 Inadequate father			.16	.29	.27	.63	-.61	.40	-.49	.25	.31	.12	.13	-.02	.39	.41
3 Number of brothers				.02	.00	.33	-.21	.10	.15	-.04	.09	.01	.16	.07	.24	.23
4 Broken home					.10	.13	-.31	.15	.15	-.04	.18	.20	.19	-.22	.32	.32
5 Unprotective father						.21	-.26	.20	.24	.08	.12	-.04	.00	-.06	.30	.26
6 Detached-hostile father							-.53	.31	.47	.13	.26	.14	.05	-.12	.41	.38
7 Identification with father								-.15	-.39	-.20	-.32	-.06	-.14	.07	-.41	-.41
8 Enjoyment of girls' activities									.28	-.01	.30	.14	.20	-.10	.46	.41
9 Childhood gender nonconformity										.19	.26	.23	.50	-.11	.55	.53
10 Isolation from other boys, grade school											-.10	.11	-.14	-.08	.18	.18
11 Homosexual activities in childhood												.16	.07	.11	.51	.39
12 First ejaculated during a homosexual encounter													.08	-.14	.36	.35
13 Felt different for gender reasons, grade school														.00	.22	.30
14 Heterosexual activities in childhood															-.17	-.27
15 Homosexual activities in adolescence																.88
16 Adult homosexuality																

Variable Number:	(1)	(2)	(3)	(4)	(5)	(6)	(7)	(8)	(9)	(10)	(11)	(12)	(13)	(14)	(15)	(16)
Mean	1.61	.00	1.52	.48	3.76	-.07	.01	1.29	-.71	.00	.88	.20	.28	1.41	1.43	.64
Standard Deviation	1.56	.94	1.52	.50	1.72	1.81	.91	1.10	1.67	2.10	.97	.40	.45	.97	.88	.47

Effects of Childhood and Adolescent Experiences on the Development of Adult
Homosexuality: BLACK MALES. R = .90.

Variable	Total Effects	Standardized Path Coefficient (β)	Unstandardized Path Coefficient (b)
Homosexual activities in adolescence	.835	.835***	.444***
Homosexual activities in childhood	.255	--	--
First ejaculated during a homosexual encounter	.152	--	--
Heterosexual activities in childhood	-.123	-.123*	-.060*
Childhood gender nonconformity	.315	--	--
Enjoyment of girls' activities	.232	--	--
Felt different for gender reasons, grade school	.123	.123*	.127*
Isolation from other boys, grade school	.107	--	--
Inadequate father	.337	--	--
Broken home	.170	--	--
Number of brothers	.154	--	--
Unprotective father	.124	--	--
Detached-hostile father	.101	--	--
Identification with father	-.071	--	--
Unsuccessful mother	.024	--	--

NOTE: "Total Effects" refers to the sum of all the pathways from a given variable to adult
sexual preference which are shown in Diagram 3. This value represents the portion of
the zero-order correlation (r) which is accounted for by the paths in Diagram 3; the
unaccounted-for portion is regarded as "extraneous" effects -- i.e., those which are
spurious or due to variables not included in the model.

*p < .05.
***p < .001.

Effects of Earlier Childhood Experiences on Later Childhood and Adolescent
Experiences As Demonstrated in Diagram 3 : BLACK MALES.

DEPENDENT VARIABLE: Homosexual activities in adolescence (R = .78).

Independent variable	Total Effects	Standardized Path Coefficient (β)	Unstandardized Path Coefficient (b)
Homosexual activities in childhood	.305	.305***	.276***
First ejaculated in a homosexual encounter	.182	.182**	.402**
Heterosexual activities in childhood	--	--	--
Childhood gender nonconformity	.304	.267***	.141***
Enjoyment of girls' activities	.278	.199**	.160**
Felt different for gender reasons, grade school	--	--	--
Isolation from other boys, grade school	.128	.128*	.054*
Inadequate father	.370	--	--
Broken home	.182	.137*	.242*
Number of brothers	.180	.159**	.092**
Unprotective father	.148	.148*	.076*
Detached-hostile father	.102	--	--
Identification with father	-.085	--	--
Unsuccessful mother	.025	--	--

DEPENDENT VARIABLE: Homosexual activities in childhood (R = .41).

Independent variable	Total Effects	Standardized Path Coefficient (β)	Unstandardized Path Coefficient (b)
Enjoyment of girls' activities	.259	.259***	.230***
Childhood gender nonconformity	--	--	--
Identification with father	-.279	-.279***	-.296***
Inadequate father	.253	--	--
Detached-hostile father	.071	--	--
Broken home	.045	--	--
Unsuccessful mother	.017	--	--
Number of brothers	.015	--	--
Unprotective father	--	--	--

DEPENDENT VARIABLE: First ejaculated in a homosexual encounter (R = .28).

Independent variable	Total Effects	Standardized Path Coefficient (β)	Unstandardized Path Coefficient (b)
Childhood gender nonconformity	.202	.202*	.048*
Enjoyment of girls' activities	--	--	--
Broken home	.170	.170*	.135*
Inadequate father	.093	--	--
Detached-hostile father	.053	--	--
Unsuccessful mother	.013	--	--
Number of brothers	.011	--	--
Identification with father	--	--	--
Unprotective father	--	--	--

DEPENDENT VARIABLE: Heterosexual activities in childhood (R = .22).

Independent variable	Total Effects	Standardized Path Coefficient (β)	Unstandardized Path Coefficient (b)
Childhood gender nonconformity	--	--	--
Enjoyment of girls' activities	--	--	--
Broken home	-.215	-.215**	-.416**
Identification with father	--	--	--
Detached-hostile father	--	--	--
Unprotective father	--	--	--
Number of brothers	--	--	--
Unsuccessful mother	--	--	--
Inadequate father	--	--	--

DEPENDENT VARIABLE: Childhood gender nonconformity (R = .53).

Independent variable	Total Effects	Standardized Path Coefficient (β)	Unstandardized Path Coefficient (b)
Inadequate father	.460	.321**	.570**
Detached-hostile father	.263	.263*	.243*
Unsuccessful mother	.064	--	--
Number of brothers	.054	--	--
Identification with father	--	--	--
Unprotective father	--	--	--
Broken home	--	--	--

DEPENDENT VARIABLE: Enjoyment of girls' activities (R = .40).

Independent variable	Total Effects	Standardized Path Coefficient (β)	Unstandardized Path Coefficient (b)
Inadequate father	.401	.401***	.467***
Identification with father	--	--	--
Detached-hostile father	--	--	--
Unprotective father	--	--	--
Number of brothers	--	--	--
Broken home	--	--	--
Unsuccessful mother	--	--	--

DEPENDENT VARIABLE: Felt different for gender reasons, grade school (R = .50).

Independent variable	Total Effects	Standardized Path Coefficient (β)	Unstandardized Path Coefficient (b)
Childhood gender nonconformity	.502	.502***	.136***
Enjoyment of girls' activities	--	--	--
Inadequate father	.231	--	--
Detached-hostile father	.132	--	--
Unsuccessful mother	.032	--	--
Number of brothers	.027	--	--
Identification with father	--	--	--
Unprotective father	--	--	--
Broken home	--	--	--

DEPENDENT VARIABLE: Isolation from other boys, grade school (R = .25).

Independent variable	Total Effects	Standardized Path Coefficient (β)	Unstandardized Path Coefficient (b)
Childhood gender nonconformity	--	--	--
Enjoyment of girls' activities	--	--	--
Inadequate father	.255	.255**	.570**
Identification with father	--	--	--
Detached-hostile father	--	--	--
Unprotective father	--	--	--
Number of brothers	--	--	--
Broken home	--	--	--
Unsuccessful mother	--	--	--

DEPENDENT VARIABLE: Detached-hostile father (R = .71).

Independent variable	Total Effects	Standardized Path Coefficient (β)	Unstandardized Path Coefficient (b)
Inadequate father	.527	.527***	1.015***
Unsuccessful mother	.242	.242***	.281***
Number of brothers	.207	.207**	.247**
Broken home	--	--	--

DEPENDENT VARIABLE: Unprotective father (R = .27).

Independent variable	Total Effects	Standardized Path Coefficient (β)	Unstandardized Path Coefficient (b)
Inadequate father	.275	.275***	.303***
Number of brothers	--	--	--
Broken home	--	--	--
Unsuccessful mother	--	--	--

DEPENDENT VARIABLE: Identification with father (R = .65).

Independent variable	Total Effects	Standardized Path Coefficient (β)	Unstandardized Path Coefficient (b)
Inadequate father	-.534	-.400***	-.391***
Detached-hostile father	-.254	-.254**	-.129**
Broken home	-.161	-.161*	-.295*
Unsuccessful mother	-.061	--	--
Number of brothers	-.053	--	--
Unprotective father	--	--	--

NOTE: Number of Brothers and Broken Home do not appear as dependent variables in this table because the diagram illustrates no antecedents for them.

*p < .05.
**p < .01.
***p < .001.

Selected Statistics from Fully Recursive Path Model: BLACK MALES[a]. R = .90.

Variable	Total Effects[b]	Standardized Path Coefficient (∂)	Unstandardized Path Coefficient (b)
Homosexual activities in adolescence	.844	.844***	.449***
Homosexual activities in childhood	.221	-.048	.106
Heterosexual activities in childhood	-.198	-.123	-.096
First ejaculated in a homosexual encounter	.174	.032	.205
Childhood gender nonconformity	.359	-.055**	.101**
Enjoyment of girls' activities	.260	-.021*	.111*
Felt different for gender reasons, grade school	.103	.145	.107
Isolation from other boys, grade school	.136	.023	.030
Inadequate father	.377	.091**	.188**
Broken home	.219	-.024	.205
Number of brothers	.172	.011	.053
Detached-hostile father	.169	-.017	.044
Unprotective father	.158	-.007	.043
Identification with father	-.144	-.041	-.073
Unsuccessful mother	.095	-.020	.028

[a]The fully recursive path model allows paths from every "upstream" variable to each "downstream" variable, including those paths which fail to meet our criteria of statistical and/or substantive significance.

[b]"Total Effects" refers to the sum of all the influences which the given variable would have on adult sexual preference if it had paths to every "downstream" variable in Diagram 3. This value represents the portion of the zero-order correlation (r) which would be accounted for by such an all-possible-paths diagram; the unaccounted-for portion is "extraneous" effects--i.e., those that are spurious or due to variables not included in the model.

*p < .05.
**p < .01.
***p < .001.

Overlap between Subsamples of White Homosexual Males. Number Given Is the Percentage of the White Homosexual Males in Both Subsamples (N=575).

Subsample	(1)	(2)	(3)	(4)	(5)	(6)	Subsample N
1. "Effeminate" WHMs	--						253
2. Noneffeminate WHMs	--	--					322
3. Bisexual WHMs	2.1%	6.3%	--				46
4. Exclusively homosexual WHMs	28.3	25.7	--	--			316
5. WHMs who have had psycho-therapy or counseling	28.3	29.7	4.9%	30.6%	--		336
6. WHMs who have never been in psychotherapy or counseling	16.0	25.4	3.5	24.0	--	--	239
7. Close-coupled WHMs	4.2	5.0	0.3	5.6	5.4%	3.8%	67
8. Open-coupled WHMs	7.5	10.3	0.7	11.1	9.9	7.8	120
9. "Functional" WHMs	5.9	7.1	0.5	7.0	7.8	5.4	102
10. Dysfunctional WHMs	5.6	7.5	1.0	6.8	8.9	4.3	86
11. Asexual WHMs	7.8	9.9	3.0	9.6	9.6	8.2	110

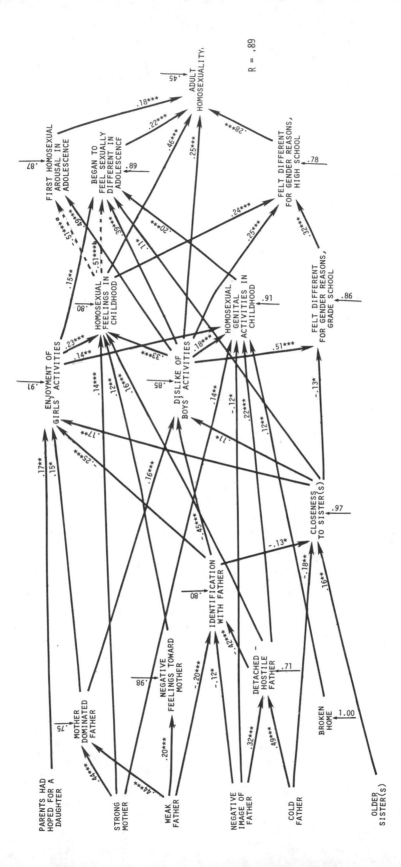

DIAGRAM 4. THE DEVELOPMENT OF SEXUAL PREFERENCE IN EFFEMINATE WHITE HOMOSEXUAL MALES.

* p < .05.
** p < .01.
*** p < .001.
a. This path is not very meaningful because it connects mutually exclusive variables. For a fuller explanation, see page xiii.
b. Ibid.

Correlations, Means, and Standard Deviations for Variables in the Model: EFFEMINATE HOMOSEXUAL AND ALL HETEROSEXUAL, WHITE MALES.

	(1)	(2)	(3)	(4)	(5)	(6)	(7)	(8)	(9)	(10)	(11)	(12)	(13)	(14)	(15)	(16)	(17)	(18)	(19)	(20)	(21)
1 Strong mother		.03	-.07	.04	.12	-.22	-.05	.49	.02	-.16	.02	.06	.09	.12	.14	-.01	.17	.04	-.08	.12	.15
2 Older sister(s)			.02	-.12	.03	-.01	-.05	.07	.03	.08	-.10	.17	.15	.08	.10	-.02	.10	.01	.03	.09	.12
3 Negative image of father				.06	.37	.49	.07	.09	.10	.56	-.43	-.05	.12	.27	.07	.13	.15	.11	.14	.22	.24
4 Parents had hoped for a daughter					.18	.04	-.05	.06	-.04	.07	-.10	-.08	.22	.14	.12	.10	.13	.12	.06	.14	.19
5 Weak father						.26	-.01	.49	.20	.33	-.38	-.05	.21	.28	.06	.18	.20	.15	.05	.24	.26
6 Cold father							-.02	-.03	.00	.65	-.40	-.13	.11	.26	.08	.08	.15	.08	.12	.13	.24
7 Broken home								-.08	.07	.06	-.11	.06	.03	.06	.13	-.08	.11	.00	-.04	.01	.11
8 Mother dominated father									.17	-.01	-.15	.06	.20	.23	.12	.12	.24	.04	-.03	.22	.22
9 Negative feelings toward mother										.13	-.09	.04	.07	.15	.06	.05	.21	.00	-.03	.04	.18
10 Detached-hostile father											-.56	-.07	.17	.35	.22	.08	.31	.14	-.10	.22	.37
11 Identification with father												-.07	-.30	-.48	-.23	-.20	-.32	-.20	-.16	-.33	-.48
12 Closeness to sister(s)													.21	.15	.16	-.05	.17	.14	.04	.14	.20
13 Enjoyment of girls' activities														.43	.26	.20	.42	.18	.07	.36	.51
14 Dislike of boys' activities															.31	.49	.52	.27	.23	.53	.74
15 Homosexual genital activities in childhood																.02	.60	.16	-.14	.25	.46
16 Felt different for gender reasons, grade school																	.20	.07	.12	.49	.42
17 Homosexual feelings in childhood																		-.11	-.26	.42	.65
18 Began to feel sexually different in adolescence																			.32	.23	.36
19 First homosexual arousal in adolescence																				.11	.22
20 Felt different for gender reasons, high school																					.68
21 Adult homosexuality																					
	(1)	(2)	(3)	(4)	(5)	(6)	(7)	(8)	(9)	(10)	(11)	(12)	(13)	(14)	(15)	(16)	(17)	(18)	(19)	(20)	(21)
Variable Number:	(1)	(2)	(3)	(4)	(5)	(6)	(7)	(8)	(9)	(10)	(11)	(12)	(13)	(14)	(15)	(16)	(17)	(18)	(19)	(20)	(21)
Mean	15.50	.55	1.27	.25	-.00	2.86	.29	.91	.30	1.84	-.15	.48	1.05	1.28	1.01	.50	.00	.20	.16	.61	.47
Standard Deviation	5.07	.98	.83	.53	.94	1.72	.45	.84	.46	1.79	1.79	.50	1.07	1.21	1.59	.50	1.74	.40	.37	.49	.50

221

Effects of Childhood and Adolescent Experiences on the Development of Adult Homosexuality: EFFEMINATE HOMOSEXUAL AND ALL HETEROSEXUAL WHITE MALES. R = .89.

Variable	Total Effects	Standardized Path Coefficient (β)	Unstandardized Path Coefficient (b)
Homosexual feelings in childhood	.327	.465***	.134***
Began to feel sexually different in adolescence	.219	.219***	.271***
First homosexual arousal in adolescence	.182	.182***	.248***
Homosexual genital activities in childhood	.044	--	--
Dislike of boys' activities	.658	.252***	.104***
Felt different for gender reasons, high school	.284	.284***	.290***
Enjoyment of girls' activities	.113	--	--
Felt different for gender reasons, grade school	.090	--	--
Identification with father	-.339	--	--
Detached-hostile father	.206	--	--
Weak father	.127	--	--
Mother dominated father	.120	--	--
Closeness to sister(s)	.103	--	--
Negative image of father	.103	--	--
Strong mother	.103	--	--
Cold father	.082	--	--
Negative feelings toward mother	.038	--	--
Parents had hoped for a daughter	.019	--	--
Older sister(s)	.016	--	--
Broken home	.005	--	--

NOTE: "Total Effects" refers to the sum of all the pathways from a given variable to adult sexual preference which are shown in Diagram 4. This value represents the portion of the zero-order correlation (r) which is accounted for by the paths in Diagram 4; the unaccounted-for portion is regarded as "extraneous" effects--i.e., those which are spurious or due to variables not included in the model.

***p < .001.

Effects of Earlier Childhood Experiences on Later Childhood and Adolescent Experiences As Demonstrated in Diagram 4: EFFEMINATE HOMOSEXUAL AND ALL HETEROSEXUAL WHITE MALES.

DEPENDENT VARIABLE: Homosexual feelings in childhood (R = .60).

Independent variable	Total Effects	Standardized Path Coefficient (β)	Unstandardized Path Coefficient (b)
Dislike of boys' activities	.326	.326***	.470***
Enjoyment of girls' activities	.228	.228***	.369***
Detached-hostile father	.252	.162***	.153***
Identification with father	-.214	--	--
Strong mother	.173	.136***	.047***
Negative feelings toward mother	.117	.117**	.441**
Cold father	.110	--	--
Negative image of father	.108	--	--
Weak father	.103	--	--
Mother dominated father	.085	--	--
Closeness to sister(s)	.074	--	--
Parents had hoped for a daughter	.039	--	--
Older sister(s)	.012	--	--
Broken home	--	--	--

DEPENDENT VARIABLE: Began to feel sexually different in adolescence (R = .46).

Independent variable	Total Effects	Standardized Path Coefficient (β)	Unstandardized Path Coefficient (b)
Homosexual feelings in childhood	-.508	-.508***	-.118***
Homosexual genital activities in childhood	.200	.200***	.051***
Dislike of boys' activities	.263	.392***	.131***
Enjoyment of girls' activities	.058	.146**	.055**
Felt different for gender reasons, grade school	--	--	--
Identification with father	-.152	--	--
Closeness to sister(s)	.145	.106*	.085*
Negative feelings toward mother	-.059	--	--
Mother dominated father	.050	--	--
Weak father	.040	--	--
Detached-hostile father	.025	--	--
Broken home	.023	--	--
Older sister(s)	.023	--	--
Strong mother	-.019	--	--
Cold father	-.014	--	--
Parents had hoped for a daughter	.010	--	--
Negative image of father	.003	--	--

DEPENDENT VARIABLE: First homosexual arousal in adolescence (R = .49).			
Independent variable	Total Effects	Standardized Path Coefficient (β)	Unstandardized Path Coefficient (b)
Homosexual feelings in childhood	-.511	-.511***	-.108***
Homosexual genital activities in childhood	--	--	--
Dislike of boys' activities	.324	.491***	.150***
Enjoyment of girls' activities	-.117	--	--
Felt different for gender reasons, grade school	--	--	--
Identification with father	-.119	--	--
Negative feelings toward mother	-.060	--	--
Strong mother	-.055	--	--
Mother dominated father	.034	--	--
Detached-hostile father	-.033	--	--
Weak father	.026	--	--
Parents had hoped for a daughter	-.020	--	--
Cold father	-.019	--	--
Closeness to sister(s)	.016	--	--
Negative image of father	.004	--	--
Older sister(s)	.003	--	--
Broken home	--	--	--

DEPENDENT VARIABLE: Homosexual genital activities in childhood (R = .41).			
Independent variable	Total Effects	Standardized Path Coefficient (β)	Unstandardized Path Coefficient (b)
Dislike of boys' activities	.182	.182***	.240***
Enjoyment of girls' activities	.139	.139**	.206**
Detached-hostile father	.270	.218***	.188***
Strong mother	.160	.138**	.043**
Cold father	.124	--	--
Identification with father	-.123	--	--
Broken home	.115	.115**	.403**
Mother dominated father	.049	--	--
Weak father	.046	--	--
Closeness to sister(s)	.044	--	--
Parents had hoped for a daughter	.023	--	--
Negative image of father	-.017	-.119*	-.227*
Older sister(s)	.007	--	--
Negative feelings toward mother	--	--	--

DEPENDENT VARIABLE: Dislike of boys' activities (R = .52).			
Independent variable	Total Effects	Standardized Path Coefficient (β)	Unstandardized Path Coefficient (b)
Identification with father	-.446	-.452***	-.306***
Detached-hostile father	.197	--	--
Weak father	.161	--	--
Mother dominated father	.157	.157***	.226***
Negative image of father	.121	--	--
Closeness to sister(s)	.110	.110*	.266*
Cold father	.076	--	--
Strong mother	.069	--	--
Older sister(s)	.017	--	--
Negative feelings toward mother	--	--	--
Broken home	--	--	--
Parents had hoped for a daughter	--	--	--

DEPENDENT VARIABLE: Felt different for gender reasons, high school (R = .62).			
Independent variable	Total Effects	Standardized Path Coefficient (β)	Unstandardized Path Coefficient (b)
Homosexual feelings in childhood	.235	.235***	.066***
Homosexual genital activities in childhood	--	--	--
Dislike of boys' activities	.487	.247***	.100***
Felt different for gender reasons, grade school	.318	.318***	.311***
Enjoyment of girls' activities	.054	--	--
Identification with father	-.236	--	--
Detached-hostile father	.138	--	--
Weak father	.089	--	--
Mother dominated father	.084	--	--
Negative image of father	.074	--	--
Strong mother	.069	--	--
Cold father	.064	--	--
Negative feelings toward mother	.028	--	--
Closeness to sister(s)	.021	--	--
Parents had hoped for a daughter	.009	--	--
Older sister(s)	.003	--	--
Broken home	--	--	--

DEPENDENT VARIABLE: Enjoyment of girls' activities (R = .42).			
Independent variable	Total Effects	Standardized Path Coefficient (β)	Unstandardized Path Coefficient (b)
Identification with father	-.272	-.250***	-.150***
Closeness to sister(s)	.169	.169**	.362**
Parents had hoped for a daughter	.169	.169**	.342**
Mother dominated father	.147	.147*	.188*
Weak father	.118	--	--
Detached-hostile father	.115	--	--
Negative image of father	.070	--	--
Strong mother	.065	--	--
Older sister(s)	.027	--	--
Cold father	.026	--	--
Negative feelings toward mother	--	--	--
Broken home	--	--	--

DEPENDENT VARIABLE: Felt different for gender reasons, grade school (R = .51).			
Independent variable	Total Effects	Standardized Path Coefficient (β)	Unstandardized Path Coefficient (b)
Dislike of boys' activities	.514	.514***	.213***
Enjoyment of girls' activities	--	--	--
Identification with father	-.223	--	--
Detached-hostile father	.094	--	--
Mother dominated father	.081	--	--
Weak father	.079	--	--
Closeness to sister(s)	-.073	-.130*	-.130*
Cold father	.059	--	--
Negative image of father	.058	--	--
Strong mother	.036	--	--
Older sister(s)	-.012	--	--
Negative feelings toward mother	--	--	--
Broken home	--	--	--
Parents had hoped for a daughter	--	--	--

DEPENDENT VARIABLE: Identification with father (R = .60).			
Independent variable	Total Effects	Standardized Path Coefficient (β)	Unstandardized Path Coefficient (b)
Detached-hostile father	-.422	-.422***	-.409***
Negative image of father	-.259	-.122*	-.263*
Cold father	-.206	--	--
Weak father	-.198	-.198***	-.374***
Negative feelings toward mother	--	--	--
Mother dominated father	--	--	--
Broken home	--	--	--
Parents had hoped for a daughter	--	--	--
Older sister(s)	--	--	--
Strong mother	--	--	--

DEPENDENT VARIABLE: Detached-hostile father (R = .71).			
Independent variable	Total Effects	Standardized Path Coefficient (β)	Unstandardized Path Coefficient (b)
Cold father	.489	.489***	.651***
Negative image of father	.324	.324***	.720***
Mother dominated father	--	--	--
Broken home	--	--	--
Parents had hoped for a daughter	--	--	--
Older sister(s)	--	--	--
Strong mother	--	--	--
Weak father	--	--	--

DEPENDENT VARIABLE: Mother dominated father (R = .66).			
Independent variable	Total Effects	Standardized Path Coefficient (β)	Unstandardized Path Coefficient (b)
Strong mother	.440	.440***	.073***
Weak father	.436	.436***	.386***
Parents had hoped for a daughter	--	--	--
Older sister(s)	--	--	--
Cold father	--	--	--
Negative image of father	--	--	--

DEPENDENT VARIABLE: Closeness to sister(s) (R = .25).			
Independent variable	Total Effects	Standardized Path Coefficient (β)	Unstandardized Path Coefficient (b)
Older sister(s)	.158	.158**	.082**
Cold father	-.153	-.180**	-.052**
Identification with father	-.130	-.130*	-.036*
Detached-hostile father	.055	--	--
Negative image of father	.034	--	--
Weak father	.026	--	--
Negative feelings toward mother	--	--	--
Mother dominated father	--	--	--
Broken home	--	--	--
Parents had hoped for a daughter	--	--	--
Strong mother	--	--	--

DEPENDENT VARIABLE: Negative feelings toward mother (R = .20).			
Independent variable	Total Effects	Standardized Path Coefficient (β)	Unstandardized Path Coefficient (b)
Weak father	.200	.200***	.097***
Mother dominated father	--	--	--
Broken home	--	--	--
Parents had hoped for a daughter	--	--	--
Older sister(s)	--	--	--
Cold father	--	--	--
Negative image of father	--	--	--
Strong mother	--	--	--

NOTE: Broken Home does not appear as a dependent variable in this table because the diagram illustrates no antecedents for it.

*p < .05.
**p < .01.
***p < .001.

Selected Statistics from Fully Recursive Path Model: EFFEMINATE HOMOSEXUAL AND
ALL HETEROSEXUAL WHITE MALES[a]. R = .91.

Variable	Total Effects[b]	Standardized Path Coefficient (ß)	Unstandardized Path Coefficient (b)
Homosexual feelings in childhood	.219	.371***	.063***
Began to feel sexually different in adolescence	.191	.191***	.236***
First homosexual arousal in adolescence	.174	.174***	.236***
Homosexual genital activities in childhood	.109	.066*	.034*
Dislike of boys' activities	.545	.204***	.225***
Felt different for gender reasons, high school	.279	.279***	.285***
Enjoyment of girls' activities	.192	.073***	.089***
Felt different for gender reasons, grade school	.143	.039**	.143**
Identification with father	-.354	-.061***	-.099***
Detached-hostile father	.308	.017***	.084***
Cold father	.199	.051*	.058*
Strong mother	.173	.055*	.017*
Parents had hoped for a daughter	.162	.010*	.153*
Closeness to sister(s)	.158	.005*	.157*
Older sister(s)	.137	.019*	.071*
Weak father	.120	-.021	.064
Mother dominated father	.115	-.044	.069
Broken home	.110	.030	.120
Negative feelings toward mother	.108	.054	.117
Negative image of father	.092	-.052	.056

[a]The fully recursive path model allows paths from every "upstream" variable to each "downstream" variable, including those paths which fail to meet our criteria of statistical and/or substantive significance.

[b]"Total Effects" refers to the sum of all the influences which the given variable would have on adult sexual preference if it had paths to every "downstream" variable in Diagram 4. This value represents the portion of the zero-order correlation (r) which would be accounted for by such an all-possible-paths diagram; the unaccounted-for portion is "extraneous" effects--i.e., those that are spurious or due to variables not included in the model.

*p < .05.
**p < .01.
***p < .001.

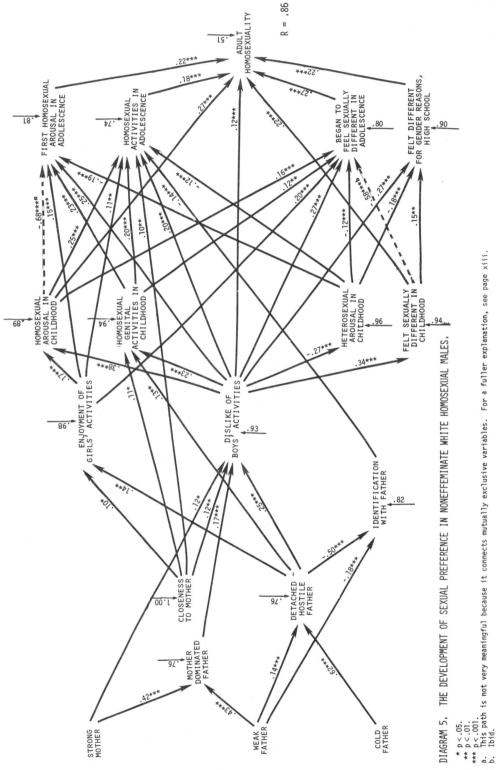

DIAGRAM 5. THE DEVELOPMENT OF SEXUAL PREFERENCE IN NONEFFEMINATE WHITE HOMOSEXUAL MALES.

* p < .05.
** p < .01.
*** p < .001.
a. This path is not very meaningful because it connects mutually exclusive variables. For a fuller explanation, see page xiii.
b. Ibid.

Correlations, Means, and Standard Deviations for Variables in the Model: NONEFFEMINATE HOMOSEXUAL AND ALL HETEROSEXUAL WHITE MALES.

	(1)	(2)	(3)	(4)	(5)	(6)	(7)	(8)	(9)	(10)	(11)	(12)	(13)	(14)	(15)	(16)	(17)	(18)
1 Strong mother		-.24	.17	.50	.07	-.15	-.04	.18	.05	-.12	.10	.13	.14	.16	.06	.19	.03	.21
2 Cold father			.15	-.03	.04	.63	-.40	.16	.07	-.03	.11	.10	.13	.02	.07	.13	.02	.12
3 Weak father				.50	-.08	.27	-.32	.22	.07	-.01	.11	.16	.16	.10	.05	.20	.00	.11
4 Mother dominated father					-.01	-.00	-.15	.23	.10	-.10	.10	.18	.17	.10	.03	.24	.05	.22
5 Closeness to mother						.13	-.06	.16	.12	-.11	.16	.14	.17	.15	.11	.25	.04	.30
6 Detached-hostile father							-.55	.25	.16	-.01	.20	.14	.21	.15	.15	.28	.04	.22
7 Identification with father								-.24	-.16	-.10	-.19	-.14	-.18	.09	-.15	-.31	-.07	-.27
8 Dislike of boys' activities									.27	-.27	.28	.34	.43	-.15	.26	.48	.11	.57
9 Enjoyment of girls' activities										-.11	.13	.17	.28	.36	.24	.30	.08	.37
10 Heterosexual arousal in childhood											-.01	-.14	-.02	.21	-.13	-.22	-.26	-.34
11 Homosexual genital activities in childhood												.31	.54	-.27	-.13	.46	-.05	.44
12 Felt sexually different in childhood													.45	.20	-.32	.32	-.11	.39
13 Homosexual arousal in childhood														.27	.14	.52	-.40	.52
14 Felt different for gender reasons, high school															.20	.42	-.18	.57
15 Began to feel sexually different in adolescence																.35	.31	.45
16 Homosexual activities in adolescence																	.32	.71
17 First homosexual arousal in adolescence																		.28
18 Adult homosexuality																		

Variable Number:	(1)	(2)	(3)	(4)	(5)	(6)	(7)	(8)	(9)	(10)	(11)	(12)	(13)	(14)	(15)	(16)	(17)	(18)
Mean	15.78	2.68	-.14	.92	.36	.04	.19	1.10	.88	.49	1.10	.22	.39	.56	.28	1.39	.21	.53
Standard Deviation	4.57	1.70	1.69	.82	.48	1.85	1.68	1.10	.90	.50	1.68	.41	.49	.50	.45	.88	.40	.50

Effects of Childhood and Adolescent Experiences on the Development of
Adult Homosexuality: NONEFFEMINATE HOMOSEXUAL AND ALL HETEROSEXUAL
WHITE MALES. R = .86.

Variable	Total Effects	Standardized Path Coefficient (β)	Unstandardized Path Coefficient (b)
Began to feel sexually different in adolescence	.272	.272***	.303***
First homosexual arousal in adolescence	.223	.223***	.276***
Homosexual arousal in childhood	.208	.272***	.279***
Homosexual activities in adolescence	.178	.178***	.101***
Heterosexual arousal in childhood	-.134	--	--
Homosexual genital activities in childhood	.121	--	--
Felt sexually different in childhood	.100	.223***	.271***
Dislike of boys' activities	.520	.119***	.054***
Felt different for gender reasons, high school	.223	.223***	.224***
Enjoyment of girls' activities	.143	--	--
Detached-hostile father	.181	--	--
Cold father	.112	--	--
Closeness to mother	.109	--	--
Strong mother	.100	--	--
Mother dominated father	.090	--	--
Weak father	.069	--	--
Identification with father	-.025	--	--

NOTE: "Total Effects" refers to the sum of all the pathways from a given variable to adult
sexual preference which are shown in Diagram 5. This value represents the portion of
the zero-order correlation (r) which is accounted for by the paths in Diagram 5; the
unaccounted-for portion is regarded as "extraneous" effects -- i.e., those which are
spurious or due to variables not included in the model.

***p < .001.

Effects of Earlier Childhood Experiences on Later Childhood and Adolescent
Experiences As Demonstrated in Diagram 5: NONEFFEMINATE HOMOSEXUAL AND ALL
HETEROSEXUAL WHITE MALES.

DEPENDENT VARIABLE: Began to feel sexually different in adolescence (R = .60).

Independent variable	Total Effects	Standardized Path Coefficient (β)	Unstandardized Path Coefficient (b)
Felt sexually different in childhood	-.577	-.577***	-.628***
Homosexual arousal in childhood	.158	.158***	.145***
Homosexual genital activities in childhood	.123	.123**	.033**
Heterosexual arousal in childhood	-.116	-.116***	-.104***
Enjoyment of girls' activities	.224	.196***	.097***
Dislike of boys' activities	.197	.272***	.110***
Detached-hostile father	.098	--	--
Cold father	.061	--	--
Closeness to mother	.060	--	--
Strong mother	.038	--	--
Mother dominated father	.034	--	--
Weak father	.029	--	--
Identification with father	--	--	--

DEPENDENT VARIABLE: First homosexual arousal in adolescence (R = .59).

Independent variable	Total Effects	Standardized Path Coefficient (β)	Unstandardized Path Coefficient (b)
Homosexual arousal in childhood	-.682	-.682***	-.567***
Homosexual genital activities in childhood	.229	.229***	.055***
Heterosexual arousal in childhood	-.187	-.187***	-.151***
Felt sexually different in childhood	--	--	--
Dislike of boys' activities	.087	.246***	.090***
Enjoyment of girls' activities	.036	.155***	.069***
Detached-hostile father	.057	--	--
Closeness to mother	.040	--	--
Cold father	.035	--	--
Strong mother	.017	--	--
Mother dominated father	.015	--	--
Weak father	.015	--	--
Identification with father	--	--	--

DEPENDENT VARIABLE: Homosexual arousal in childhood (R = .46).			
Independent variable	Total Effects	Standardized Path Coefficient (β)	Unstandardized Path Coefficient (b)
Dislike of boys' activities	.383	.383***	.168***
Enjoyment of girls' activities	.175	.175***	.095***
Detached-hostile father	.122	--	--
Cold father	.075	--	--
Strong mother	.073	--	--
Mother dominated father	.066	--	--
Closeness to mother	.064	--	--
Weak father	.046	--	--
Identification with father	--	--	--

DEPENDENT VARIABLE: Homosexual activities in adolescence (R = .67).			
Independent variable	Total Effects	Standardized Path Coefficient (β)	Unstandardized Path Coefficient (b)
Homosexual arousal in childhood	.251	.251***	.453***
Homosexual genital activities in childhood	.203	.203***	.106***
Heterosexual arousal in childhood	-.118	-.118***	-.207***
Felt sexually different in childhood	--	--	--
Dislike of boys' activities	.376	.202***	.161***
Enjoyment of girls' activities	.150	.106**	.103**
Detached-hostile father	.215	--	--
Closeness to mother	.187	.104**	.191**
Identification with father	-.143	-.143***	-.075***
Cold father	.133	--	--
Weak father	.085	--	--
Strong mother	.072	--	--
Mother dominated father	.065	--	--

DEPENDENT VARIABLE: Heterosexual arousal in childhood (R = .27).			
Independent variable	Total Effects	Standardized Path Coefficient (β)	Unstandardized Path Coefficient (b)
Dislike of boys' activities	-.265	-.265***	-.120***
Enjoyment of girls' activities	--	--	--
Detached-hostile father	-.067	--	--
Strong mother	-.051	--	--
Mother dominated father	-.046	--	--
Cold father	-.041	--	--
Closeness to mother	-.032	--	--
Weak father	-.029	--	--
Identification with father	--	--	--

DEPENDENT VARIABLE: Homosexual genital activities in childhood (R = .33).

Independent variable	Total Effects	Standardized Path Coefficient (β)	Unstandardized Path Coefficient (b)
Dislike of boys' activities	.232	.232***	.353***
Enjoyment of girls' activities	--	--	--
Detached-hostile father	.190	.131**	.119**
Closeness to mother	.139	.111*	.391*
Cold father	.117	--	--
Strong mother	.044	--	--
Weak father	.044	--	--
Mother dominated father	.040	--	--
Identification with father	--	--	--

DEPENDENT VARIABLE: Felt sexually different in childhood (R = .34).

Independent variable	Total Effects	Standardized Path Coefficient (β)	Unstandardized Path Coefficient (b)
Dislike of boys' activities	.337	.337***	.125***
Enjoyment of girls' activities	--	--	--
Detached-hostile father	.085	--	--
Strong mother	.057	--	--
Cold father	.053	--	--
Closeness to mother	.041	--	--
Mother dominated father	.040	--	--
Weak father	.029	--	--
Identification with father	--	--	--

DEPENDENT VARIABLE: Dislike of boys' activities (R = .38).

Independent variable	Total Effects	Standardized Path Coefficient (β)	Unstandardized Path Coefficient (b)
Detached-hostile father	.253	.253***	.151***
Strong mother	.191	.118*	.029*
Mother dominated father	.173	.173***	.233***
Cold father	.156	--	--
Closeness to mother	.121	.121**	.278**
Weak father	.111	--	--
Identification with father	--	--	--

DEPENDENT VARIABLE: Felt different for gender reasons, high school (R = .43).

Independent variable	Total Effects	Standardized Path Coefficient (β)	Unstandardized Path Coefficient (b)
Heterosexual arousal in childhood	-.180	-.180***	-.178***
Felt sexually different in childhood	.150	.150**	.150**·
Homosexual genital activities in childhood	--	--	--
Homosexual arousal in childhood	--	--	--
Dislike of boys' activities	.364	.266***	.120***
Enjoyment of girls' activities	--	--	--
Detached-hostile father	.092	--	--
Strong mother	.070	--	--
Mother dominated father	.063	--	--
Cold father	.057	--	--
Closeness to mother	.044	--	--
Weak father	.040	--	--
Identification with father	--	--	--

DEPENDENT VARIABLE: Enjoyment of girls' activities (R = .19).

Independent variable	Total Effects	Standardized Path Coefficient (β)	Unstandardized Path Coefficient (b)
Detached-hostile father	.145	.145**	.071**
Closeness to mother	.100	.100*	.187*
Cold father	.090	--	--
Weak father	.021	--	--
Identification with father	--	--	--
Mother dominated father	--	--	--
Strong mother	--	--	--

DEPENDENT VARIABLE: Detached-hostile father (R = .65).

Independent variable	Total Effects	Standardized Path Coefficient (β)	Unstandardized Path Coefficient (b)
Cold father	.618	.618***	.674***
Weak father	.143	.143***	.159***
Mother dominated father	--	--	--
Strong mother	--	--	--

DEPENDENT VARIABLE: Mother dominated father (R = .65).

Independent variable	Total Effects	Standardized Path Coefficient (β)	Unstandardized Path Coefficient (b)
Weak father	.431	.431***	.209***
Strong mother	.424	.424***	.076***
Cold father	--	--	--

DEPENDENT VARIABLE: Identification with father (R = .58).			
Independent variable	Total Effects	Standardized Path Coefficient (β)	Unstandardized Path Coefficient (b)
Detached-hostile father	-.499	-.499***	-.453***
Cold father	-.308	--	--
Weak father	-.253	-.182***	-.180***
Closeness to mother	--	--	--
Mother dominated father	--	--	--
Strong mother	--	--	--

NOTE: Closeness to Mother does not appear as a dependent variable in this table because the diagram illustrates no antecedents for it.

*p < .05.
**p < .01.
***p < .001.

Selected Statistics from Fully Recursive Path Model: NONEFFEMINATE HOMOSEXUAL
AND ALL HETEROSEXUAL WHITE MALES[a]. R = .87.

Variable	Total Effects[b]	Standardized Path Coefficient (β)	Unstandardized Path Coefficient (b)
Began to feel sexually different in adolescence	.256	.256***	.285***
Heterosexual arousal in childhood	-.202	-.086***	-.202***
First homosexual arousal in adolescence	.195	.195***	.241***
Homosexual arousal in childhood	.187	.234***	.192***
Homosexual genital activities in childhood	.179	.073***	.053***
Homosexual activities in adolescence	.148	.148**	.084**
Felt sexually different in childhood	.066	.199	.081
Dislike of boys' activities	.441	.106***	.199***
Felt different for gender reasons, high school	.203	.203***	.204***
Enjoyment of girls' activities	.200	.045***	.111***
Closeness to mother	.264	.082***	.275***
Strong mother	.238	.010***	.026***
Detached-hostile father	.197	-.044**	.053**
Identification with father	-.175	-.042**	-.052**
Cold father	.166	.023**	.049**
Mother dominated father	.146	.044	.089
Weak father	.049	-.076	.014

[a]The fully recursive path model allows paths from every "upstream" variable to each "downstream" variable, including those paths which fail to meet our criteria of statistical and/or substantive significance.

[b]"Total Effects" refers to the sum of all the influences which the given variable would have on adult sexual preference if it had paths to every "downstream" variable in Diagram 5. This value represents the portion of the zero-order correlation (r) which would be accounted for by such an all-possible-paths diagram; the unaccounted-for portion is "extraneous" effects--i.e., those that are spurious or due to variables not included in the model.

**p < .01.
***p < .001.

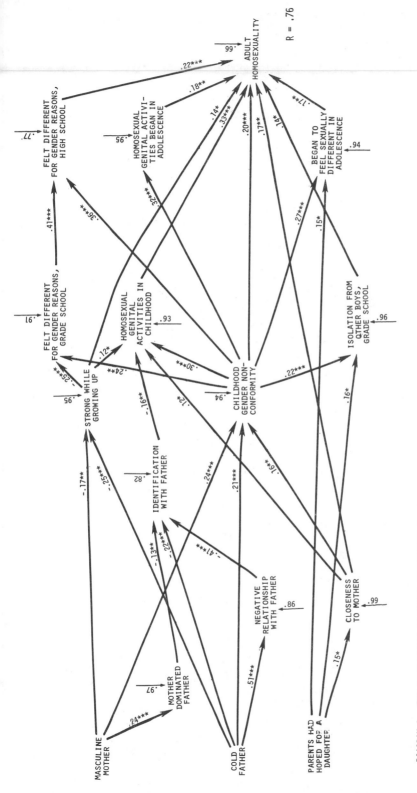

DIAGRAM 6. THE DEVELOPMENT OF SEXUAL PREFERENCE IN BISEXUAL WHITE MALES.

* p < .05.
** p < .01.
*** p < .001.

Correlations, Means, and Standard Deviations for Variables in the Model: BISEXUAL AND HETEROSEXUAL WHITE MALES.

	(1)	(2)	(3)	(4)	(5)	(6)	(7)	(8)	(9)	(10)	(11)	(12)	(13)	(14)	(15)	(16)
1 Cold father		.03	.08	-.01	.51	.03	-.43	-.25	.22	.11	.18	.10	.12	.22	.09	.17
2 Masculine mother			.03	.24	.09	-.04	-.05	-.18	.23	.02	.10	.06	.06	.18	.15	.13
3 Parents had hoped for a daughter				.01	.02	.15	-.06	-.08	.13	.08	.07	.19	-.11	.02	.19	.15
4 Mother dominated father					.06	-.05	-.15	-.13	.14	.12	.06	.05	.06	.18	.02	.17
5 Negative relationship with father						.11	-.52	-.22	.17	.18	.23	.12	.19	.23	.16	.15
6 Closeness to mother							.02	-.03	.15	.16	-.05	.11	.07	.10	.07	.31
7 Identification with father								.13	-.17	-.19	-.04	-.13	-.16	-.11	-.17	-.19
8 Relatively strong while growing up									-.47	-.19	-.36	-.11	-.14	-.30	-.15	-.11
9 Childhood gender nonconformity										.29	.36	.24	.32	.51	.29	.51
10 Homosexual genital activities in childhood											.07	.07	.07	.18	.13	.49
11 Felt different for gender reasons, grade school												.14	.25	.54	.16	.19
12 Isolation from other boys, grade school													.20	.07	.20	.29
13 Homosexual genital activities begun in adolescence														.29	.30	.40
14 Felt different for gender reasons, high school															.13	.44
15 Began to feel sexually different in adolescence																.37
16 Adult homosexuality																

Variable Number:	(1)	(2)	(3)	(4)	(5)	(6)	(7)	(8)	(9)	(10)	(11)	(12)	(13)	(14)	(15)	(16)
Mean	2.58	1.31	.19	.79	1.81	.26	.53	20.36	-.56	.58	.26	-.58	.54	.26	.11	.15
Standard Deviation	1.70	1.27	.50	.82	1.30	.44	1.69	4.74	.53	1.33	.44	1.34	1.22	.44	.32	.35

240

Effects of Childhood and Adolescent Experiences on the Development of Adult Homosexuality: BISEXUAL AND HETEROSEXUAL WHITE MALES. R = .76.

Variable	Total Effects	Standardized Path Coefficient (a)	Unstandardized Path Coefficient (b)
Homosexual genital activities in childhood	.330	.330***	.087***
Homosexual genital activities begun in adolescence	.177	.177**	.051**
Began to feel sexually different in adolescence	.166	.166**	.183**
Childhood gender nonconformity	.534	.199**	.131**
Felt different for gender reasons, high school	.221	.221***	.177***
Felt different for gender reasons, grade school	.091	--	--
Isolation from other boys, grade school	.136	.136*	.036*
Closeness to mother	.294	.172**	.137**
Relatively strong while growing up	.156	.138*	.010*
Masculine mother	.101	--	--
Cold father	.095	--	--
Parents had hoped for a daughter	.090	--	--
Identification with father	-.052	--	--
Negative relationship with father	.021	--	--
Mother dominated father	.007	--	--

NOTE: "Total Effects" refers to the sum of all the pathways from a given variable to adult sexual preference which are shown in Diagram 6. This value represents the portion of the zero-order correlation (r) which is accounted for by the paths in Diagram 6; the unaccounted-for portion is regarded as "extraneous" effects -- i.e., those which are spurious or due to variables not included in the model.

*p < .05.
**p < .01.
***p < .001.

Effects of Earlier Childhood Experiences on Later Childhood and Adolescent Experiences As Demonstrated in Diagram 6: BISEXUAL AND HETEROSEXUAL WHITE MALES.

DEPENDENT VARIABLE: Homosexual genital activities in childhood (R = .36).

Independent variable	Total Effects	Standardized Path Coefficient (β)	Unstandardized Path Coefficient (b)
Childhood gender nonconformity	.304	.304***	.756***
Closeness to mother	.167	.120*	.361*
Identification with father	-.159	-.159**	-.125**
Relatively strong while growing up	.123	.123*	.035*
Cold father	.101	--	--
Negative relationship with father	.064	--	--
Masculine mother	.056	--	--
Parents had hoped for a daughter	.025	--	--
Mother dominated father	.021	--	--

DEPENDENT VARIABLE: Homosexual activities begun in adolescence (R = .32).

Independent variable	Total Effects	Standardized Path Coefficient (β)	Unstandardized Path Coefficient (b)
Homosexual genital activities in childhood	--	--	--
Childhood gender nonconformity	.324	.324***	.738***
Felt different for gender reasons, grade school	--	--	--
Isolation from other boys, grade school	--	--	--
Masculine mother	.076	--	--
Cold father	.067	--	--
Closeness to mother	.050	--	--
Parents had hoped for a daughter	.007	--	--
Relatively strong while growing up	--	--	--
Identification with father	--	--	--
Negative relationship with father	--	--	--
Mother dominated father	--	--	--

DEPENDENT VARIABLE: Began to feel sexually different in adolescence (R = .33).

Independent variable	Total Effects	Standardized Path Coefficient (β)	Unstandardized Path Coefficient (b)
Homosexual genital activities in childhood	--	--	--
Childhood gender nonconformity	.271	.271***	.162***
Felt different for gender reasons, grade school	--	--	--
Isolation from other boys, grade school	--	--	--
Parents had hoped for a daughter	.156	.150*	.096*
Masculine mother	.064	--	--
Cold father	.056	--	--
Closeness to mother	.042	--	--
Relatively strong while growing up	--	--	--
Identification with father	--	--	--
Negative relationship with father	--	--	--
Mother dominated father	--	--	--

DEPENDENT VARIABLE: Childhood gender nonconformity (R = .35).

Independent variable	Total Effects	Standardized Path Coefficient (β)	Unstandardized Path Coefficient (b)
Masculine mother	.236	.236***	.099***
Cold father	.208	.208***	.065***
Closeness to mother	.155	.155**	.188**
Parents had hoped for a daughter	.023	--	--
Identification with father	--	--	--
Negative relationship with father	--	--	--
Mother dominated father	--	--	--

DEPENDENT VARIABLE: Felt different for gender reasons, high school (R = .64).

Independent variable	Total Effects	Standardized Path Coefficient (β)	Unstandardized Path Coefficient (b)
Homosexual genital activities in childhood	--	--	--
Childhood gender nonconformity	.463	.364***	.300***
Felt different for gender reasons, grade school	.414	.414***	.414***
Isolation from other boys, grade school	--	--	--
Masculine mother	.127	--	--
Cold father	.122	--	--
Relatively strong while growing up	-.104	--	--
Closeness to mother	.072	--	--
Parents had hoped for a daughter	.011	--	--
Identification with father	--	--	--
Negative relationship with father	--	--	--
Mother dominated father	--	--	--

DEPENDENT VARIABLE: Felt different for gender reasons, grade school (R = .42).

Independent variable	Total Effects	Standardized Path Coefficient (β)	Unstandardized Path Coefficient (b)
Childhood gender nonconformity	.239	.239**	.197**
Relatively strong while growing up	-.251	-.251**	-.023**
Cold father	.111	--	--
Masculine mother	.100	--	--
Closeness to mother	.037	--	--
Parents had hoped for a daughter	.005	--	--
Identification with father	--	--	--
Negative relationship with father	--	--	--
Mother dominated father	--	--	--

DEPENDENT VARIABLE: Isolation from other boys, grade school (R = .29).

Independent variable	Total Effects	Standardized Path Coefficient (β)	Unstandardized Path Coefficient (b)
Childhood gender nonconformity	.219	.219***	.551***
Parents had hoped for a daughter	.166	.161*	.433*
Masculine mother	.052	--	--
Cold father	.046	--	--
Closeness to mother	.034	--	--
Relatively strong while growing up	--	--	--
Identification with father	--	--	--
Negative relationship with father	--	--	--
Mother dominated father	--	--	--

DEPENDENT VARIABLE: Closeness to mother (R = .15).

Independent variable	Total Effects	Standardized Path Coefficient (β)	Unstandardized Path Coefficient (b)
Parents had hoped for a daughter	.147	.147*	.130*
Mother dominated father	--	--	--
Cold father	--	--	--
Masculine mother	--	--	--

DEPENDENT VARIABLE: Relatively strong while growing up (R = .30).

Independent variable	Total Effects	Standardized Path Coefficient (β)	Unstandardized Path Coefficient (b)
Cold father	-.246	-.246***	-.684***
Masculine mother	-.172	-.172**	-.643**
Identification with father	--	--	--
Negative relationship with father	--	--	--
Closeness to mother	--	--	--
Mother dominated father	--	--	--
Parents had hoped for a daughter	--	--	--

DEPENDENT VARIABLE: Identification with father (R = .57).			
Independent variable	Total Effects	Standardized Path Coefficient (β)	Unstandardized Path Coefficient (b)
Cold father	-.428	-.221***	-.220***
Negative relationship with father	-.403	-.403***	-.525***
Mother dominated father	-.131	-.131**	-.269**
Masculine mother	-.032	--	--
Closeness to mother	--	--	--
Parents had hoped for a daughter	--	--	--

DEPENDENT VARIABLE: Negative relationship with father (R = .51).			
Independent variable	Total Effects	Standardized Path Coefficient (β)	Unstandardized Path Coefficient (b)
Cold father	.513	.513***	.391***
Mother dominated father	--	--	--
Masculine mother	--	--	--
Parents had hoped for a daughter	--	--	--

DEPENDENT VARIABLE: Mother dominated father (R = .24).			
Independent variable	Total Effects	Standardized Path Coefficient (β)	Unstandardized Path Coefficient (b)
Masculine mother	.242	.242***	.157***
Cold father	--	--	--
Parents had hoped for a daughter	--	--	--

*p < .05.
**p < .01.
***p < .001.

Selected Statistics from Fully Recursive Path Model: BISEXUAL AND HETEROSEXUAL
WHITE MALES[a]. R = .77.

Variable	Total Effects[b]	Standardized Path Coefficient (β)	Unstandardized Path Coefficient (b)
Homosexual genital activities in childhood	.330	.329***	.088***
Homosexual genital activities begun in adolescence	.190	.190*	.055*
Began to feel sexually different in adolescence	.176	.176*	.194*
Childhood gender nonconformity	.503	.180***	.332***
Felt different for gender reasons, high school	.244	.244**	.196**
Felt different for gender reasons, grade school	.082	-.060	.066
Isolation from other boys, grade school	.155	.140*	.041*
Closeness to mother	.304	.184***	.243***
Relatively strong while growing up	.186	.127*	.014*
Cold father	.160	.079	.033
Mother dominated father	.152	.071	.065
Identification with father	-.127	-.027	-.026
Masculine mother	.119	.013	.033
Negative relationship with father	.014	-.118	.004

[a]The fully recursive path model allows paths from every "upstream" variable to each "down-stream" variable, including those paths which fail to meet our criteria of statistical and/or substantive significance.

[b]"Total Effects" refers to the sum of all the influences which the given variable would have on adult sexual preference if it had paths to every "downstream" variable in Diagram 6. This value represents the portion of the zero-order correlation (r) which would be accounted for by such an all-possible-paths diagram; the unaccounted-for portion is "extraneous" effects--i.e., those that are spurious or due to variables not included in the model.

*p < .05.
**p < .01.
***p < .001.

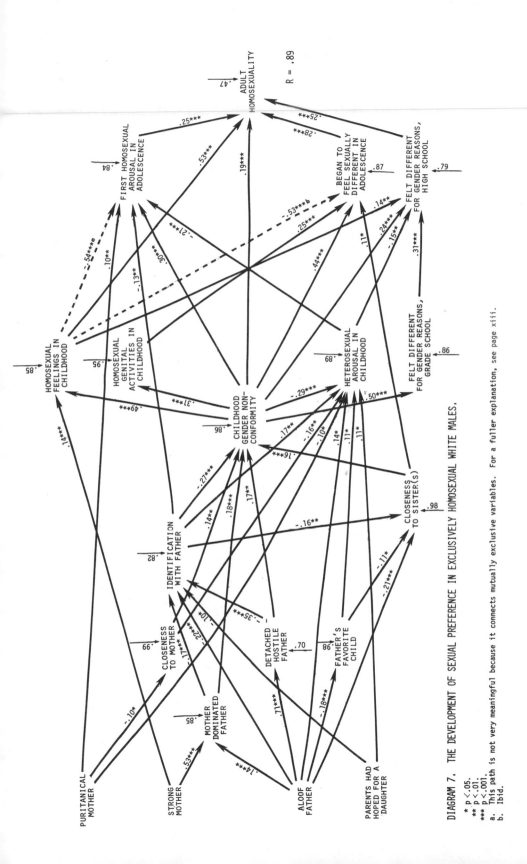

DIAGRAM 7. THE DEVELOPMENT OF SEXUAL PREFERENCE IN EXCLUSIVELY HOMOSEXUAL WHITE MALES.

* p < .05.
** p < .01.
*** p < .001.
a. This path is not very meaningful because it connects mutually exclusive variables. For a fuller explanation, see page xiii.
b. Ibid.

Correlations, Means, and Standard Deviations for Variables in the Model: EXCLUSIVELY HOMOSEXUAL AND ALL HETEROSEXUAL WHITE MALES.

Variable Number:	(1)	(2)	(3)	(4)	(5)	(6)	(7)	(8)	(9)	(10)	(11)	(12)	(13)	(14)	(15)	(16)	(17)	(18)	(19)
1 Parents had hoped for a daughter		.01	-.02	.11	.09	-.07	.09	.02	-.12	.11	.17	.15	.01	.11	.10	.13	.03	.04	.14
2 "Puritanical" mother			.01	.11	.04	-.03	-.10	.07	-.03	-.03	.02	-.05	-.09	.05	.03	.04	.11	.05	.14
3 Aloof father				-.15	.06	-.18	.02	.71	-.48	-.11	.25	.16	-.04	-.07	.10	.10	.11	.14	.18
4 Strong mother					.51	-.06	.10	-.15	-.02	.12	.15	.00	-.12	.14	.21	.04	-.04	.10	.21
5 Mother dominated father						-.07	.03	.00	-.19	.06	.25	-.11	-.10	.09	.23	-.11	.02	-.17	.22
6 Was father's favorite child							-.10	-.26	.21	-.11	-.20	.11	.19	-.07	-.14	.03	-.06	-.21	-.21
7 Closeness to mother								.09	-.06	.04	.18	.10	-.21	.10	.14	.14	.07	.11	.25
8 Detached-hostile father									-.51	-.07	.31	.13	-.11	.16	.19	.16	.11	.13	.25
9 Identification with father										-.09	-.41	-.18	.25	-.21	-.27	-.15	-.16	-.29	-.43
10 Closeness to sister(s)											.19	.08	-.14	.14	.14	.15	.02	.03	.19
11 Childhood gender nonconformity												.50	-.36	.31	.51	.27	.16	.52	.71
12 Felt different for gender reasons, grade school													-.20	.06	.21	.14	.08	.49	.40
13 Heterosexual arousal in childhood														-.13	-.22	-.17	-.24	-.33	-.47
14 Homosexual genital activities in childhood															.56	.11	-.11	.21	.45
15 Homosexual feelings in childhood																-.15	-.30	.36	.60
16 Began to feel sexually different in adolescence																	.33	.20	.38
17 First homosexual arousal in adolescence																		.18	.26
18 Felt different for gender reasons, high school																			.64
19 Adult homosexuality																			
Mean	.22	1.35	.02	15.83	.92	.23	.33	.01	-.10	.48	-.10	.51	.43	1.08	.00	.24	.19	.61	.53
Standard Deviation	.49	2.03	4.52	4.87	.83	.42	.47	1.85	1.75	.50	.78	.50	.50	1.62	1.73	.43	.39	.49	.50

Effects of Childhood and Adolescent Experiences on the Development of Adult
Homosexuality: EXCLUSIVELY HOMOSEXUAL AND ALL HETEROSEXUAL WHITE MALES.
R = .89.

Variable	Total Effects	Standardized Path Coefficient (β)	Unstandardized Path Coefficient (b)
Homosexual feelings in childhood	.281	.529***	.153***
Began to feel sexually different in adolescence	.276	.276***	.324***
First homosexual arousal in adolescence	.254	.254***	.321***
Heterosexual arousal in childhood	-.091	--	--
Homosexual genital activities in childhood	.070	--	--
Childhood gender nonconformity	.675	.191***	.124***
Felt different for gender reasons, high school	.250	.250***	.256***
Felt different for gender reasons, grade school	.076	--	--
Identification with father	-.250	--	--
Detached-hostile father	.204	--	--
Aloof father	.186	--	--
Mother dominated father	.166	--	--
Closeness to sister(s)	.140	--	--
Strong mother	.127	--	--
Closeness to mother	.107	--	--
Was father's favorite child	-.026	--	--
"Puritanical" mother	.024	--	--
Parents had hoped for a daughter	.016	--	--

NOTE: "Total Effects" refers to the sum of all the pathways from a given variable to adult
sexual preference which are shown in Diagram 7. This value represents the portion of
the zero-order correlation (r) which is accounted for by the paths in Diagram 7; the
unaccounted-for portion is regarded as "extraneous" effects--i.e., those which are
spurious or due to variables not included in the model.

***p < .001.

Effects of Earlier Childhood Experiences on Later Childhood and Adolescent Experiences As Demonstrated in Diagram 7: EXCLUSIVELY HOMOSEXUAL AND ALL HETEROSEXUAL WHITE MALES.

DEPENDENT VARIABLE: Homosexual feelings in childhood (R = .53).

Independent Variable	Total Effects	Standardized Path Coefficient (β)	Unstandardized Path Coefficient (b)
Childhood gender nonconformity	.490	.490***	1.099***
Strong mother	.200	.140***	.050***
Identification with father	-.144	--	--
Detached-hostile father	.135	--	--
Aloof father	.129	--	--
Mother dominated father	.114	--	--
Closeness to sister(s)	.080	--	--
Closeness to mother	.068	--	--
Parents had hoped for a daughter	-.015	--	--
Was father's favorite child	-.009	--	--
"Puritanical" mother	-.007	--	--

DEPENDENT VARIABLE: Began to feel sexually different in adolescence (R = .49).

Independent Variable	Total Effects	Standardized Path Coefficient (β)	Unstandardized Path Coefficient (b)
Homosexual feelings in childhood	-.529	-.529***	-.130***
Homosexual genital activities in childhood	.252	.252***	.066***
Heterosexual arousal in childhood	--	--	--
Childhood gender nonconformity	.260	.441***	.243***
Felt different for gender reasons, grade school	--	--	--
Closeness to sister(s)	.150	.108*	.092*
Identification with father	-.094	--	--
Detached-hostile father	.078	--	--
Mother dominated father	.064	--	--
Aloof father	.057	--	--
Strong mother	-.040	--	--
Closeness to mother	.036	--	--
Was father's favorite child	-.016	--	--
Parents had hoped for a daughter	.010	--	--
"Puritanical" mother	-.004	--	--

DEPENDENT VARIABLE: First homosexual arousal in adolescence (R = .54).

Independent Variable	Total Effects	Standardized Path Coefficient (β)	Unstandardized Path Coefficient (b)
Homosexual feelings in childhood	-.538	-.538***	-.123***
Heterosexual arousal in childhood	-.212	-.212***	-.169***
Homosexual genital activities in childhood	--	--	--
Childhood gender nonconformity	.098	.301***	.154***
Felt different for gender reasons, grade school	--	--	--
Identification with father	-.192	-.127**	-.029**
"Puritanical" mother	.117	.100**	.020**
Detached-hostile father	.084	--	--
Aloof father	.081	--	--
Mother dominated father	.051	--	--
Strong mother	-.048	--	--
Closeness to mother	.047	--	--
Was father's favorite child	-.026	--	--
Closeness to sister(s)	.016	--	--
Parents had hoped for a daughter	-.004	--	--

DEPENDENT VARIABLE: Heterosexual arousal in childhood (R = .45).

Independent Variable	Total Effects	Standardized Path Coefficient (β)	Unstandardized Path Coefficient (b)
Childhood gender nonconformity	-.288	-.288***	-.184***
Identification with father	.255	.171**	.048**
Closeness to mother	-.197	-.157**	-.166**
Detached-hostile father	-.139	--	--
Was father's favorite child	.119	.114*	.135*
Mother dominated father	-.096	--	--
Parents had hoped for a daughter	.083	.110*	.111*
"Puritanical" mother	-.082	-.102*	-.025*
Strong mother	-.051	--	--
Closeness to sister(s)	-.047	--	--
Aloof father	.039	.141*	.002*

DEPENDENT VARIABLE: Homosexual genital activities in childhood (R = .31).			
Independent Variable	Total Effects	Standardized Path Coefficient (β)	Unstandardized Path Coefficient (b)
Childhood gender nonconformity	.310	.310***	.652***
Identification with father	-.091	--	--
Detached-hostile father	.085	--	--
Aloof father	.081	--	--
Mother dominated father	.072	--	--
Closeness to sister(s)	.051	--	--
Closeness to mother	.043	--	--
Strong mother	.038	--	--
Parents had hoped for a daughter	.009	--	--
Was father's favorite child	-.006	--	--
"Puritanical" mother	-.004	--	--

DEPENDENT VARIABLE: Childhood gender nonconformity (R = .51).			
Independent Variable	Total Effects	Standardized Path Coefficient (β)	Unstandardized Path Coefficient (b)
Identification with father	-.293	-.266***	-.117***
Detached-hostile father	.275	.172**	.072**
Aloof father	.262	--	--
Mother dominated father	.233	.183***	.171***
Closeness to sister(s)	.163	.163***	.251***
Closeness to mother	.138	.138**	.227**
Strong mother	.123	--	--
Parents had hoped for a daughter	.030	--	--
Was father's favorite child	-.018	--	--
"Puritanical" mother	-.014	--	--

DEPENDENT VARIABLE: Felt different for gender reasons, high school (R = .62).			
Independent Variable	Total Effects	Standardized Path Coefficient (β)	Unstandardized Path Coefficient (b)
Heterosexual arousal in childhood	-.149	-.149**	-.147**
Homosexual feelings in childhood	.143	.143**	.040**
Homosexual genital activities in childhood	--	--	--
Childhood gender nonconformity	.511	.244***	.154***
Felt different for gender reasons, grade school	.305	.305***	.297***
Identification with father	-.175	--	--
Detached-hostile father	.149	--	--
Aloof father	.128	--	--
Mother dominated father	.123	--	--
Closeness to mother	.094	--	--
Strong mother	.085	--	--
Closeness to sister(s)	.083	--	--
Was father's favorite child	-.026	--	--
"Puritanical" mother	.006	--	--
Parents had hoped for a daughter	.002	--	--

DEPENDENT VARIABLE: Felt different for gender reasons, grade school (R = .50).

Independent Variable	Total Effects	Standardized Path Coefficient (β)	Unstandardized Path Coefficient (b)
Childhood gender nonconformity	.504	.504***	.327***
Identification with father	-.148	--	--
Detached-hostile father	.138	--	--
Aloof father	.132	--	--
Mother dominated father	.117	--	--
Closeness to sister(s)	.082	--	--
Closeness to mother	.070	--	--
Strong mother	.062	--	--
Parents had hoped for a daughter	.015	--	--
Was father's favorite child	-.009	--	--
"Puritanical" mother	-.007	--	--

DEPENDENT VARIABLE: Identification with father (R = .58).

Independent Variable	Total Effects	Standardized Path Coefficient (β)	Unstandardized Path Coefficient (b)
Aloof father	-.496	-.224***	-.010***
Detached-hostile father	-.350	-.350***	-.330***
Mother dominated father	-.170	-.170***	-.359***
Parents had hoped for a daughter	-.104	-.104*	-.373*
Strong mother	-.090	--	--
Closeness to mother	--	--	--
Was father's favorite child	--	--	--
"Puritanical" mother	--	--	--

DEPENDENT VARIABLE: Detached-hostile father (R = .71).

Independent Variable	Total Effects	Standardized Path Coefficient (β)	Unstandardized Path Coefficient (b)
Aloof father	.710	.710***	.032***
Mother dominated father	--	--	--
"Puritanical" mother	--	--	--
Parents had hoped for a daughter	--	--	--
Strong mother	--	--	--

DEPENDENT VARIABLE: Mother dominated father (R = .53).

Independent Variable	Total Effects	Standardized Path Coefficient (β)	Unstandardized Path Coefficient (b)
Strong mother	.529	.529***	.090***
Aloof father	.136	.136***	.003***
"Puritanical" mother	--	--	--
Parents had hoped for a daughter	--	--	--

DEPENDENT VARIABLE: Closeness to sister(s) (R = .22).			
Independent Variable	Total Effects	Standardized Path Coefficient (β)	Unstandardized Path Coefficient (b)
Identification with father	-.165	-.165**	-.047**
Was father's favorite child	-.109	-.109*	-.130*
Aloof father	-.105	-.206***	-.003***
Detached-hostile father	.058	--	--
Mother dominated father	.028	--	--
Parents had hoped for a daughter	.017	--	--
Strong mother	.015	--	--
Closeness to mother	--	--	--
"Puritanical" mother	--	--	--

DEPENDENT VARIABLE: Closeness to mother (R = .10).			
Independent Variable	Total Effects	Standardized Path Coefficient (β)	Unstandardized Path Coefficient (b)
"Puritanical" mother	-.100	-.100*	-.023*
Mother dominated father	--	--	--
Aloof father	--	--	--
Strong mother	--	--	--
Parents had hoped for a daughter	--	--	--

DEPENDENT VARIABLE: Was father's favorite child (R = .18).			
Independent Variable	Total Effects	Standardized Path Coefficient (β)	Unstandardized Path Coefficient (b)
Aloof father	-.176	-.176***	-.002***
Mother dominated father	--	--	--
"Puritanical" mother	--	--	--
Parents had hoped for a daughter	--	--	--
Strong mother	--	--	--

*p < .05.
**p < .01.
***p < .001.

Selected Statistics from Fully Recursive Path Model: EXCLUSIVELY HOMOSEXUAL
AND ALL HETEROSEXUAL WHITE MALES[a]. R = .90.

Variable	Total Effects[b]	Standardized Path Coefficient (β)	Unstandardized Path Coefficient (b)
Began to feel sexually different in adolescence	.254	.254***	.298***
Homosexual feelings in childhood	.217	.447***	.063***
First homosexual arousal in adolescence	.209	.209***	.264***
Heterosexual arousal in childhood	-.185	-.091***	-.187***
Homosexual genital activities in childhood	.142	.064**	.044**
Childhood gender nonconformity	.594	.151***	.384***
Felt different for gender reasons, high school	.218	.218***	.224***
Felt different for gender reasons, grade school	.107	.044*	.107*
Identification with father	-.354	-.081***	-.101***
Strong mother	.225	.044***	.023***
Closeness to mother	.212	.090***	.226***
Aloof father	.210	-.004**	.003**
Detached-hostile father	.187	-.039*	.051*
"Puritanical" mother	.135	.083*	.033*
Closeness to sister(s)	.129	.014*	.129*
Was father's favorite child	-.121	.004	-.144
Mother dominated father	.114	-.024	.069
Parents had hoped for a daughter	.114	-.018	.116

[a]The fully recursive path model allows paths from every "upstream" variable to each "downstream" variable, including those paths which fail to meet our criteria of statistical
and/or substantive significance.

[b]"Total Effects" refers to the sum of all the influences which the given variable would have
on adult sexual preference if it had paths to every "downstream" variable in Diagram 7.
This value represents the portion of the zero-order correlation (r) which would be accounted
for by such an all-possible-paths diagram; the unaccounted-for portion is "extraneous"
effects--i.e., those that are spurious or due to variables not included in the model.

*p < .05.
**p < .01.
***p < .001.

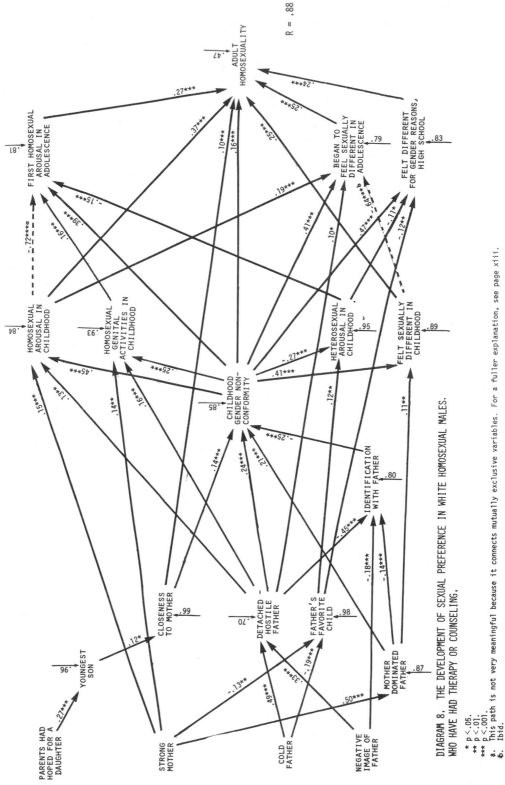

DIAGRAM 8. THE DEVELOPMENT OF SEXUAL PREFERENCE IN WHITE HOMOSEXUAL MALES, WHO HAVE HAD THERAPY OR COUNSELING.

* p < .05.
** p < .01.
*** p < .001.
a. This path is not very meaningful because it connects mutually exclusive variables. For a fuller explanation, see page xiii.
b. Ibid.

Correlations, Means, and Standard Deviations for Variables in the Model: WHITE HOMOSEXUAL MALES WHO HAVE HAD THERAPY OR COUNSELING AND ALL HETEROSEXUAL MALES.

Variable	(2)	(3)	(4)	(5)	(6)	(7)	(8)	(9)	(10)	(11)	(12)	(13)	(14)	(15)	(16)	(17)	(18)	(19)
1 Negative image of father	.49	-.07	.02	.05	-.01	.57	-.12	.02	-.44	.24	.10	.15	.13	-.05	.08	.08	.19	.23
2 Cold father		-.21	-.01	-.02	-.07	.65	-.16	.06	-.38	.27	.10	.14	.16	-.04	.09	.07	.11	.24
3 Strong mother			.04	.50	.08	-.14	-.09	.05	-.03	.13	.15	.19	.13	-.09	-.02	.06	.14	.20
4 Parents had hoped for a daughter				.01	.27	.05	-.06	.04	-.11	.16	.08	.12	.05	.00	.02	.11	.11	.12
5 Mother dominated father					.03	.02	-.08	-.03	-.16	.25	.12	.22	.21	-.09	.02	.03	.19	.24
6 Was the youngest son						-.03	.01	.12	-.04	.12	.11	.12	.06	-.10	.02	.04	.14	.12
7 Detached-hostile father							-.24	.11	-.56	.40	.24	.29	.25	-.13	.08	.16	.19	.38
8 Was father's favorite child								-.08	.22	-.21	-.06	-.13	-.10	.18	-.06	-.12	-.24	-.19
9 Closeness to mother									-.06	-.18	-.06	-.14	-.12	-.14	-.04	-.07	.10	.27
10 Identification with father										-.43	-.22	-.24	-.24	-.21	-.11	-.16	-.24	-.40
11 Childhood gender nonconformity											.33	.52	.44	-.29	.11	.27	.53	.70
12 Homosexual genital activities in childhood												.58	.38	-.07	-.12	.08	.18	.45
13 Homosexual arousal in childhood													.48	-.09	-.41	.13	.33	.59
14 Felt sexually different in childhood														-.19	-.11	-.35	.26	.45
15 Heterosexual arousal in childhood															-.21	-.10	-.26	-.36
16 First homosexual arousal in adolescence																.30	.14	.22
17 Began to feel sexually different in adolescence																	.21	.40
18 Felt different for gender reasons, high school																		.61
19 Adult homosexuality																		

Variable Number:	(1)	(2)	(3)	(4)	(5)	(6)	(7)	(8)	(9)	(10)	(11)	(12)	(13)	(14)	(15)	(16)	(17)	(18)	(19)
Mean	1.29	2.92	15.87	.22	.94	.40	1.85	.23	.34	-.11	-.08	1.15	.43	.26	.48	.18	.25	.61	.54
Standard Deviation	.82	1.74	4.93	.52	.84	.49	1.85	.42	.48	1.77	.77	1.71	.50	.44	.50	.38	.44	.49	.50

257

Effects of Childhood and Adolescent Experiences on the Development of Adult Homosexuality: WHITE HOMOSEXUAL MALES WHO HAVE HAD THERAPY OR COUNSELING AND ALL WHITE HETEROSEXUAL MALES. R = .88.

Variable	Total Effects	Standardized Path Coefficient (β)	Unstandardized Path Coefficient (b)
First homosexual arousal in adolescence	.270	.270***	.353***
Began to feel sexually different in adolescence	.255	.255***	.291***
Homosexual arousal in childhood	.225	.369***	.371***
Felt sexually different in childhood	.084	.248***	.282***
Heterosexual arousal in childhood	-.066	--	--
Homosexual genital activities in childhood	.043	--	--
Childhood gender nonconformity	.646	.156***	.100***
Felt different for gender reasons, high school	.243	.243***	.249***
Detached-hostile father	.291	--	--
Closeness to mother	.197	.105***	.110***
Mother dominated father	.167	--	--
Identification with father	-.161	--	--
Cold father	.151	--	--
Strong mother	.127	--	--
Negative image of father	.124	--	--
Was father's favorite child	-.038	--	--
Was the youngest son	.024	--	--
Parents had hoped for a daughter	.006	--	--

NOTE: "Total Effects" refers to the sum of all the pathways from a given variable to adult sexual preference which are shown in Diagram 8. This value represents the portion of the zero-order correlation (r) which is accounted for by the paths in Diagram 8; the unaccounted-for portion is regarded as "extraneous" effects--i.e., those which are spurious or due to variables not included in the model.

***p < .001.

Effects of Earlier Childhood Experiences on Later Childhood and Adolescent
Experiences as Demonstrated in Diagram 8: WHITE HOMOSEXUAL MALES WHO HAVE
HAD THERAPY OR COUNSELING AND ALL WHITE HETEROSEXUAL MALES.

DEPENDENT VARIABLE: First homosexual arousal in adolescence (R = .59).

Independent variable	Total Effects	Standardized Path Coefficient (β)	Unstandardized Path Coefficient (b)
Homosexual arousal in childhood	-.717	-.717***	-.553***
Homosexual genital activities in childhood	.160	.160***	.036***
Heterosexual arousal in childhood	-.150	-.150***	-.115***
Felt sexually different in childhood	--	--	--
Childhood gender nonconformity	.310	.391***	.193***
Identification with father	-.077	--	--
Mother dominated father	.076	--	--
Closeness to mother	.044	--	--
Detached-hostile father	.043	--	--
Strong mother	-.042	--	--
Negative image of father	.028	--	--
Cold father	.025	--	--
Was father's favorite child	-.018	--	--
Was the youngest son	.005	--	--
Parents had hoped for a daughter	.001	--	--

DEPENDENT VARIABLE: Began to feel sexually different in adolescence (R = .61).

Independent variable	Total Effects	Standardized Path Coefficient (β)	Unstandardized Path Coefficient (b)
Felt sexually different in childhood	-.644	-.644***	-.639***
Homosexual arousal in childhood	.193	.193***	.170***
Homosexual genital activities in childhood	--	--	--
Heterosexual arousal in childhood	--	--	--
Childhood gender nonconformity	.235	.412***	.232***
Detached-hostile father	.208	.100*	.023*
Cold father	.103	--	--
Negative image of father	.078	--	--
Identification with father	-.059	--	--
Closeness to mother	.033	--	--
Strong mother	.022	--	--
Mother dominated father	-.011	--	--
Was the youngest son	.004	--	--
Parents had hoped for a daughter	.001	--	--
Was father's favorite child	--	--	--

DEPENDENT VARIABLE: Homosexual arousal in childhood (R = .55).			
Independent variable	Total Effects	Standardized Path Coefficient (β)	Unstandardized Path Coefficient (b)
Childhood gender nonconformity	.452	.452***	.290***
Detached-hostile father	.289	.129**	.035**
Strong mother	.201	.145***	.015***
Cold father	.143	--	--
Negative image of father	.114	--	--
Identification with father	-.113	--	--
Mother dominated father	.111	--	--
Closeness to mother	.064	--	--
Was the youngest son	.008	--	--
Parents had hoped for a daughter	.002	--	--
Was father's favorite child	--	--	--

DEPENDENT VARIABLE: Felt sexually different in childhood (R = .45).			
Independent variable	Total Effects	Standardized Path Coefficient (β)	Unstandardized Path Coefficient (b)
Childhood gender nonconformity	.411	.411***	.234***
Mother dominated father	.207	.107**	.057**
Detached-hostile father	.146	--	--
Strong mother	.104	--	--
Identification with father	-.102	--	--
Cold father	.072	--	--
Negative image of father	.066	--	--
Closeness to mother	.058	--	--
Was the youngest son	.007	--	--
Parents had hoped for a daughter	.002	--	--
Was father's favorite child	--	--	--

DEPENDENT VARIABLE: Heterosexual arousal in childhood (R = .31).			
Independent variable	Total Effects	Standardized Path Coefficient (β)	Unstandardized Path Coefficient (b)
Childhood gender nonconformity	-.265	-.265***	-.172***
Was father's favorite child	.120	.120**	.143**
Identification with father	.066	--	--
Mother dominated father	-.065	--	--
Strong mother	-.048	--	--
Closeness to mother	-.038	--	--
Cold father	-.038	--	--
Detached-hostile father	-.030	--	--
Negative image of father	-.022	--	--
Was the youngest son	-.005	--	--
Parents had hoped for a daughter	-.001	--	--

DEPENDENT VARIABLE: Homosexual genital activities in childhood (R = .38).

Independent variable	Total Effects	Standardized Path Coefficient (β)	Unstandardized Path Coefficient (b)
Childhood gender nonconformity	.251	.251***	.554***
Detached-hostile father	.250	.161***	.149***
Strong mother	.167	.137**	.047**
Cold father	.124	--	--
Negative image of father	.093	--	--
Identification with father	-.062	--	--
Mother dominated father	.061	--	--
Closeness to mother	.036	--	--
Was the youngest son	.004	--	--
Parents had hoped for a daughter	.001	--	--
Was father's favorite child	--	--	--

DEPENDENT VARIABLE: Childhood gender nonconformity (R = .53).

Independent variable	Total Effects	Standardized Path Coefficient (β)	Unstandardized Path Coefficient (b)
Detached-hostile father	.355	.242***	.101***
Identification with father	-.249	-.249***	-.109***
Mother dominated father	.245	.210***	.195***
Cold father	.175	--	--
Negative image of father	.160	--	--
Closeness to mother	.142	.142***	.231***
Strong mother	.122	--	--
Was the youngest son	.018	--	--
Parents had hoped for a daughter	.005	--	--
Was father's favorite child	--	--	--

DEPENDENT VARIABLE: Felt different for gender reasons, high school (R = .56).

Independent variable	Total Effects	Standardized Path Coefficient (β)	Unstandardized Path Coefficient (b)
Heterosexual arousal in childhood	-.105	-.105*	-.103*
Homosexual genital activities in childhood	--	--	--
Homosexual arousal in childhood	--	--	--
Felt sexually different in childhood	--	--	--
Childhood gender nonconformity	.501	.473***	.299***
Detached-hostile father	.178	--	--
Was father's favorite child	-.135	-.122**	-.142**
Identification with father	-.125	--	--
Mother dominated father	.123	--	--
Cold father	.113	--	--
Negative image of father	.080	--	--
Strong mother	.079	--	--
Closeness to mother	.071	--	--
Was the youngest son	.009	--	--
Parents had hoped for a daughter	.002	--	--

DEPENDENT VARIABLE: Detached-hostile father (R = .71).			
Independent variable	Total Effects	Standardized Path Coefficient (β)	Unstandardized Path Coefficient (b)
Cold father	.494	.494***	.527***
Negative image of father	.326	.326***	.735***
Mother dominated father	--	--	--
Was the youngest son	--	--	--
Strong mother	--	--	--
Parents had hoped for a daughter	--	--	--

DEPENDENT VARIABLE: Closeness to mother (R = .12).			
Independent variable	Total Effects	Standardized Path Coefficient (β)	Unstandardized Path Coefficient (b)
Was the youngest son	.124	.124*	.120*
Parents had hoped for a daughter	.033	--	--
Mother dominated father	--	--	--
Strong mother	--	--	--
Cold father	--	--	--
Negative image of father	--	--	--

DEPENDENT VARIABLE: Mother dominated father (R = .50).			
Independent variable	Total Effects	Standardized Path Coefficient (β)	Unstandardized Path Coefficient (b)
Strong mother	.500	.500***	.085***
Cold father	--	--	--
Negative image of father	--	--	--
Parents had hoped for a daughter	--	--	--

DEPENDENT VARIABLE: Identification with father (R = .59).			
Independent variable	Total Effects	Standardized Path Coefficient (β)	Unstandardized Path Coefficient (b)
Detached-hostile father	-.452	-.452***	-.431***
Negative image of father	-.326	-.179***	-.383***
Cold father	-.223	--	--
Mother dominated father	-.139	-.139***	-.294***
Strong mother	-.070	--	--
Was father's favorite child	--	--	--
Closeness to mother	--	--	--
Was the youngest son	--	--	--
Parents had hoped for a daughter	--	--	--

DEPENDENT VARIABLE: Was father's favorite child (R = .21).			
Independent variable	Total Effects	Standardized Path Coefficient (β)	Unstandardized Path Coefficient (b)
Cold father	-.188	-.188***	-.046***
Strong mother	-.131	-.131**	-.011**
Mother dominated father	--	--	--
Was the youngest son	--	--	--
Negative image of father	--	--	--
Parents had hoped for a daughter	--	--	--

DEPENDENT VARIABLE: Was the youngest son (R = .27).			
Independent variable	Total Effects	Standardized Path Coefficient (β)	Unstandardized Path Coefficient (b)
Parents had hoped for a daughter	.268	.268***	.254***
Cold father	--	--	--
Strong mother	--	--	--
Negative image of father	--	--	--

*p < .05.
**p < .01.
***p < .001.

Selected Statistics from Fully Recursive Path Model: WHITE HOMOSEXUAL MALES WHO HAVE HAD THERAPY OR COUNSELING AND ALL WHITE HETEROSEXUAL MALES.[a] R = .90.

Variable	Total Effects [b]	Standardized Path Coefficient (β)	Unstandardized Path Coefficient (b)
Began to feel sexually different in adolescence	.245	.245***	.280***
First homosexual arousal in adolescence	.240	.240***	.313***
Homosexual arousal in childhood	.205	.323***	.206***
Heterosexual arousal in childhood	-.166	-.086***	-.166***
Homosexual genital activities in childhood	.123	.073**	.036**
Felt sexually different in childhood	.043	.215	.049
Childhood gender nonconformity	.579	.126***	.374***
Felt different for gender reasons, high school	.250	.250***	.256***
Detached-hostile father	.323	-.001***	.087***
Strong mother	.257	.054***	.026***
Cold father	.237	.054***	.068***
Identification with father	-.215	-.060***	-.061***
Closeness to mother	.208	.102***	.218***
Mother dominated father	.141	-.015*	.084*
Negative image of father	.128	-.021*	.078*
Parents had hoped for a daughter	.105	-.020	.102
Was the youngest son	.101	-.021	.102
Was father's favorite child	-.060	.049	-.071

[a] The fully recursive path model allows paths from every "upstream" variable to each "downstream" variable, including those paths which fail to meet our criteria of statistical and/or substantive significance.

[b] "Total Effects" refers to the sum of all the influences which the given variable would have on adult sexual preference if it had paths to every "downstream" variable in Diagram 8. This value represents the portion of the zero-order correlation (r) which would be accounted for by such an all-possible-paths diagram; the unaccounted-for portion is "extraneous" effects--i.e., those that are spurious or due to variables not included in the model.

*p < .05.
**p < .01.
***p < .001.

264

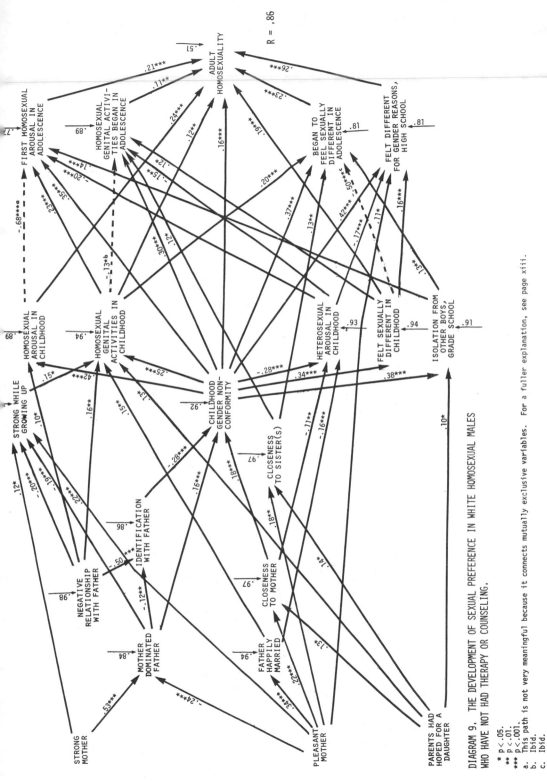

DIAGRAM 9. THE DEVELOPMENT OF SEXUAL PREFERENCE IN WHITE HOMOSEXUAL MALES
WHO HAVE NOT HAD THERAPY OR COUNSELING.

* p < .05.
** p < .01.
*** p < .001.
a. This path is not very meaningful because it connects mutually exclusive variables. For a fuller explanation, see page xiii.
b. Ibid.
c. Ibid.

Correlations, Means, and Standard Deviations for Variables in the Model: WHITE HOMOSEXUAL MALES WITH NO THERAPY OR COUNSELING AND ALL WHITE HETEROSEXUAL MALES.

Variable	(1)	(2)	(3)	(4)	(5)	(6)	(7)	(8)	(9)	(10)	(11)	(12)	(13)	(14)	(15)	(16)	(17)	(18)	(19)	(20)	(21)
1 Strong mother		.18	.05	.06	.49	-.08	.10	.03	.05	.08	.04	.08	.13	.10	-.09	.05	-.01	.05	.04	.13	.14
2 Pleasant mother			-.04	.34	-.15	-.15	.21	.03	.17	.30	-.05	.12	.03	-.03	-.14	.00	.02	.02	.03	.12	.11
3 Parents had hoped for a daughter				-.01	-.07	-.07	.12	-.10	.13	-.04	.18	.17	.14	.03	.01	.17	.08	.13	.00	.05	.17
4 Father happily married					-.07	-.21	.05	.11	.03	-.10	.01	-.13	.00	.02	-.17	.00	.09	.08	.17	.15	.15
5 Mother dominated father						.03	.01	-.13	-.01	-.17	.20	-.10	.17	.14	-.08	.10	.07	.06	.13	.18	.21
6 Negative relationship with father							.12	-.50	-.08	-.25	.22	.15	.19	.16	.02	.07	.03	.08	.12	.11	.16
7 Closeness to mother								-.06	.08	-.05	.20	.14	.09	.14	-.18	.11	.12	.09	-.17	.12	.28
8 Identification with father									-.07	.19	-.31	-.18	-.21	-.15	.14	-.11	-.12	-.16	-.18	-.24	-.31
9 Closeness to sister(s)										.05	-.15	-.13	-.14	-.10	-.10	-.16	-.06	-.12	-.15	-.07	-.17
10 Relatively strong while growing up											-.52	-.01	-.20	-.4	.14	.03	-.06	-.15	.38	-.26	-.23
11 Childhood gender nonconformity												.23	.44	.34	-.30	-.20	-.22	.32	.01	.52	.65
12 Homosexual genital activities in childhood													.57	.34	-.06	.40	-.05	.15	.17	.27	.45
13 Homosexual arousal in childhood														.48	-.06	.06	-.36	.11	.22	.36	.53
14 Felt sexually different in childhood															-.17	.15	-.06	-.28	-.27	.33	.43
15 Heterosexual arousal in childhood																.08	-.09	-.17	.24	-.34	-.41
16 Isolation from other boys, grade school																	-.30	.26	.43	.22	.37
17 First homosexual arousal in adolescence																		.35	.28	.16	.30
18 Began to feel sexually different in adolescence																				.20	.43
19 Homosexual genital activities begun in adolescence																				.27	.48
20 Felt different for gender reasons, high school																					.63
21 Adult homosexuality																					
Mean	15.40	16.71	.24	3.06	.88	1.92	.32	.19	.45	19.42	-.27	.96	.35	.20	.49	-.22	.20	.23	1.06	.55	.46
Standard Deviation	4.66	4.42	.51	1.35	.82	1.30	.47	1.69	.50	5.35	.68	1.56	.48	4.0	.50	1.53	.40	.42	1.64	.50	.50

266

Effects of Childhood and Adolescent Experiences on the Development of Adult Homosexuality: WHITE HOMOSEXUAL MALES WITH NO THERAPY OR COUNSELING AND ALL WHITE HETEROSEXUAL MALES. R = .86.

Variable	Total Effects	Standardized Path Coefficient (β)	Unstandardized Path Coefficient (b)
Began to feel sexually different in adolescence	.226	.226***	.267***
First homosexual arousal in adolescence	.208	.208***	.261***
Homosexual genital activities in childhood	.200	.120**	.038**
Felt sexually different in childhood	.131	.187***	.231***
Homosexual genital activities begun in adolescence	.109	.109**	.033**
Heterosexual arousal in childhood	-.103	--	--
Homosexual arousal in childhood	.098	.239***	.250***
Childhood gender nonconformity	.549	.161***	.118***
Felt different for gender reasons, high school	.262	.262***	.262***
Isolation from other boys, grade school	.060	--	--
Identification with father	-.153	--	--
Negative relationship with father	.112	--	--
Closeness to mother	.110	--	--
Mother dominated father	.100	--	--
Strong mother	.056	--	--
Parents had hoped for a daughter	.053	--	--
Pleasant mother	.051	--	--
Closeness to sister(s)	.042	--	--
Relatively strong while growing up	.029	--	--
Father happily married	.024	--	--

NOTE: "Total Effects" refers to the sum of all the pathways from a given variable to adult sexual preference which are shown in Diagram 9. This value represents the portion of the zero-order correlation (r) which is accounted for by the paths in Diagram 9; the unaccounted-for portion is regarded as "extraneous" effects--i.e., those which are spurious or due to variables not included in the model.

**p < .01.
***p < .001.

Effects of Earlier Childhood Experiences on Later Childhood and Adolescent Experiences as Demonstrated in Diagram 9: WHITE HOMOSEXUAL MALES WITH NO THERAPY OR COUNSELING AND ALL WHITE HETEROSEXUAL MALES.

DEPENDENT VARIABLE: Began to feel sexually different in adolescence (R = .58).

Independent Variable	Total Effects	Standardized Path Coefficient (β)	Unstandardized Path Coefficient (b)
Felt sexually different in childhood	-.495	-.495***	-.519***
Homosexual genital activities in childhood	.199	.199***	.054***
Homosexual arousal in childhood	--	--	--
Heterosexual arousal in childhood	--	--	--
Childhood gender nonconformity	.302	.371***	.230***
Isolation from other boys, grade school	.132	.132**	.036**
Closeness to sister(s)	.127	.127**	.108**
Identification with father	-.084	--	--
Negative relationship with father	.068	--	--
Parents had hoped for a daughter	.064	--	--
Closeness to mother	.054	--	--
Mother dominated father	.052	--	--
Pleasant mother	.035	--	--
Strong mother	.031	--	--
Relatively strong while growing up	.029	--	--
Father happily married	.017	--	--

DEPENDENT VARIABLE: First homosexual arousal in adolescence (R = .63).

Independent Variable	Total Effects	Standardized Path Coefficient (β)	Unstandardized Path Coefficient (b)
Homosexual arousal in childhood	-.680	-.680***	-.566***
Homosexual genital activities in childhood	.234	.234***	.059***
Heterosexual arousal in childhood	-.195	-.195***	-.155***
Felt sexually different in childhood	--	--	--
Childhood gender nonconformity	.236	.351***	.205***
Isolation from other boys, grade school	.143	.143***	.038***
Father happily married	.069	--	--
Identification with father	-.066	--	--
Closeness to mother	.064	--	--
Parents had hoped for a daughter	.053	--	--
Mother dominated father	.039	--	--
Pleasant mother	.035	--	--
Relatively strong while growing up	.034	--	--
Strong mother	.025	--	--
Negative relationship with father	-.006	--	--
Closeness to sister(s)	--	--	--

DEPENDENT VARIABLE: Homosexual genital activities in childhood (R = .35).

Independent Variable	Total Effects	Standardized Path Coefficient (β)	Unstandardized Path Coefficient (b)
Childhood gender nonconformity	.250	.250***	.573***
Negative relationship with father	.167	.161**	.194**
Relatively strong while growing up	.146	.146*	.043*
Parents had hoped for a daughter	.131	.125*	.386*
Father happily married	.119	.155**	.178**
Pleasant mother	.077	--	--
Identification with father	-.070	--	--
Closeness to mother	.045	--	--
Strong mother	.028	--	--
Mother dominated father	.020	--	--
Closeness to sister(s)	--	--	--

DEPENDENT VARIABLE: Felt sexually different in childhood (R = .34).

Independent Variable	Total Effects	Standardized Path Coefficient (β)	Unstandardized Path Coefficient (b)
Childhood gender nonconformity	.342	.342***	.202***
Identification with father	-.095	--	--
Mother dominated father	.066	--	--
Closeness to mother	.061	--	--
Negative relationship with father	.047	--	--
Strong mother	.035	--	--
Father happily married	-.010	--	--
Parents had hoped for a daughter	.008	--	--
Pleasant mother	.006	--	--
Relatively strong while growing up	--	--	--
Closeness to sister(s)	--	--	--

DEPENDENT VARIABLE: Homosexual activities begun in adolescence (R = .45).

Independent Variable	Total Effects	Standardized Path Coefficient (β)	Unstandardized Path Coefficient (b)
Heterosexual arousal in childhood	-.153	-.153**	-.501**
Homosexual genital activities in childhood	-.127	-.127*	-.134*
Felt sexually different in childhood	.124	.124*	.506*
Homosexual arousal in childhood	--	--	--
Childhood gender nonconformity	.353	.300***	.724***
Isolation from other boys, grade school	--	--	--
Closeness to sister(s)	.121	.121*	.399*
Identification with father	-.098	--	--
Closeness to mother	.081	--	--
Mother dominated father	.071	--	--
Strong mother	.035	--	--
Negative relationship with father	.032	--	--
Relatively strong while growing up	-.018	--	--
Pleasant mother	.018	--	--
Parents had hoped for a daughter	.012	--	--
Father happily married	-.002	--	--

DEPENDENT VARIABLE: Heterosexual arousal in childhood (R = .36).

Independent Variable	Total Effects	Standardized Path Coefficient (β)	Unstandardized Path Coefficient (b)
Childhood gender nonconformity	-.279	-.279***	-.205***
Closeness to mother	-.164	-.114**	-.121**
Father happily married	-.155	-.163***	-.060***
Identification with father	.078	--	--
Pleasant mother	-.078	--	--
Mother dominated father	-.054	--	--
Negative relationship with father	-.039	--	--
Strong mother	-.029	--	--
Parents had hoped for a daughter	-.022	--	--
Relatively strong while growing up	--	--	--
Closeness to sister(s)	--	--	--

DEPENDENT VARIABLE: Homosexual arousal in childhood (R = .45).			
Independent variable	Total Effects	Standardized Path Coefficient (β)	Unstandardized Path Coefficient (b)
Childhood gender nonconformity	.415	.415***	.291***
Negative relationship with father	.160	.102*	.038*
Identification with father	-.116	--	--
Mother dominated father	.080	--	--
Closeness to mother	.074	--	--
Strong mother	.042	--	--
Father happily married	-.034	--	--
Pleasant mother	-.014	--	--
Parents had hoped for a daughter	.010	--	--
Relatively strong while growing up	--	--	--
Closeness to sister(s)	--	--	--

DEPENDENT VARIABLE: Childhood gender nonconformity (R = .39).			
Independent variable	Total Effects	Standardized Path Coefficient (β)	Unstandardized Path Coefficient (b)
Identification with father	-.279	-.279***	-.113***
Mother dominated father	.192	.160***	.133***
Closeness to mother	.179	.179***	.260***
Negative relationship with father	.138	--	--
Strong mother	.102	--	--
Father happily married	-.029	--	--
Parents had hoped for a daughter	.024	--	--
Pleasant mother	-.017	--	--
Closeness to sister(s)	--	--	--

DEPENDENT VARIABLE: Felt different for gender reasons, high school (R = .58).			
Independent variable	Total Effects	Standardized Path Coefficient (β)	Unstandardized Path Coefficient (b)
Heterosexual arousal in childhood	-.170	-.170***	-.170***
Felt sexually different in childhood	.160	.160***	.198***
Homosexual genital activities in childhood	--	--	--
Homosexual arousal in childhood	--	--	--
Childhood gender nonconformity	.519	.417***	.306***
Isolation from other boys, grade school	--	--	--
Identification with father	-.145	--	--
Pleasant mother	.117	.112*	.013*
Closeness to mother	.112	--	--
Mother dominated father	.100	--	--
Negative relationship with father	.072	--	--
Strong mother	.053	--	--
Parents had hoped for a daughter	.015	--	--
Father happily married	.013	--	--
Relatively strong while growing up	--	--	--
Closeness to sister(s)	--	--	--

DEPENDENT VARIABLE: Isolation from other boys, grade school (R = .41).

Independent Variable	Total Effects	Standardized Path Coefficient (β)	Unstandardized Path Coefficient (b)
Childhood gender nonconformity	.381	.381***	.839***
Parents had hoped for a daughter	.112	.103*	.315*
Identification with father	-.106	--	--
Mother dominated father	.073	--	--
Closeness to mother	.068	--	--
Negative relationship with father	.053	--	--
Strong mother	.039	--	--
Father happily married	-.011	--	--
Pleasant mother	-.006	--	--
Relatively strong while growing up	--	--	--
Closeness to sister(s)	--	--	--

DEPENDENT VARIABLE: Identification with father (R = .51).

Independent Variable	Total Effects	Standardized Path Coefficient (β)	Unstandardized Path Coefficient (b)
Negative relationship with father	-.496	-.496***	-.644***
Mother dominated father	-.115	-.115**	-.238**
Father happily married	.106	--	--
Pleasant mother	.063	--	--
Strong mother	-.061	--	--
Closeness to mother	--	--	--
Parents had hoped for a daughter	--	--	--

DEPENDENT VARIABLE: Negative relationship with father (R = .21).

Independent Variable	Total Effects	Standardized Path Coefficient (β)	Unstandardized Path Coefficient (b)
Father happily married	-.213	-.213***	-.205***
Mother dominated father	--	--	--
Strong mother	--	--	--
Pleasant mother	--	--	--
Parents had hoped for a daughter	--	--	--

DEPENDENT VARIABLE: Closeness to mother (R = .25).

Independent Variable	Total Effects	Standardized Path Coefficient (β)	Unstandardized Path Coefficient (b)
Pleasant mother	.219	.219***	.023***
Parents had hoped for a daughter	.134	.134**	.124**
Mother dominated father	--	--	--
Father happily married	--	--	--
Strong mother	--	--	--

DEPENDENT VARIABLE: Closeness to sister(s) (R = .22).			
Independent Variable	Total Effects	Standardized Path Coefficient (β)	Unstandardized Path Coefficient (b)
Pleasant mother	.180	.180**	.020**
Parents had hoped for a daughter	.142	.142*	.140*
Identification with father	--	--	--
Negative relationship with father	--	--	--
Closeness to mother	--	--	--
Mother dominated father	--	--	--
Father happily married	--	--	--
Strong mother	--	--	--

DEPENDENT VARIABLE: Relatively strong while growing up (R = .40).			
Independent Variable	Total Effects	Standardized Path Coefficient (β)	Unstandardized Path Coefficient (b)
Pleasant mother	.281	.221***	.267***
Negative relationship with father	-.198	-.198***	-.814***
Mother dominated father	-.192	-.192***	-1.250***
Father happily married	.042	--	--
Strong mother	.008	.120*	.138*
Closeness to sister(s)	--	--	--
Identification with father	--	--	--
Closeness to mother	--	--	--
Parents had hoped for a daughter	--	--	--

DEPENDENT VARIABLE: Father happily married (R = .34).			
Independent Variable	Total Effects	Standardized Path Coefficient (β)	Unstandardized Path Coefficient (b)
Pleasant mother	.335	.335***	.103***
Strong mother	--	--	--
Parents had hoped for a daughter	--	--	--

*p < .05.
**p < .01.
***p < .001.

Selected Statistics from Fully Recursive Path Model: WHITE HOMOSEXUAL MALES
WITH NO THERAPY OR COUNSELING AND ALL WHITE HETEROSEXUAL MALES.[a] R =.88.

Variable	Total Effects[b]	Standardized Path Coefficient (β)	Unstandardized Path Coefficient (b)
Began to feel sexually different in adolescence	.210	.210***	.247***
Heterosexual arousal in childhood	-.192	-.089***	-.191***
Homosexual arousal in childhood	.173	.241**	.181**
Homosexual genital activities in childhood	.170	.109**	.054**
First homosexual arousal in adolescence	.165	.165**	.207**
Homosexual genital activities begun in adolescence	.104	.104*	.032*
Felt sexually different in childhood	.091	.170	.112
Childhood gender nonconformity	.616	.155***	.451***
Felt different for gender reasons, high school	.235	.235***	.236***
Isolation from other boys, grade school	.132	.072**	.043**
Identification with father	-.274	-.057***	-.081***
Closeness to mother	.216	.090**	.229**
Mother dominated father	.216	.000**	.131**
Parents had hoped for a daughter	.166	.009*	.163*
Negative relationship with father	.161	-.062*	.062*
Father happily married	.127	.024	.047
Strong mother	.119	.010	.013
Closeness to sister(s)	.116	-.028	.116
Relatively strong while growing up	.104	.062	.010
Pleasant mother	.099	-.007	.011

[a]The fully recursive path model allows paths from every "upstream" variable to each "downstream" variable, including those paths which fail to meet our criteria of statistical and/
or substantive significance.

[b]"Total Effects" refers to the sum of all the influences which the given variable would have
on adult sexual preference if it had paths to every "downstream" variable in Diagram 9.
This value represents the portion of the zero-order correlation (r) which would be accounted
for by such an all-possible-paths diagram; the unaccounted-for portion is "extraneous"
effects--i.e., those that are spurious or due to variables not included in the model.

*p $<$ .05.
**p $<$ .01.
***p $<$ .001.

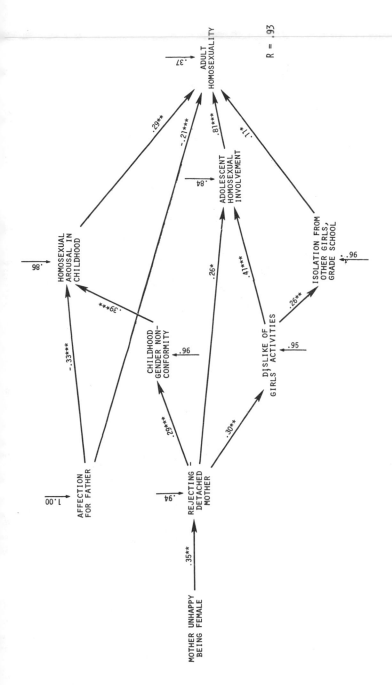

DIAGRAM 10. THE DEVELOPMENT OF SEXUAL PREFERENCE IN BLACK FEMALES.

* p < .05.
** p < .01.
*** p < .001.

Correlations, Means, and Standard Deviations for Variables in the Model: BLACK FEMALES.

	(1)	(2)	(3)	(4)	(5)	(6)	(7)	(8)	(9)
1 Mother unhappy being a woman		-.14	.35	-.03	.21	.00	.28	.22	.28
2 Affection for father			-.06	-.04	-.00	-.07	-.33	.02	-.30
3 Rejecting-detached mother				.30	.29	.12	.17	.38	.35
4 Dislike of girls' activities					.52	.26	.20	.48	.49
5 Childhood gender nonconformity						.01	.39	.44	.47
6 Isolation from other girls, grade school							.11	.05	.20
7 Homosexual arousal in childhood								.05	.41
8 Adolescent homosexual involvement									.82
9 Adult homosexuality									

Variable Number:	(1)	(2)	(3)	(4)	(5)	(6)	(7)	(8)	(9)
Mean	.54	.43	-.02	1.16	.00	.49	.25	.14	.62
Standard Deviation	.74	.50	.87	1.14	.82	.50	.44	2.53	.49

Effects of Childhood and Adolescent Experiences on the Development of Adult Homosexuality: BLACK FEMALES. R = .93.

Variable	Total Effects	Standardized Path Coefficient (β)	Unstandardized Path Coefficient (b)
Adolescent homosexual involvement	.806	.806***	.155***
Homosexual arousal in childhood	.288	.288***	.322***
Dislike of girls' activities	.355	--	--
Childhood gender nonconformity	.111	--	--
Isolation from other girls, grade school	.109	.109*	.106*
Rejecting-detached mother	.347	--	--
Affection for father	-.305	-.210***	-.206***
Mother unhappy being female	.120	--	--

NOTE: "Total Effects" refers to the sum of all the pathways from a given variable to adult sexual preference which are shown in Diagram 10. This value represents the portion of the zero-order correlation (r) which is accounted for by the paths in Diagram 10; the unaccounted-for portion is regarded as "extraneous" effects -- i.e., those which are spurious or due to variables not included in the model.

*p < .05.
***p < .001.

Effects of Earlier Childhood Experiences on Later Childhood and Adolescent Experiences As Demonstrated In Diagram 10: BLACK FEMALES.

DEPENDENT VARIABLE: Adolescent homosexual involvement (R = .54).			
Independent variable	Total Effects	Standardized Path Coefficient (β)	Unstandardized Path Coefficient (b)
Homosexual arousal in childhood	--	--	--
Dislike of girls' activities	.405	.405***	.896***
Childhood gender nonconformity	--	--	--
Isolation from other girls, grade school	--	--	--
Rejecting-detached mother	.380	.257*	.744*
Mother unhappy being female	.132	--	--
Affection for father	--	--	--

DEPENDENT VARIABLE: Homosexual arousal in childhood (R = .51).			
Independent variable	Total Effects	Standardized Path Coefficient (β)	Unstandardized Path Coefficient (b)
Childhood gender nonconformity	.387	.387***	.206***
Dislike of girls' activities	--	--	--
Affection for father	-.330	-.330***	-.289***
Rejecting-detached mother	.113	--	--
Mother unhappy being female	.039	--	--

DEPENDENT VARIABLE: Dislike of girls' activities (R = .30).			
Independent variable	Total Effects	Standardized Path Coefficient (β)	Unstandardized Path Coefficient (b)
Rejecting-detached mother	.303	.303**	.398**
Mother unhappy being female	.105	--	--
Affection for father	--	--	--

DEPENDENT VARIABLE: Childhood gender nonconformity (R = .29).			
Independent variable	Total Effects	Standardized Path Coefficient (β)	Unstandardized Path Coefficient (b)
Rejecting-detached mother	.293	.293**	.275***
Mother unhappy being female	.102	--	--
Affection for father	--	--	--

DEPENDENT VARIABLE: Isolation from other girls, grade school (R = .26).			
Independent variable	Total Effects	Standardized Path Coefficient (ß)	Unstandardized Path Coefficient (b)
Dislike of girls' activities	.260	.260**	.114**
Childhood gender nonconformity	--	--	--
Rejecting-detached mother	.079	--	--
Mother unhappy being female	.027	--	--
Affection for father	--	--	--

DEPENDENT VARIABLE: Rejecting-detached mother (R = .35).			
Independent variable	Total Effects	Standardized Path Coefficient (ß)	Unstandardized Path Coefficient (b)
Mother unhappy being female	.347	.347**	.411**

NOTE: Affection for Father does not appear as a dependent variable in this table because the diagram illustrates no antecedents for it.

*p < .05.
**p < .01.
***p < .001.

Selected Statistics from Fully Recursive Path Model: BLACK FEMALES[a]. R = .93.

Variable	Total Effects[b]	Standardized Path Coefficient (β)	Unstandardized Path Coefficient (b)
Adolescent homosexual involvement	.812	.812***	.157***
Homosexual arousal in childhood	.138	.293	.154
Dislike of girls' activities	.344	.029**	.147**
Childhood gender nonconformity	.217	-.014	.130
Isolation from other girls, grade school	.071	.107	.069
Mother unhappy being female	.282	.010*	.186*
Rejecting-detached mother	.281	.044*	.157*
Affection for father	-.263	-.209*	-.257*

[a]The fully recursive path model allows paths from every "upstream" variable to each "downstream" variable, including those paths which fail to meet our criteria of statistical and/or substantive significance.

[b]"Total Effects" refers to the sum of all the influences which the given variable would have on adult sexual preference if it had paths to every "downstream" variable in Diagram 10. This value represents the portion of the zero-order correlation (r) which would be accounted for by such an all-possible-paths diagram; the unaccounted-for portion is "extraneous" effects--i.e., those that are spurious or due to variables not included in the model.

*p < .05.
**p < .01.
***p < .001.

Overlap between Subsamples of White Homosexual Females. Number Given Is the Percentage of the White Homosexual Females in Both Subsamples (N=229).

Subsample	(1)	(2)	(3)	(4)	(5)	(6)	Subsample N
1. "Masculine" WHFs	--						124
2. Nonmasculine WHFs	--	--					105
3. Bisexual WHFs	2.6%	10.5%	--				30
4. Exclusively homosexual WHFs	31.4	12.7	--	--			103
5. WHFs who have had psychotherapy or counseling	34.5	33.6	10.9	25.8	--		156
6. WHFs who have never been in psychotherapy or counseling	18.8	12.7	2.2	18.8	--	--	73
7. Close-coupled WHFs	16.6	2.2	0.9	16.6	18.8	10.5	81
8. Open-coupled WHFs	8.7	7.9	2.6	8.3	11.4	5.2	51
9. "Functional" WHFs	3.1	7.0	2.2	4.8	6.1	3.9	30
10. Dysfunctional WHFs	2.2	3.1	1.3	0.9	4.4	0.9	16
11. Asexual WHFs	6.6	4.4	1.7	3.9	8.7	2.2	33

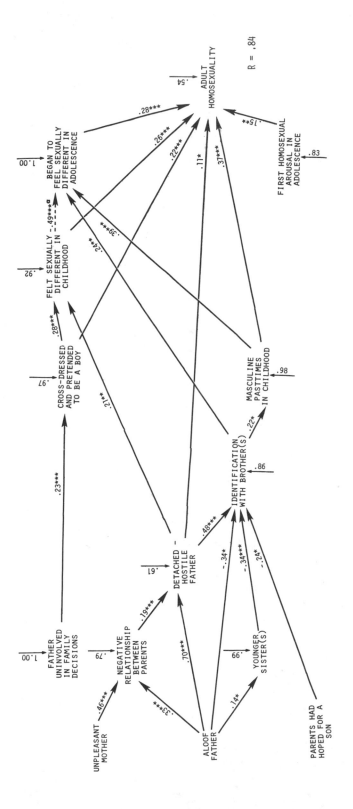

DIAGRAM 11. THE DEVELOPMENT OF SEXUAL PREFERENCE IN THE MORE MASCULINE WHITE HOMOSEXUAL FEMALES.

* p < .05.
** p < .01.
*** p < .001.
a. This path is not very meaningful because it connects mutually exclusive variables. For a fuller explanation, see page xiii.

Correlations, Means, and Standard Deviations for Variables in the Model: MORE MASCULINE HOMOSEXUAL AND ALL HETEROSEXUAL WHITE FEMALES.

	(1)	(2)	(3)	(4)	(5)	(6)	(7)	(8)	(9)	(10)	(11)	(12)	(13)	(14)
1 Unpleasant mother		.16	.21	.05	.05	.53	.21	.03	.16	.23	.18	.22	.24	.36
2 Parents had hoped for a son			.15	-.07	.07	.09	.19	-.22	.09	.17	.05	.07	.12	.20
3 Aloof father				-.01	.14	.42	.78	-.05	.16	.20	.19	.01	.03	.27
4 Father uninvolved in family decisions					-.08	.08	.07	.06	.23	.19	.14	.16	.11	.26
5 Younger sister(s)						.06	.09	-.36	-.11	-.14	.03	-.08	-.12	-.17
6 Negative interparental relationship							.48	.03	.18	.24	.17	.17	.16	.32
7 Detached-hostile father								.14	.27	.18	.29	.03	.02	.32
8 Identification with brother(s)									.27	.22	.18	.16	.24	.23
9 "Cross-dressed" and pretended to be a boy										.49	.34	.14	.17	.58
10 Masculine pastimes in childhood											.34	.32	.28	.70
11 Felt sexually different in childhood												.15	-.31	.42
12 First homosexual arousal in adolescence													.38	.44
13 Began to feel sexually different in adolescence														.40
14 Adult homosexuality														
Variable Number:	(1)	(2)	(3)	(4)	(5)	(6)	(7)	(8)	(9)	(10)	(11)	(12)	(13)	(14)
Mean	.00	.38	-.01	2.08	.56	5.08	-.01	.52	.38	-.00	.25	.24	.23	.55
Standard Deviation	.94	.64	1.75	2.32	.96	4.26	1.87	.50	.49	1.73	.43	.43	.42	.50

Effects of Childhood and Adolescent Experiences on the Development of Adult Homosexuality: MORE MASCULINE HOMOSEXUAL AND ALL HETEROSEXUAL WHITE FEMALES. R = .84.

Variable	Total Effects	Standardized Path Coefficient (β)	Unstandardized Path Coefficient (b)
Began to feel sexually different in adolescence	.282	.282***	.332***
First homosexual arousal in adolescence	.147	.147**	.172**
Felt sexually different in childhood	.117	.256***	.296***
Masculine pastimes in childhood	.476	.365***	.105***
"Cross-dressed" and pretended to be a boy	.248	.215***	.220***
Detached-hostile father	.220	.113*	.030*
Identification with brother(s)	.171	--	--
Aloof father	.101	--	--
Younger sister(s)	-.059	--	--
Father uninvolved in family decisions	.056	--	--
Negative interparental relationship	.041	--	--
Parents had hoped for a son	-.041	--	--
Unpleasant mother	.019	--	--

NOTE: "Total Effects" refers to the sum of all the pathways from a given variable to adult sexual preference which are shown in Diagram 11. This value represents the portion of the zero-order correlation (r) which is accounted for by the paths in Diagram 11; the unaccounted-for portion is regarded as "extraneous" effects -- i.e., those which are spurious or due to variables not included in the model.

*p < .05.
**p < .01.
***p < .001.

Effects of Earlier Childhood Experiences on Later Childhood and
Adolescent Experiences as Demonstrated in Diagram 11: MORE MASCULINE
HOMOSEXUAL AND ALL HETEROSEXUAL WHITE FEMALES.

DEPENDENT VARIABLE: Began to feel sexually different in adolescence (R = .57).

Independent variable	Total Effects	Standardized Path Coefficient (β)	Unstandardized Path Coefficient (b)
Felt sexually different in childhood	-.490	-.490***	-.480***
Masculine pastimes in childhood	.393	.393***	.096***
"Cross-dressed" and pretended to be a boy	-.138	--	--
Identification with brother(s)	.325	.239**	.202**
Younger sister(s)	-.112	--	--
Aloof father	-.084	--	--
Parents had hoped for a son	-.079	--	--
Detached-hostile father	.054	--	--
Father uninvolved in family decisions	-.031	--	--
Negative interparental relationship	.010	--	--
Unpleasant mother	.005	--	--

DEPENDENT VARIABLE: Felt sexually different in childhood (R = .40).

Independent Variable	Total Effects	Standardized Path Coefficient (β)	Unstandardized Path Coefficient (b)
"Cross-dressed" and pretended to be a boy	.282	.282***	.250***
Masculine pastimes in childhood	--	--	--
Detached-hostile father	.211	.211**	.049**
Aloof father	.160	--	--
Father uninvolved in family decisions	.064	--	--
Negative interparental relationship	.040	--	--
Unpleasant mother	.018	--	--
Identification with brother(s)	--	--	--
Younger sister(s)	--	--	--
Parents had hoped for a son	--	--	--

DEPENDENT VARIABLE: Masculine pastimes in childhood (R = .22).

Independent variable	Total Effects	Standardized Path Coefficient (β)	Unstandardized Path Coefficient (b)
Identification with brother(s)	.218	.218*	.754*
Detached-hostile father	.105	--	--
Younger sister(s)	-.075	--	--
Parents had hoped for a son	-.053	--	--
Negative interparental relationship	.020	--	--
Unpleasant mother	.009	--	--
Aloof father	-.004	--	--
Father uninvolved in family decisions	--	--	--

DEPENDENT VARIABLE: "Cross-dressed" and pretended to be a boy (R = .23).

Independent variable	Total Effects	Standardized Path Coefficient (β)	Unstandardized Path Coefficient (b)
Father uninvolved in family decisions	.226	.226***	.047***
Identification with brother(s)	--	--	--
Detached-hostile father	--	--	--
Negative interparental relationship	--	--	--
Younger sister(s)	--	--	--
Unpleasant mother	--	--	--
Aloof father	--	--	--
Parents had hoped for a son	--	--	--

DEPENDENT VARIABLE: Detached-hostile father (R = .79).

Independent variable	Total Effects	Standardized Path Coefficient (β)	Unstandardized Path Coefficient (b)
Aloof father	.757	.696***	.747***
Negative interparental relationship	.188	.188***	.082***
Unpleasant mother	.086	--	--
Father uninvolved in family decisions	--	--	--
Younger sister(s)	--	--	--
Parents had hoped for a son	--	--	--

DEPENDENT VARIABLE: Identification with brother(s) (R = .51).

Independent variable	Total Effects	Standardized Path Coefficient (β)	Unstandardized Path Coefficient (b)
Detached-hostile father	.483	.483***	.129***
Younger sister(s)	-.344	-.344***	-.180***
Parents had hoped for a son	-.242	-.242*	-.189*
Negative interparental relationship	.091	--	--
Unpleasant mother	.042	--	--
Aloof father	-.019	-.337*	-.097*
Father uninvolved in family decisions	--	--	--

DEPENDENT VARIABLE: Younger sister(s) (R = .14).

Independent variable	Total Effects	Standardized Path Coefficient (β)	Unstandardized Path Coefficient (b)
Aloof father	.138	.138*	.076*
Unpleasant mother	--	--	--
Parents had hoped for a son	--	--	--

DEPENDENT VARIABLE: Negative interparental relationship (R = .62).

Independent variable	Total Effects	Standardized Path Coefficient (β)	Unstandardized Path Coefficient (b)
Unpleasant mother	.458	.458***	2.069***
Aloof father	.326	.326***	.796***
Parents had hoped for a son	--	--	--

NOTE: First Homosexual Arousal in Adolescence and Father Uninvolved in Family Decisions do not appear as dependent variables in this table because the diagram illustrates no antecedents for them.

*p< .05.
**p< .01.
***p< .001.

Selected Statistics from Fully Recursive Path Model: MORE MASCULINE HOMOSEXUAL AND ALL HETEROSEXUAL WHITE FEMALES[a]. R = .85.

Variable	Total Effects[b]	Standardized Path Coefficient (β)	Unstandardized Path Coefficient (b)
Began to feel sexually different in adolescence	.278	.278***	.328***
First homosexual arousal in adolescence	.138	.138*	.161*
Felt sexually different in childhood	.119	.262	.137
Masculine pastimes in childhood	.478	.344***	.138***
"Cross-dressed" and pretended to be a boy	.247	.216**	.253**
Unpleasant mother	.300	.088**	.159***
Father uninvolved in family decisions	.231	.043*	.049*
Younger sister(s)	-.209	-.117**	-.109*
Identification with brother(s)	.191	.103	.190
Aloof father	.189	.017	.054
Detached-hostile father	.156	.113	.042
Parents had hoped for a son	.118	.012	.092
Negative interparental relationship	.087	-.020	.011

[a]The fully recursive path model allows paths from every "upstream" variable to each "downstream" variable, including those paths which fall to meet our criteria of statistical and/or substantive significance.

[b]"Total Effects" refers to the sum of all the influences which the given variable would have on adult sexual preference if it had paths to every "downstream" variable in Diagram 11. This value represents the portion of the zero-order correlation (r) which would be accounted for by such an all-possible-paths diagram; the unaccounted-for portion is "extraneous" effects--i.e., those that are spurious or due to variables not included in the model.

*p < .05.
**p < .01.
***p < .001.

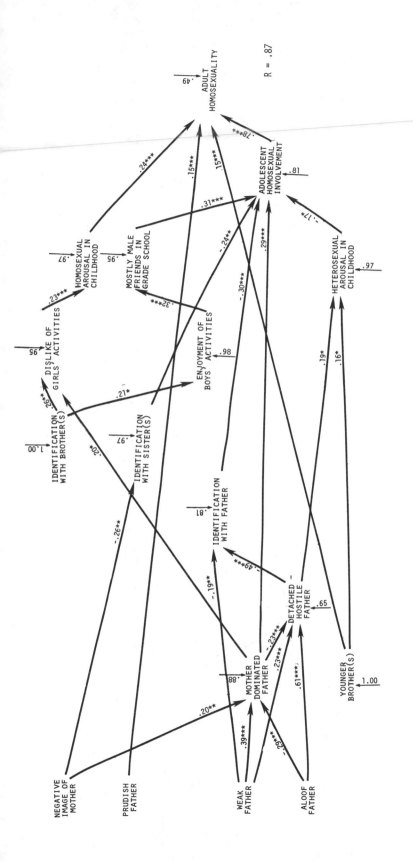

DIAGRAM 12. THE DEVELOPMENT OF SEXUAL PREFERENCE IN THE NONMASCULINE WHITE HOMOSEXUAL FEMALES.

* p < .05.
** p < .01.
*** p < .001.

Correlations, Means, and Standard Deviations for Variables in the Model: LESS MASCULINE HOMOSEXUAL AND ALL HETEROSEXUAL WHITE FEMALES.

	(1)	(2)	(3)	(4)	(5)	(6)	(7)	(8)	(9)	(10)	(11)	(12)	(13)	(14)	(15)	(16)	(17)
1 Prudish father		.08	.37	.07	.05	-.12	.35	-.19	.02	-.16	-.06	.02	-.03	-.03	-.03	.03	.16
2 Weak father			.37	.32	-.04	-.35	.38	-.37	-.10	.06	.18	.19	.25	.07	-.12	.34	.31
3 Aloof father				.21	-.01	-.11	.72	-.47	.01	-.04	.09	.26	.09	.10	-.06	.20	.31
4 Negative image of mother					-.01	.27	.15	-.20	.00	-.26	.01	.24	.07	-.01	.12	.21	.26
5 Younger brother(s)						-.05	.01	-.03	.12	.11	.06	-.05	-.05	.16	.03	-.07	-.21
6 Mother dominated father							-.21	-.03	-.05	.06	.18	.18	.16	-.00	.15	.33	.26
7 Detached-hostile father								-.56	.01	-.01	.02	.21	.14	-.19	-.20	.20	.30
8 Identification with father									-.07	-.02	.07	-.09	-.09	-.10	.14	-.24	-.21
9 Identification with brother(s)										-.43	.21	.25	.08	-.03	-.00	.12	.19
10 Identification with sister(s)											-.00	.21	-.05	.08	.02	-.23	-.26
11 Enjoyment of boys' activities												.22	-.00	.05	.32	.28	.19
12 Dislike of girls' activities													.23	.06	.15	.28	.38
13 Homosexual arousal in childhood														.06	-.14	.06	.29
14 Heterosexual arousal in childhood															.07	-.15	-.14
15 Mostly male friends in grade school																.30	.16
16 Adolescent homosexual involvement																	.82
17 Adult homosexuality																	
	(1)	(2)	(3)	(4)	(5)	(6)	(7)	(8)	(9)	(10)	(11)	(12)	(13)	(14)	(15)	(16)	(17)
Mean	1.41	7.72	-.00	.80	.54	.91	-.05	1.61	.49	.39	1.86	1.09	.13	.23	2.33	.00	.51
Standard Deviation	.94	6.29	1.76	.89	.92	.82	1.88	1.02	.50	.49	1.14	1.05	.34	.42	1.49	1.78	.50

Effects of Childhood and Adolescent Experiences on the Development of Adult Homosexuality: LESS MASCULINE HOMOSEXUAL AND ALL HETEROSEXUAL WHITE FEMALES. R = .87.

Variable	Total Effects	Standardized Path Coefficient (β)	Unstandardized Path Coefficient (b)
Adolescent homosexual involvement	.785	.785***	.221***
Homosexual arousal in childhood	.238	.238***	.353***
Heterosexual arousal in childhood	-.135	--	--
Enjoyment of boys' activities	.078	--	--
Dislike of girls' activities	.055	--	--
Mostly male friends in grade school	.245	--	--
Identification with father	-.234	--	--
Mother dominated father	.220	--	--
Identification with sister(s)	-.188	--	--
Younger brother(s)	-.167	-.146***	-.079***
Weak father	.151	--	--
Prudish father	.147	.147***	.078***
Negative image of mother	.092	--	--
Detached-hostile father	.089	--	--
Identification with brother(s)	.031	--	--
Aloof father	-.010	--	--

NOTE: "Total Effects" refers to the sum of all the pathways from a given variable to adult sexual preference which are shown in Diagram 12. This value represents the portion of the zero-order correlation (r) which is accounted for by the paths in Diagram 12; the unaccounted-for portion is regarded as "extraneous" effects -- i.e., those which are spurious or due to variables not included in the model.

***p < .001.

Effects of Earlier Childhood Experiences on Later Childhood and Adolescent Experiences As Demonstrated in Diagram 12: LESS MASCULINE HOMOSEXUAL AND ALL HETEROSEXUAL WHITE FEMALES.

DEPENDENT VARIABLE: Adolescent homosexual involvement (R = .58).

Independent variable	Total Effects	Standardized Path Coefficient (β)	Unstandardized Path Coefficient (b)
Heterosexual arousal in childhood	-.172	-.172*	-.728*
Homosexual arousal in childhood	--	--	--
Enjoyment of boys' activities	.100	--	--
Dislike of girls' activities	--	--	--
Mostly male friends in grade school	.312	.312***	.373***
Identification with father	-.298	-.298***	-.521***
Mother dominated father	.266	.292***	.632***
Identification with sister(s)	-.240	-.240**	-.869**
Weak father	.186	--	--
Negative image of mother	.115	--	--
Detached-hostile father	.113	--	--
Younger brother(s)	-.027	--	--
Identification with brother(s)	.021	--	--
Aloof father	-.009	--	--
Prudish father	--	--	--

DEPENDENT VARIABLE: Homosexual arousal in childhood (R = .23).

Independent variable	Total Effects	Standardized Path Coefficient (β)	Unstandardized Path Coefficient (b)
Dislike of girls' activities	.231	.231***	.074***
Enjoyment of boys' activities	--	--	--
Identification with brother(s)	.061	--	--
Mother dominated father	.046	--	--
Weak father	.018	--	--
Aloof father	-.013	--	--
Negative image of mother	.009	--	--
Identification with sister(s)	--	--	--
Identification with father	--	--	--
Detached-hostile father	--	--	--
Younger brother(s)	--	--	--
Prudish father	--	--	--

DEPENDENT VARIABLE: Heterosexual arousal in childhood (R = .24).

Independent variable	Total Effects	Standardized Path Coefficient (β)	Unstandardized Path Coefficient (b)
Dislike of girls' activities	--	--	--
Enjoyment of boys' activities	--	--	--
Detached-hostile father	.185	.185*	.041*
Younger brother(s)	.159	.159*	.072*
Aloof father	.125	--	--
Mother dominated father	-.042	--	--
Weak father	.034	--	--
Negative image of mother	-.008	--	--
Identificiation with brother(s)	--	--	--
Identification with sister(s)	--	--	--
Identification with father	--	--	--
Prudish father	--	--	--

DEPENDENT VARIABLE: Enjoyment of boys' activities (R = .21).

Independent variable	Total Effects	Standardized Path Coefficient (β)	Unstandardized Path Coefficient (b)
Identification with brother(s)	.206	.206*	.467*
Identification with sister(s)	--	--	--
Identification with father	--	--	--
Detached-hostile father	--	--	--
Younger brother(s)	--	--	--
Mother dominated father	--	--	--
Prudish father	--	--	--
Weak father	--	--	--
Aloof father	--	--	--
Negative image of mother	--	--	--

DEPENDENT VARIABLE: Dislike of girls' activities (R = .32).

Independent variable	Total Effects	Standardized Path Coefficient (β)	Unstandardized Path Coefficient (b)
Identification with brother(s)	.265	.265**	.556**
Mother dominated father	.199	.199*	.255*
Weak father	.078	--	--
Aloof father	-.058	--	--
Negative image of mother	.040	--	--
Identification with sister(s)	--	--	--
Identification with father	--	--	--
Detached-hostile father	--	--	--
Younger brother(s)	--	--	--
Prudish father	--	--	--

DEPENDENT VARIABLE: Mostly male friends in grade school (R = .32).

Independent variable	Total Effects	Standardized Path Coefficient (β)	Unstandardized Path Coefficient (b)
Enjoyment of boys' activities	.320	.320***	.418***
Dislike of girls' activities	--	--	--
Identification with brother(s)	.066	--	--
Identification with sister(s)	--	--	--
Identification with father	--	--	--
Detached-hostile father	--	--	--
Younger brother(s)	--	--	--
Mother dominated father	--	--	--
Prudish father	--	--	--
Weak father	--	--	--
Aloof father	--	--	--
Negative image of mother	--	--	--

DEPENDENT VARIABLE: Identification with father (R = .58).

Independent variable	Total Effects	Standardized Path Coefficient (β)	Unstandardized Path Coefficient (b)
Detached-hostile father	-.487	-.487***	-.263***
Aloof father	-.329	--	--
Weak father	-.256	-.186**	-.030**
Mother dominated father	.110	--	--
Negative image of mother	.022	--	--
Younger brother(s)	--	--	--
Prudish father	--	--	--

DEPENDENT VARIABLE: Mother dominated father (R = .47).

Independent variable	Total Effects	Standardized Path Coefficient (β)	Unstandardized Path Coefficient (b)
Weak father	.393	.393***	.051***
Aloof father	-.292	-.292***	-.136***
Negative image of mother	.200	.200**	.185**
Prudish father	--	--	--

DEPENDENT VARIABLE: Identification with sister(s) (R = .26).

Independent variable	Total Effects	Standardized Path Coefficient (β)	Unstandardized Path Coefficient (b)
Negative image of mother	-.258	-.258**	-.142**
Identification with father	--	--	--
Detached-hostile father	--	--	--
Younger brother(s)	--	--	--
Mother dominated father	--	--	--
Prudish father	--	--	--
Weak father	--	--	--
Aloof father	--	--	--

DEPENDENT VARIABLE: Detached-hostile father (R = .76).			
Independent variable	Total Effects	Standardized Path Coefficient (β)	Unstandardized Path Coefficient (b)
Aloof father	.675	.609***	.651***
Mother dominated father	-.226	-.226***	-.518***
Weak father	.143	.232***	.070***
Negative image of mother	-.045	--	--
Younger brother(s)	--	--	--
Prudish father	--	--	--

NOTE: Identification with Brother(s) and Younger Brother(s) do not appear as dependent variables in this table because the diagram illustrates no antecedents for them.

*p < .05.
**p < .01.
***p < .001.

Selected Statistics from Fully Recursive Path Model: LESS MASCULINE
HOMOSEXUAL AND ALL HETEROSEXUAL WHITE FEMALES[a]. R = .89.

Variable	Total Effects[b]	Standardized Path Coefficient (ß)	Unstandardized Path Coefficient (b)
Adolescent homosexual involvement	.786	.786***	.221***
Heterosexual arousal in childhood	-.194	-.019	-.231
Homosexual arousal in childhood	.193	.215	.285
Dislike of girls' activities	.163	.063	.078
Enjoyment of boys' activities	.087	-.036	.038
Mostly male friends in grade school	.197	-.037	.066
Mother dominated father	.226	-.005	.138
Detached-hostile father	.215	.060	.057
Younger brother(s)	-.195	-.153	-.106
Weak father	.193	-.053	.015
Aloof father	.183	.082	.052
Identification with brother(s)	.163	.105	.163
Identification with sister(s)	-.160	.060	-.164
Negative image of mother	.152	.083	.086
Prudish father	.063	.114	.034
Identification with father	.025	.103	.012

[a]The fully recursive path model allows paths from every "upstream" variable to each "downstream" variable, including those paths which fail to meet our criteria of statistical and/or
substantive significance.

[b]"Total Effects" refers to the sum of all the influences which the given variable would have
on adult sexual preference if it had paths to every "downstream" variable in Diagram 12.
This value represents the portion of the zero-order correlation (r) which would be accounted
for by such an all-possible-paths diagram; the unaccounted-for portion is "extraneous" ef-
fects--i.e., those that are spurious or due to variables not included in the model.

***p < .001.

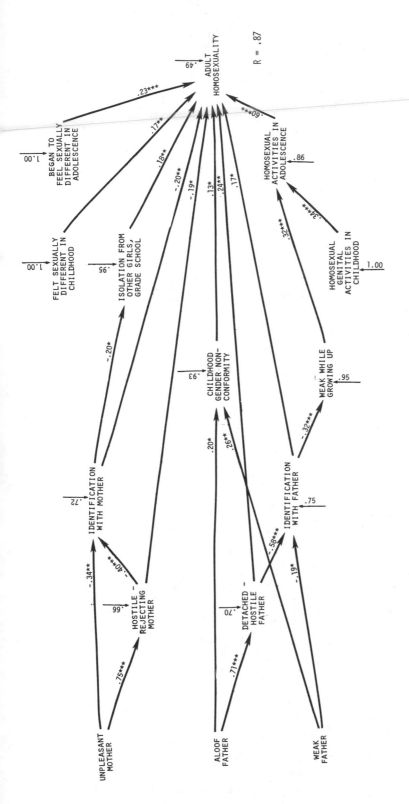

DIAGRAM 13. THE DEVELOPMENT OF SEXUAL PREFERENCE IN BISEXUAL WHITE FEMALES.

* p < .05.
** p < .01.
*** p < .001.

Correlations, Means, and Standard Deviations for Variables in the Model: BISEXUAL AND HETEROSEXUAL WHITE FEMALES.

	(1)	(2)	(3)	(4)	(5)	(6)	(7)	(8)	(9)	(10)	(11)	(12)	(13)	(14)	(15)
1 Weak father		.25	.36	.29	.29	-.36	-.21	.22	.33	.07	.04	.15	.21	.25	.28
2 Unpleasant mother			.30	.23	.75	-.13	-.64	.37	.19	.15	.15	.09	.17	.33	.32
3 Aloof father				.71	.28	-.48	.30	-.30	.29	.05	.20	.18	.10	.25	.39
4 Detached-hostile father					.26	-.64	.18	-.29	.18	-.03	.05	.05	.13	.22	.31
5 Hostile-rejecting mother						-.16	-.66	-.37	.22	-.15	.22	-.04	.23	.29	.30
6 Identification with father							-.28	.32	-.09	-.05	-.07	-.09	-.15	-.29	-.25
7 Identification with mother								-.30	-.14	-.23	-.06	-.17	-.14	-.23	-.31
8 Relatively weak while growing up									-.02	.04	.23	.21	.08	.40	.35
9 Childhood gender nonconformity										.23	-.02	-.02	.35	.28	.43
10 Isolation from other girls, grade school											.09	.14	.12	.20	.37
11 Felt sexually different in childhood												.27	-.12	.21	.25
12 Homosexual genital activities in childhood													-.02	.41	.32
13 Began to feel sexually different in adolescence														.30	.44
14 Homosexual activities in adolescence															.77
15 Adult homosexuality															

Variable Number:	(1)	(2)	(3)	(4)	(5)	(6)	(7)	(8)	(9)	(10)	(11)	(12)	(13)	(14)	(15)
Mean	6.64	-.00	-.00	-1.19	-.01	.67	-.03	-.02	-.66	-.21	.09	.18	.12	.46	.23
Standard Deviation	5.73	.95	1.80	4.13	1.82	1.64	1.79	1.78	.68	.62	.28	.72	.33	.84	.42

Effects of Childhood and Adolescent Experiences on the Development of Adult
Homosexuality: BISEXUAL AND HETEROSEXUAL WHITE FEMALES. R = .87.

Variable	Total Effects	Standardized Path Coefficient (β)	Unstandardized Path Coefficient (b)
Homosexual activities in adolescence	.596	.596***	.298***
Began to feel sexually different in adolescence	.229	.229***	.291***
Homosexual genital activities in childhood	.204	--	--
Felt sexually different in childhood	.172	.172**	.258**
Childhood gender nonconformity	.164	.128*	.080*
Isolation from other girls, grade school	.179	.179**	.121**
Identification with mother	-.237	-.201**	-.047**
Relatively weak while growing up	.193	--	--
Detached-hostile father	.177	.238**	.024**
Aloof father	.159	--	--
Identification with father	.104	.167*	.043*
Hostile-rejecting mother	-.095	-.189*	-.044*
Weak father	.023	--	--
Unpleasant mother	.010	--	--

NOTE: "Total Effects" refers to the sum of all the pathways from a given variable to adult
sexual preference which are shown in Diagram 13. This value represents the portion of
the zero-order correlation (r) which is accounted for by the paths in Diagram 13; the
unaccounted-for portion is regarded as "extraneous" effects--i.e., those which are
spurious or due to variables not included in the model.

*p $<$ .05.
**p $<$ .01.
***p $<$ .001.

Effects of Earlier Childhood Experiences on Later Childhood and Adolescent Experiences As Demonstrated in Diagram 13: BISEXUAL AND HETEROSEXUAL WHITE FEMALES.

DEPENDENT VARIABLE: Homosexual activities in adolescence (R = .52).

Independent variable	Total Effects	Standardized Path Coefficient (β)	Unstandardized Path Coefficient (b)
Homosexual genital activities in childhood	.342	.342***	.400***
Felt sexually different in childhood	--	--	--
Childhood gender nonconformity	--	--	--
Isolation from other girls, grade school	--	--	--
Relatively weak while growing up	.323	.323***	.153***
Identification with father	-.105	--	--
Detached-hostile father	.061	--	--
Aloof father	.043	--	--
Weak father	.020	--	--
Identification with mother	--	--	--
Hostile-rejecting mother	--	--	--
Unpleasant mother	--	--	--

DEPENDENT VARIABLE: Childhood gender nonconformity (R = .38).

Independent variable	Total Effects	Standardized Path Coefficient (β)	Unstandardized Path Coefficient (b)
Weak father	.261	.261**	.031**
Aloof father	.198	.198*	.074*
Identification with mother	--	--	--
Identification with father	--	--	--
Hostile-rejecting mother	--	--	--
Detached-hostile father	--	--	--
Unpleasant mother	--	--	--

DEPENDENT VARIABLE: Isolation from other girls, grade school (R = .31).

Independent variable	Total Effects	Standardized Path Coefficient (β)	Unstandardized Path Coefficient (b)
Childhood gender nonconformity	.202	.202*	.185*
Identification with mother	-.202	-.202*	-.070*
Unpleasant mother	.130	--	--
Hostile-rejecting mother	.080	--	--
Weak father	.053	--	--
Aloof father	.040	--	--
Relatively weak while growing up	--	--	--
Identification with father	--	--	--
Detached-hostile father	--	--	--

DEPENDENT VARIABLE: Identification with mother (R = .69).

Independent variable	Total Effects	Standardized Path Coefficient (β)	Unstandardized Path Coefficient (b)
Unpleasant mother	-.642	-.343**	-.648**
Hostile-rejecting mother	-.397	-.397***	-.392***
Detached-hostile father	--	--	--
Aloof father	--	--	--
Weak father	--	--	--

DEPENDENT VARIABLE: Relatively weak while growing up (R = .32).

Independent variable	Total Effects	Standardized Path Coefficient (β)	Unstandardized Path Coefficient (b)
Identification with father	-.324	-.324***	-.352***
Detached-hostile father	.189	--	--
Aloof father	.135	--	--
Weak father	.062	--	--
Identification with mother	--	--	--
Hostile-rejecting mother	--	--	--
Unpleasant mother	--	--	--

DEPENDENT VARIABLE: Detached-hostile father (R = .71).

Independent variable	Total Effects	Standardized Path Coefficient (β)	Unstandardized Path Coefficient (b)
Aloof father	.713	.713***	1.634***
Weak father	--	--	--
Unpleasant mother	--	--	--

DEPENDENT VARIABLE: Identification with father (R = .66).

Independent variable	Total Effects	Standardized Path Coefficient (β)	Unstandardized Path Coefficient (b)
Detached-hostile father	-.582	-.582***	-.231***
Aloof father	-.415	--	--
Weak father	-.191	-.191*	-.055*
Hostile-rejecting mother	--	--	--
Unpleasant mother	--	--	--

DEPENDENT VARIABLE: Hostile-rejecting mother (R = .75).

Independent variable	Total Effects	Standardized Path Coefficient (β)	Unstandardized Path Coefficient (b)
Unpleasant mother	.754	.754***	1.439***
Aloof father	--	--	--
Weak father	--	--	--

NOTE: Began to Feel Sexually Different in Adolescence, Felt Sexually Different in Childhood, and Homosexual Genital Activities in Childhood do not appear as dependent variables in this table because the diagram illustrates no antecedents for them.

*p < .05.
**p < .01.
***p < .001.

Selected Statistics from Fully Recursive Path Model: BISEXUAL AND HETEROSEXUAL WHITE FEMALES[a]. R = .88.

Variable	Total Effects[b]	Standardized Path Coefficient (β)	Unstandardized Path Coefficient (b)
Homosexual activities in adolescence	.600	.600***	.300***
Began to feel sexually different in adolescence	.229	.229***	.291***
Homosexual genital activities in childhood	.182	-.039*	.106*
Felt sexually different in childhood	.131	.160	.197
Childhood gender nonconformity	.371	.112***	.232***
Isolation from other girls, grade school	.235	.184**	.160**
Aloof father	.278	.086*	.065*
Relatively weak while growing up	.257	.058*	.061*
Unpleasant mother	-.204	.044	-.090
Weak father	.134	.027	.010
Identification with mother	-.104	-.204	.025
Hostile-rejecting mother	.072	-.185	-.016
Detached-hostile father	.036	.181	.004
Identification with father	-.025	.191	-.007

[a]The fully recursive path model allows paths from every "upstream" variable to each "downstream" variable, including those paths which fail to meet our criteria of statistical and/or substantive significance.

[b]"Total Effects" refers to the sum of all the influences which the given variable would have on adult sexual preference if it had paths to **every** "downstream" variable in Diagram 13. This value represents the portion of the zero-order correlation (r) which would be accounted for by such an all-possible-paths diagram; the unaccounted-for portion is "extraneous" effects—i.e., those that are spurious or due to variables not included in the model.

*p < .05.
**p < .01.
***p < .001.

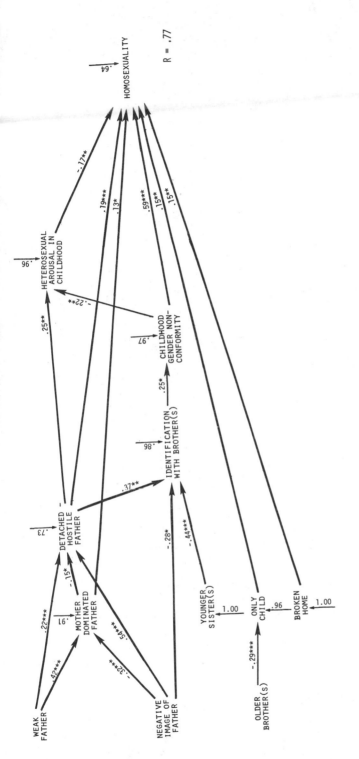

DIAGRAM 14. THE DEVELOPMENT OF SEXUAL PREFERENCE IN EXCLUSIVELY HOMOSEXUAL WHITE FEMALES.

* p < .05.
** p < .01.
*** p < .001.

Correlations, Means, and Standard Deviations for Variables in the Model: EXCLUSIVELY HOMOSEXUAL AND ALL HETEROSEXUAL WHITE FEMALES.

	(1)	(2)	(3)	(4)	(5)	(6)	(7)	(8)	(9)	(10)	(11)	(12)
1 Older brother(s)		.07	-.06	.02	-.09	-.06	-.29	.07	.12	.16	-.02	.14
2 Weak father			.43	.06	.10	.29	.04	.41	-.04	.33	-.07	.30
3 Negative image of father				.05	.07	-.14	-.10	.66	-.06	.27	-.08	.26
4 Broken home					.01	-.01	-.04	.10	-.04	.05	.01	.20
5 Younger sister(s)						-.05	-.26	.10	-.42	-.13	.04	-.18
6 Mother dominated father							.14	-.16	.01	.17	-.03	.22
7 Was an only child								.01	--a	-.05	-.08	.16
8 Detached-hostile father									.15	.26	.19	.31
9 Identification with brother(s)										.25	-.07	.22
10 Childhood gender nonconformity											-.16	.69
11 Heterosexual arousal in childhood												-.24
12 Adult homosexuality												

Variable Number:	(1)	(2)	(3)	(4)	(5)	(6)	(7)	(8)	(9)	(10)	(11)	(12)
Mean	.66	7.62	.98	.34	.57	.88	.17	-.04	.50	-.15	.19	.50
Standard Deviation	1.00	6.50	.92	.48	.98	.82	.37	1.87	.50	.96	.39	.50

aCorrelation coefficient cannot be computed.

304

Effects of Childhood Experiences on the Development of Adult Homosexuality:
EXCLUSIVELY HOMOSEXUAL AND ALL HETEROSEXUAL WHITE FEMALES. R = .77.

Variable	Total Effects	Standardized Path Coefficient (β)	Unstandardized Path Coefficient (b)
Heterosexual arousal in childhood	-.170	-.170**	-.216**
Childhood gender nonconformity	.624	.586***	.306***
Detached-hostile father	.210	.193***	.052***
Identification with brother(s)	.156	--	--
Broken home	.151	.151**	.159**
Was an only child	.149	.149**	.199**
Mother dominated father	.097	.130*	.079*
Weak father	.089	--	--
Younger sister(s)	-.069	--	--
Older brother(s)	-.044	--	--
Negative image of father	.041	--	--

NOTE: "Total Effects" refers to the sum of all the pathways from a given variable to adult
sexual preference which are shown in Diagram 14. This value represents the portion of
the zero-order correlation (r) which is accounted for by the paths in Diagram 14; the
unaccounted-for portion is regarded as "extraneous" effects -- i.e., those which are
spurious or due to variables not included in the model.

*p < .05.
**p < .01.
***p < .001.

Effects of Earlier Childhood Experiences on Later Childhood and Adolescent Experiences as Demonstrated in Diagram 14: EXCLUSIVELY HOMOSEXUAL AND ALL HETEROSEXUAL WHITE FEMALES.

DEPENDENT VARIABLE: Heterosexual arousal in childhood (R = .29).

Independent variable	Total Effects	Standardized Path Coefficient (β)	Unstandardized Path Coefficient (b)
Childhood gender nonconformity	-.223	-.223**	-.092**
Detached-hostile father	.226	.247**	.052**
Negative image of father	.149	--	--
Identification with brother(s)	-.056	--	--
Mother dominated father	-.035	--	--
Weak father	.035	--	--
Younger sister(s)	.024	--	--
Broken home	--	--	--
Was an only child	--	--	--
Parents had hoped for a son	--	--	--
Older brother(s)	--	--	--

DEPENDENT VARIABLE: Childhood gender nonconformity (R = .25).

Independent variable	Total Effects	Standardized Path Coefficient (β)	Unstandardized Path Coefficient (b)
Identification with brother(s)	.250	.250*	.477*
Younger sister(s)	-.109	--	--
Detached-hostile father	.093	--	--
Weak father	.015	--	--
Mother dominated father	-.014	--	--
Negative image of father	-.014	--	--
Broken home	--	--	--
Was an only child	--	--	--
Parents had hoped for a son	--	--	--
Older brother(s)	--	--	--

DEPENDENT VARIABLE: Detached-hostile father (R = .69).

Independent variable	Total Effects	Standardized Path Coefficient (β)	Unstandardized Path Coefficient (b)
Negative image of father	.592	.543***	1.103***
Weak father	.157	.222**	.064**
Mother dominated father	-.153	-.153*	-.350*
Younger sister(s)	--	--	--
Broken home	--	--	--
Was an only child	--	--	--
Parents had hoped for a son	--	--	--
Older brother(s)	--	--	--

DEPENDENT VARIABLE: Identification with brother(s) (R = .50).			
Independent variable	Total Effects	Standardized Path Coefficient (β)	Unstandardized Path Coefficient (b)
Younger sister(s)	-.436	-.436***	-.224***
Detached-hostile father	.373	.373**	.100**
Weak father	.059	--	--
Mother dominated father	-.057	--	--
Negative image of father	-.054	-.275*	-.150*
Broken home	--	--	--
Was an only child	--	--	--
Parents had hoped for a son	--	--	--
Older brother(s)	--	--	--

DEPENDENT VARIABLE: Was an only child (R = .29).			
Independent variable	Total Effects	Standardized Path Coefficient (β)	Unstandardized Path Coefficient (b)
Older brother(s)	-.293	-.293***	-.108***
Parents had hoped for a son	--	--	--
Negative image of father	--	--	--
Weak father	--	--	--

DEPENDENT VARIABLE: Mother dominated father (R = .41).			
Independent variable	Total Effects	Standardized Path Coefficient (β)	Unstandardized Path Coefficient (b)
Weak father	.423	.423***	.053***
Negative image of father	-.317	-.317***	-.282***
Older brother(s)	--	--	--
Parents had hoped for a son	--	--	--

NOTE: Younger Sister(s) and Broken Home do not appear as dependent variables in this table because the diagram illustrates no antecedents for them.

*p < .05.
**p < .01.
***p < .001.

Selected Statistics from Fully Recursive Path Model: EXCLUSIVELY HOMOSEXUAL
AND ALL HETEROSEXUAL WHITE FEMALES[a]. R = .77.

Variable	Total Effects[b]	Standardized Path Coefficient (β)	Unstandardized Path Coefficient (b)
Heterosexual arousal in childhood	-.174	-.174*	-.221*
Childhood gender nonconformity	.596	.562***	.294***
Weak father	.246	-.048	-.004
Detached-hostile father	.216	.186	.050
Mother dominated father	.193	.155	.094
Broken home	.177	.153	.161
Identification with brother(s)	.165	.015	.015
Was an only child	.153	.159	.214
Negative image of father	.151	.053	.029
Older brother(s)	.149	.076	.038
Younger sister(s)	-.147	-.055	-.028

[a]The fully recursive path model allows paths from every "upstream" variable to each "down-stream" variable, including those paths which fail to meet our criteria of statistical and/or substantive significance.

[b]"Total Effects" refers to the sum of all the influences which the given variable would have on adult sexual preference if it had paths to every "downstream" variable in Diagram 14. This value represents the portion of the zero-order correlation (r) which would be accounted for by such an all-possible-paths diagram; the unaccounted-for portion is "extraneous" effects--i.e., those that are spurious or due to variables not included in the model.

*p < .05.
***p < .01.

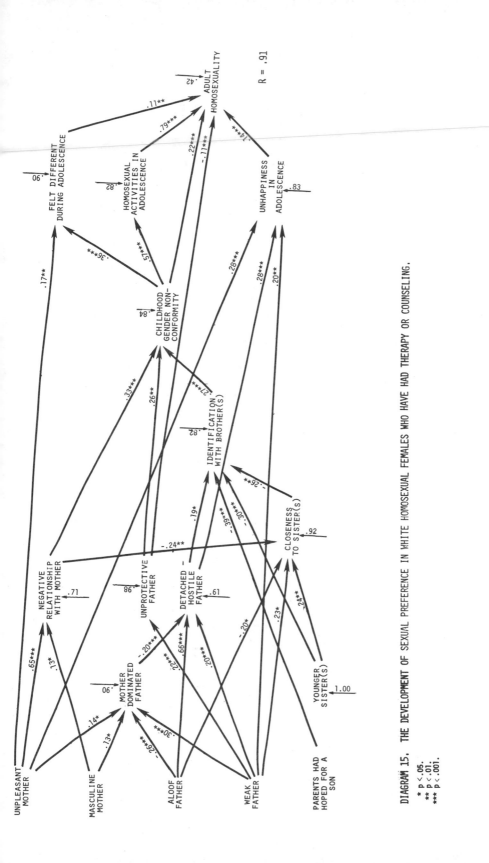

DIAGRAM 15. THE DEVELOPMENT OF SEXUAL PREFERENCE IN WHITE HOMOSEXUAL FEMALES WHO HAVE HAD THERAPY OR COUNSELING.

* p < .05.
** p < .01.
*** p < .001.

Correlations, Means, and Standard Deviations for Variables in the Model: WHITE HOMOSEXUAL FEMALES WHO HAVE HAD THERAPY OR COUNSELING AND ALL WHITE HETEROSEXUAL FEMALES.

	(1)	(2)	(3)	(4)	(5)	(6)	(7)	(8)	(9)	(10)	(11)	(12)	(13)	(14)	(15)	(16)	(17)
1 Parents had hoped for a son		-.04	-.01	.08	.06	.08	.15	.09	.16	.14	-.13	-.33	.13	.06	.01	.26	.23
2 Masculine mother			-.07	.25	.30	.07	.31	.08	.33	.04	-.09	-.11	.28	.22	.19	.21	.21
3 Younger sister(s)				-.02	.10	.07	.08	.09	.07	.07	.24	-.34	-.12	-.09	.02	-.12	-.15
4 Mother dominated father					.30	-.12	.25	.04	.21	-.22	.01	-.01	.19	.08	.04	.25	.23
5 Weak father						.37	.41	.22	.39	.39	.08	-.03	.31	.25	.42	.32	.31
6 Aloof father							.20	.13	.19	.76	-.14	-.07	.23	.20	.33	.23	.30
7 Unpleasant mother								.11	.69	.13	-.03	-.04	.25	.26	.40	.33	.32
8 Unprotective father									.16	.17	.01	.01	.31	.13	.16	.21	.13
9 Negative relationship with mother										.15	-.17	.07	.39	.13	.38	.39	.40
10 Detached-hostile father											-.04	.12	.25	.20	.40	.25	.33
11 Closeness to sister(s)												-.29	-.27	.15	-.08	-.16	-.23
12 Identification with brother(s)													.29	-.16	.04	.15	.22
13 Childhood gender nonconformity														.19	.26	.57	.63
14 Felt different from other girls, high school															.43	.32	.28
15 Unhappiness in adolescence																.18	.28
16 Homosexual activities in adolescence																	.88
17 Adult homosexuality																	
Variable Number:	(1)	(2)	(3)	(4)	(5)	(6)	(7)	(8)	(9)	(10)	(11)	(12)	(13)	(14)	(15)	(16)	(17)
Mean	.43	1.40	.57	.94	-.01	-.01	-.00	2.84	1.96	-.02	.66	.53	-.12	2.00	1.54	1.08	.61
Standard Deviation	.66	1.58	.94	.84	.94	1.74	.92	1.84	1.32	1.89	.48	.50	.90	.96	.89	.97	.49

Effects of Childhood and Adolescent Experiences on the Development of Adult
Homosexuality: WHITE HOMOSEXUAL FEMALES WHO HAVE HAD THERAPY OR COUNSELING
AND ALL WHITE HETEROSEXUAL FEMALES.   R = .91.

Variable	Total Effects	Standardized Path Coefficient (β)	Unstandardized Path Coefficient (b)
Homosexual activities in adolescence	.788	.788***	.397***
Childhood gender nonconformity	.713	.221***	.120***
Unhappiness in adolescence	.143	.143***	.078***
Felt different from other girls, high school	.113	.113**	.058**
Negative relationship with mother	.245	--	--
Unpleasant mother	.217	--	--
Identification with brother(s)	.193	--	--
Detached-hostile father	.077	--	--
Parents had hoped for a son	-.076	--	--
Unprotective father	.072	-.114***	-.030***
Younger sister(s)	-.069	--	--
Aloof father	.065	--	--
Closeness to sister(s)	-.050	--	--
Weak father	.043	--	--
Masculine mother	.030	--	--
Mother dominated father	-.016	--	--

NOTE: "Total Effects" refers to the sum of all the pathways from a given variable to adult
sexual preference which are shown in Diagram 15. This value represents the portion of
the zero-order correlation (r) which is accounted for by the paths in Diagram 15; the
unaccounted-for portion is regarded as "extraneous" effects--i.e., those which are
spurious or due to varaiables not included in the model.

**p<.01.
***p<.001.

Effects of Earlier Childhood Experiences on Later Childhood and Adolescent
Experiences as Demonstrated in Diagram 15: WHITE HOMOSEXUAL FEMALES WHO
HAVE HAD THERAPY OR COUNSELING AND ALL WHITE HETEROSEXUAL FEMALES.

DEPENDENT VARIABLE: Homosexual activities in adolescence (R = .57).

Independent variable	Total Effects	Standardized Path Coefficient (β)	Unstandardized Path Coefficient (b)
Childhood gender nonconformity	.572	.572***	.619***
Negative relationship with mother	.197	--	--
Identification with brother(s)	.154	--	--
Unprotective father	.149	--	--
Unpleasant mother	.128	--	--
Parents had hoped for a son	-.061	--	--
Younger sister(s)	-.055	--	--
Closeness to sister(s)	-.040	--	--
Detached-hostile father	.029	--	--
Aloof father	.029	--	--
Weak father	.028	--	--
Masculine mother	.025	--	--
Mother dominated father	-.006	--	--

DEPENDENT VARIABLE: Childhood gender nonconformity (R = .54).

Independent variable	Total Effects	Standardized Path Coefficient (β)	Unstandardized Path Coefficient (b)
Negative relationship with mother	.344	.327***	.222***
Identification with brother(s)	.270	.270***	.483***
Unprotective father	.261	.261**	.127**
Unpleasant mother	.223	--	--
Parents had hoped for a son	-.106	--	--
Younger sister(s)	-.097	--	--
Closeness to sister(s)	-.070	--	--
Detached-hostile father	.051	--	--
Aloof father	.050	--	--
Weak father	.049	--	--
Masculine mother	.043	--	--
Mother dominated father	-.010	--	--

DEPENDENT VARIABLE: Unhappiness in adolescence (R = .56).

Independent variable	Total Effects	Standardized Path Coefficient (β)	Unstandardized Path Coefficient (b)
Childhood gender nonconformity	--	--	--
Detached-hostile father	.285	.285***	.134***
Unpleasant mother	.275	.283***	.275***
Weak father	.235	.195**	.186**
Aloof father	.205	--	--
Mother dominated father	-.058	--	--
Masculine mother	-.007	--	--
Identification with brother(s)	--	--	--
Closeness to sister(s)	--	--	--
Negative relationship with mother	--	--	--

Independent variable	Total Effects	Standardized Path Coefficient (β)	Unstandardized Path Coefficient (b)
Unprotective father	--	--	--
Younger sister(s)	--	--	--
Parents had hoped for a son	--	--	--

DEPENDENT VARIABLE: Felt different from other girls, high school (R = .44).

Independent variable	Total Effects	Standardized Path Coefficient (β)	Unstandardized Path Coefficient (b)
Childhood gender nonconformity	.363	.363***	.390***
Unpleasant mother	.248	.167**	.175**
Negative relationship with mother	.125	--	--
Identification with brother(s)	.098	--	--
Unprotective father	.095	--	--
Parents had hoped for a son	-.039	--	--
Younger sister(s)	-.035	--	--
Closeness to sister(s)	-.025	--	--
Aloof father	.020	--	--
Detached-hostile father	.018	--	--
Masculine mother	.016	--	--
Weak father	.016	--	--
Mother dominated father	-.004	--	--

DEPENDENT VARIABLE: Negative relationship with mother (R = .70).

Independent variable	Total Effects	Standardized Path Coefficient (β)	Unstandardized Path Coefficient (b)
Unpleasant mother	.653	.653***	.939***
Masculine mother	.129	.129*	.108*
Younger sister(s)	--	--	--
Mother dominated father	--	--	--
Aloof father	--	--	--
Weak father	--	--	--
Parents had hoped for a son	--	--	--

DEPENDENT VARIABLE: Identification with brother(s) (R = .57).

Independent variable	Total Effects	Standardized Path Coefficient (β)	Unstandardized Path Coefficient (b)
Parents had hoped for a son	-.394	-.394***	-.300***
Younger sister(s)	-.360	-.297***	-.159***
Closeness to sister(s)	-.258	-.258**	-.272**
Detached-hostile father	.188	.188*	.050*
Aloof father	.186	--	--
Negative relationship with mother	.063	--	--
Mother dominated father	-.038	--	--
Unpleasant mother	.036	--	--
Weak father	-.033	--	--
Masculine mother	.003	--	--
Unprotective father	--	--	--

DEPENDENT VARIABLE: Detached-hostile father (R = .79).

Independent variable	Total Effects	Standardized Path Coefficient (β)	Unstandardized Path Coefficient (b)
Aloof father	.718	.664***	.722***
Mother dominated father	-.202	-.202***	-.457***
Weak father	.140	.200***	.405***
Unpleasant mother	-.028	--	--
Masculine mother	-.026	--	--
Younger sister(s)	--	--	--
Parents had hoped for a son	--	--	--

DEPENDENT VARIABLE: Unprotective father (R = .22).

Independent variable	Total Effects	Standardized Path Coefficient (β)	Unstandardized Path Coefficient (b)
Weak father	.222	.222***	.438***
Younger sister(s)	--	--	--
Mother dominated father	--	--	--
Unpleasant mother	--	--	--
Masculine mother	--	--	--
Aloof father	--	--	--
Parents had hoped for a son	--	--	--

DEPENDENT VARIABLE: Closeness to sister(s) (R = .38).

Independent variable	Total Effects	Standardized Path Coefficient (β)	Unstandardized Path Coefficient (b)
Negative relationship with mother	-.243	-.243**	-.087**
Younger sister(s)	.243	.243**	.123**
Weak father	.226	.226*	.115*
Aloof father	-.197	-.197*	-.054*
Unpleasant mother	-.159	--	--
Masculine mother	-.031	--	--
Detached-hostile father	--	--	--
Unprotective father	--	--	--
Mother dominated father	--	--	--
Parents had hoped for a son	--	--	--

DEPENDENT VARIABLE: Mother dominated father (R = .43).

Independent variable	Total Effects	Standardized Path Coefficient (β)	Unstandardized Path Coefficient (b)
Weak father	.299	.299***	.267***
Aloof father	-.265	-.265***	-.127***
Unpleasant mother	.140	.140*	.127*
Masculine mother	.129	.129*	.068*
Parents had hoped for a son	--	--	--

NOTE: Younger Sister(s) does not appear as a dependent variable in this table because the diagram illustrates no antecedents for it.

*p < .05.
**p < .01.
***p < .001.

Selected Statistics from Fully Recursive Path Model: WHITE HOMOSEXUAL FEMALES
WHO HAVE HAD THERAPY OR COUNSELING AND ALL WHITE HETEROSEXUAL FEMALES.[a] R = 92.

Variable	Total Effects[b]	Standardized Path Coefficient (β)	Unstandardized Path Coefficient (b)
Homosexual activities in adolescence	.764	.764***	.385***
Childhood gender nonconformity	.467	.188***	.255***
Unhappiness in adolescence	.126	.126*	.069*
Felt different from other girls, high school	.115	.115*	.058*
Detached-hostile father	.297	.065*	.077*
Negative relationship with mother	.278	-.003*	.103*
Aloof father	.202	.035*	.057*
Parents had hoped for a son	.192	.026*	.142*
Younger sister(s)	-.176	-.015	-.092
Identification with brother(s)	.175	.049	.171
Unpleasant mother	.161	.004	.086
Mother dominated father	.160	.040	.093
Closeness to sister(s)	-.124	-.035	-.128
Weak father	.122	-.034	.064
Masculine mother	.118	-.010	.036
Unprotective father	.030	-.105	.007

[a]The fully recursive path model allows paths from every "upstream" variable to each "down-stream" variable, including those paths which fail to meet our criteria of statistical and/or substantive significance.

[b]"Total Effects" refers to the sum of all the influences which the given variable would have on adult sexual preference if it had paths to _every_ "downstream" variable in Diagram 13. This value represents the portion of the zero-order correlation (r) which would be accounted for by such an all-possible-paths diagram; the unaccounted-for portion is "extraneous" effects -- i.e., those that are spurious or due to variables not included in the model.

*p < .05.
***p < .001.

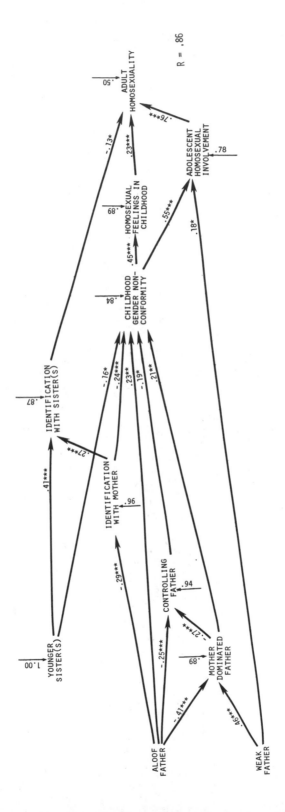

DIAGRAM 16. THE DEVELOPMENT OF SEXUAL PREFERENCE IN WHITE HOMOSEXUAL FEMALES WHO HAVE NOT HAD THERAPY OR COUNSELING.

* p < .05.
** p < .01.
*** p < .001.

Correlations, Means, and Standard Deviations for Variables in the Model: WHITE HOMOSEXUAL FEMALES WITH NO THERAPY OR COUNSELING AND ALL WHITE HETEROSEXUAL FEMALES.

	(1)	(2)	(3)	(4)	(5)	(6)	(7)	(8)	(9)	(10)	(11)
1 Weak father		.45	.01	.27	-.28	-.15	-.02	.31	.15	.35	.31
2 Aloof father			.14	-.20	-.20	-.29	.06	.27	.09	.16	.25
3 Younger sister(s)				-.11	.12	-.01	.41	-.17	-.04	-.10	-.16
4 Mother dominated father					-.22	-.07	-.04	-.24	.21	-.30	-.23
5 Controlling father						.14	.23	-.34	-.03	-.32	-.27
6 Identification with mother							.27	-.35	-.19	-.34	-.34
7 Identification with sister(s)								-.22	-.05	-.10	-.21
8 Childhood gender nonconformity									.45	.61	.67
9 Homosexual feelings in childhood										.24	.42
10 Adolescent homosexual involvement											.83
11 Adult homosexuality											

Variable Number:	(1)	(2)	(3)	(4)	(5)	(6)	(7)	(8)	(9)	(10)	(11)
Mean	7.35	-.00	.60	.85	3.04	-.00	.43	-.30	.01	.07	.42
Standard Deviation	6.13	1.77	1.02	.80	2.07	1.80	.50	.91	1.78	1.82	.49

Effects of Childhood and Adolescent Experiences on the Development of Adult Homosexuality: WHITE HOMOSEXUAL FEMALES WITH NO THERAPY OR COUNSELING AND ALL WHITE HETEROSEXUAL FEMALES. R = .86.

Variable	Total Effects	Standardized Path Coefficient (β)	Unstandardized Path Coefficient (b)
Adolescent homosexual involvement	.758	.758***	.206***
Homosexual feelings in childhood	.228	.228***	.063***
Childhood gender nonconformity	.521	--	--
Weak father	.197	--	--
Identification with mother	-.161	--	--
Mother dominated father	.137	--	--
Younger sister(s)	-.137	--	--
Aloof father	.136	--	--
Identification with sister(s)	-.130	-.130*	-.129*
Controlling father	-.101	--	--

NOTE: "Total Effects" refers to the sum of all the pathways from a given variable to adult sexual preference which are shown in Diagram 16. This value represents the portion of the zero-order correlation (r) which is accounted for by the paths in Diagram 16; the unaccounted-for portion is regarded as "extraneous" effects -- i.e., those which are spurious or due to variables not included in the model.

*p < .05.
***p < .001.

Effects of Earlier Childhood Experiences on Later Childhood and Adolescent
Experiences As Demonstrated in Diagram 16: WHITE HOMOSEXUAL FEMALES WITH NO
THERAPY OR COUNSELING AND ALL WHITE HETEROSEXUAL FEMALES.

DEPENDENT VARIABLE: Adolescent homosexual involvement (R = .63).

Independent Variable	Total Effects	Standardized Path Coefficient (β)	Unstandardized Path Coefficient (b)
Homosexual feelings in childhood	--	--	--
Childhood gender nonconformity	.552	.552***	1.109***
Weak father	.244	.178*	.053*
Mother dominated father	.145	--	--
Identification with mother	-.133	--	--
Aloof father	.133	--	--
Controlling father	-.107	--	--
Younger sister(s)	-.088	--	--
Identification with sister(s)	--	--	--

DEPENDENT VARIABLE: Homosexual feelings in childhood (R = .45).

Independent variable	Total Effects	Standardized Path Coefficient (β)	Unstandardized Path Coefficient (b)
Childhood gender nonconformity	.448	.448***	.882***
Mother dominated father	.118	--	--
Identification with mother	-.108	--	--
Aloof father	.108	--	--
Controlling father	-.086	--	--
Younger sister(s)	-.072	--	--
Weak father	.054	--	--
Identification with sister(s)	--	--	--

DEPENDENT VARIABLE: Childhood gender nonconformity (R = .54).

Independent variable	Total Effects	Standardized Path Coefficient (β)	Unstandardized Path Coefficient (b)
Mother dominated father	.263	.211**	.238**
Aloof father	.242	.231**	.118**
Identification with mother	-.241	-.241***	-.121***
Controlling father	-.193	-.193*	-.085*
Younger sister(s)	-.160	-.160*	-.143*
Weak father	.120	--	--
Identification with sister(s)	--	--	--

DEPENDENT VARIABLE: Identification with mother (R = .29).

Independent variable	Total Effects	Standardized Path Coefficient (β)	Unstandardized Path Coefficient (b)
Aloof father	-.286	-.286***	-.290***
Controlling father	--	--	--
Mother dominated father	--	--	--
Younger sister(s)	--	--	--
Weak father	--	--	--

DEPENDENT VARIABLE: Mother dominated father (R = .45).

Independent variable	Total Effects	Standardized Path Coefficient (β)	Unstandardized Path Coefficient (b)
Weak father	.455	.455***	.060***
Aloof father	-.407	-.407***	-.184***

DEPENDENT VARIABLE: Identification with sister(s) (R = .49).

Independent variable	Total Effects	Standardized Path Coefficient (β)	Unstandardized Path Coefficient (b)
Younger sister(s)	.411	.411***	.201***
Identification with mother	.273	.273***	.075***
Aloof father	-.078	--	--
Controlling father	--	--	--
Mother dominated father	--	--	--
Weak father	--	--	--

DEPENDENT VARIABLE: Controlling father (R = .33).

Independent variable	Total Effects	Standardized Path Coefficient (β)	Unstandardized Path Coefficient (b)
Mother dominated father	-.270	-.270***	-.697***
Aloof father	-.142	-.252**	-.294**
Weak father	-.123	--	--
Younger sister(s)	--	--	--

NOTE: Younger Sister(s) does not appear as a dependent variable in this table because the diagram illustrates no antecedents for it.

*p < .05.
**p < .01.
***p < .001.

Selected Statistics from Fully Recursive Path Model: WHITE HOMOSEXUAL FEMALES
WITH NO THERAPY OR COUNSELING AND ALL WHITE HETEROSEXUAL FEMALES.[a] R = .88.

Variable	Total Effects[b]	Standardized Path Coefficient (β)	Unstandardized Path Coefficient (b)
Adolescent homosexual involvement	.711	.711***	.193***
Homosexual feelings in childhood	.144	.187	.040
Childhood gender nonconformity	.560	.131***	.306***
Weak father	.255	-.043*	.021*
Identification with mother	-.248	.042*	-.068*
Mother dominated father	.226	-.015	.140
Younger sister(s)	-.173	-.034	-.084
Aloof father	.133	.130	.037
Controlling father	-.131	.039	-.031
Identification with sister(s)	-.078	-.124	-.078

[a]The fully recursive path model allows paths from every "upstream" variable to each "downstream" variable, including those paths which fail to meet our criteria of statistical and/or substantive significance.

[b]"Total Effects" refers to the sum of all the influences which the given variable would have on adult sexual preference if it had paths to every "downstream" variable in Diagram 16. This value represents the portion of the zero-order correlation (r) which would be accounted for by such an all-possible-paths diagram; the unaccounted-for portion is "extraneous" effects--i.e., those that are spurious or due to variables not included in the model.

*p $<$ .05.
***p $<$ .001.